"Our Government is the potent, the omnipresent teacher. For good or for ill, it teaches the whole people by its example. Crime is contagious. If the Government becomes a lawbreaker, it bleeds contempt for law; it invites every man to become a law unto himself; it invites anarchy. To declare that in the administration of the criminal law the end justifies the means – to declare that the Government may commit crimes in order to secure the conviction of a private criminal – would bring terrible retribution. Against that pernicious doctrine this Court should resolutely set its face."

Justice Louis D. Brandeis, dissenting in *Olmstead v. United States*, 277 U.S. 438, 485 (1928)

"It is a fair summary of history to say that the safeguards of liberty have frequently been forged in controversies involving not very nice people."

Justice Felix Frankfurter, dissenting in *United States v. Rabinowitz*, 339 U.S. 56, 69 (1950)

"What happens behind doors that are opened and closed at the sole discretion of the police is a black chapter in every country – the free as well as the despotic, the modern as well as the ancient."

Justice William O. Douglas (the longest-serving Supreme Court Justice in U.S. history), concurring in *United States v. Carignan*, 342 U.S. 36, 46 (1951)

"If a person is innocent of a crime, then he is not a suspect."

then **Attorney General Edwin Meese** explaining to the American Bar Association why the *Miranda* decision enabling those arrested to be advised of their rights was not necessary anymore (From *The 776 Stupidest Things Ever Said* (p. 100), by R. Petras and K. Petras, 1993, New York: Doubleday.)

INTERROGATIONS AND DISPUTED CONFESSIONS

A MANUAL FOR FORENSIC PSYCHOLOGICAL PRACTICE

GREGORY DeCLUE, PhD, ABPP (FORENSIC)

PROFESSIONAL RESOURCE PRESS
SARASOTA, FLORIDA

Published by
Professional Resource Press
(An imprint of Professional Resource Exchange, Inc.)
Post Office Box 15560
Sarasota, FL 34277-1560

The copy editor for this book was Vicki Kennedy, the managing editor was Debbie Fink, the production coordinator was Laurie Girsch, the typesetter was Richard Sullivan, and the cover designer was Rosebud Design Group.

Library of Congress Cataloging-in-Publication Data

DeClue, Gregory, date.
 Interrogations and disputed confessions : a manual for forensic psychological practice / Gregory DeClue.
  p. cm.
 Includes bibliographical references (p.) and index.
 ISBN 1-56887-093-0 (alk. paper)
  1. Forensic psychology. 2. Confession (Law) 3. Police questioning. I. Title.

RA1148.D43 2005
614'.15--dc22

2005043030

About the Author

Gregory DeClue, PhD, ABPP, has conducted over 1,000 criminal forensic psychological evaluations and over 1,000 evaluations of prospective or current law enforcement or corrections officers. He has written articles across a wide range of forensic psychological practice areas, including child custody, competency, malingering, sex-offender re-offense risk assessment, and confessions. Dr. DeClue is a licensed Florida psychologist and is a diplomate of the American Board of Forensic Psychology. He is 2004-2005 president of the Consortium of Police Psychologists (COPPS) and has presented workshops sponsored by COPPS, the Missouri Prevention Institute, the Florida Alcohol and Drug Abuse Association, the National Association of Alcohol and Drug Abuse Counselors, the Florida Association of Criminal Defense Lawyers, the Florida Mental Health Institute, and the American Association of Sex Educators, Counselors, and Therapists. Dr. DeClue is in independent practice in Sarasota, Florida, and is police psychologist for several law-enforcement agencies. His website is http://gregdeclue.myakkatech.com/

— DEDICATION —

This book is dedicated to law enforcement officers who seek the truth in investigating cases; judges who seek to balance detectives' need to solve cases with suspects' rights to be treated fairly; attorneys who advocate for the prosecution and the defense; juries who listen to both sides and decide questions of guilt and innocence; expert witnesses who explain matters that are beyond the common knowledge of those without specialized training and experience; and to any of us who may ever find ourselves in a small, windowless room trying to explain how our fingerprints – or DNA – came to be someplace we have never been.

— Acknowledgments —

Thanks to Alan Goldstein and Bruce Frumkin for helpful comments on a draft. I am responsible for mistakes and shortcomings that remain.

I would also like to thank Donna DeClue, Larry Ritt, Debra Fink, and the staff at Professional Resource Press.

TABLE OF CONTENTS

Part III
Conducting Psychological Assessments
And Preparing Testimony

INTERROGATIONS AND DISPUTED CONFESSIONS

A MANUAL FOR FORENSIC PSYCHOLOGICAL PRACTICE

Disputed — Confessions — In A Nutshell

Some people falsely confess to some crimes some times. Some of those people begin by denying guilt, then during police interrogation say, "I did it," but afterwards say, "No, I didn't." U.S. courts provide two opportunities to challenge confessions. At a suppression hearing the defense can present evidence challenging the voluntariness of the confession, and/or whether the defendant gave a knowing, intelligent, and voluntary waiver of his or her Constitutional rights prior to interrogation. At trial the defense can present evidence challenging the accuracy of the confession. At both stages psychologists are called upon to present expert testimony, either at the request of the defense or the prosecution. This book is designed to assist psychologists working on criminal cases involving interrogations and confessions.

— 1 —

INTRODUCTION

DNA PROFILING CAN IDENTIFY THE GUILTY AND EXONERATE THE INNOCENT

In April 1953 Watson and Crick "put forward a radically different structure for the salt of deoxyribose nucleic acid [DNA]," the now famous double helix, noting, "It has not escaped our notice that the specific pairing we have postulated immediately suggests a possible copying mechanism for the genetic material" (p. 737). Hailed as unveiling the secret of life, this work led to the granting of a Nobel Prize in 1962. Knowledge about DNA has advanced our basic understanding of life and has spawned numerous practical applications, including one of the most effective tools in modern crime detection:

It was 9am, Monday September 15, 1984 when Sir Alec [Jeffreys] removed some X-ray film from the developing tank and experienced a rare moment in science, an absolute eureka. "I thought – My God what have we got here – but it was so blindingly obvious," he says. "We'd been looking for good genetic markers for basic genetic analysis and had stumbled on a way of establishing a human's genetic identification. By the afternoon we'd named our discovery DNA fingerprinting." . . . A DNA fingerprint appears as a pattern of bands or stripes on X-ray film. The technology's applications for forensic science are obvious: It can determine whether two biological samples come from the same person. It can [also] be used to establish family relationships because the banded patterns the technology produces are simply inherited. (*1998 Australia Prize*, ¶ 2, ¶ 12; see also Jeffreys, Wilson, & Thein, 1985)

Jeffreys promptly used the new technology in an immigration case to establish both paternity and maternity (see Watson & Berry, 2003, p. 264). Then he used DNA profiling to establish the identity of a man who raped and killed two 15-year-old girls, 3 years apart, near the village of Narborough, in England. The police collected blood from all the adult males in and around Narborough and Jeffreys successfully identified the culprit. Colin Pitchfork became the first criminal ever apprehended on the basis of DNA profiling (Watson & Berry, 2003, p. 266). This same case introduces us to a central topic of this book.

When the local police contacted Jeffreys to consult on the Narborough case, they had already arrested a 17-year-old kitchen assistant who had a record of minor sex offenses. During their interrogation of him he confessed to one of the murders, but not the other. Noting similarities in the two cases, the police expected that Jeffreys would assist them in proving that the man had raped and killed both girls. Jeffreys' analysis showed that the same man had committed both rapes, but it was not the man who had confessed.

> "The police subsequently dropped the case against that man," says Sir Alec, "and he became the first person ever proven innocent by DNA analysis. If we hadn't developed the technology, I'm confident he would have been gaoled [jailed] for life." (*1998 Australia Prize*, ¶ 21)

And he is not the only one. In 1996, the FBI reported that in sexual assault cases in which DNA results could be obtained, the DNA evidence exonerated the primary suspect in 25% of the cases (Connors et al., 1996; Scheck & Neufeld, 2001). And, back to Britain:

> These days, the use of DNA profiling sees 30 per cent of accused in British rape cases exonerated. "The technology provides powerful evidence that allows courts to arrive at solid decisions in criminal cases," says Sir Alec. "It's also led to a swathe of longstanding convictions around the world being overturned. Some of these people had been in gaol for over a decade before molecular evidence proved their innocence." (*1998 Australia Prize*, ¶ 23)

SOME INNOCENT PEOPLE
CONFESS TO CRIMES

The Narborough case illustrates that in some circumstances DNA evidence can prove guilt or innocence. Although DNA testing can allow some falsely accused – and some falsely convicted – people to prove their innocence, in some cases there is no biological evidence to test. It is therefore critical to study cases where innocent people have been convicted and to identify what errors led to the wrongful convictions, so that the risk of such errors can be minimized in the future.

Bedau and colleagues have analyzed 416 cases of wrongful conviction of capital or potentially capital crimes in the United States in the 20th century (Bedau & Radelet, 1987; Radelet, Bedau, & Putnam, 1992; see also Radelet, Lofquist, & Bedau, 1996). Of the 350 cases reported in the 1987 paper, 40% of the people were sentenced to death. These miscarriages of justice were caused by a number of different errors, often in combination, the most common being perjury by prosecution witnesses and mistaken eyewitness testimony (see Gudjonsson, 2003, for a summary that includes some criticism and defense of the study). Of the 350 cases reported in 1987, 49 (14%) involved false confessions. Although a few of those were voluntary false confessions, most were the result of rigorous interrogation by the police.

Some early analyses of wrongful conviction provoked challenges to the claim that the exonerated person was truly innocent (see, e.g., Markman & Cassell, 1988). In some more recent analyses, DNA evidence provides more certain exoneration. That resolves questions about guilt and innocence, and therefore about whether a given case should be counted as a confirmed case of false confession (Scheck & Neufeld, 2001). The cases in which DNA evidence confirmed a wrongful conviction provide the best opportunity to estimate the percentage of wrongful conviction cases that involve an innocent person confessing. Scheck, Neufeld, and Dwyer (2001) found that in nearly one in four (15 of 62) cases of wrongful conviction, an innocent person had confessed.

The famous *Miranda* (1966) case has not closed the book on false confessions resulting from police interrogations. For example, Leo and Ofshe (1998) describe 60 cases of alleged false confessions in the United States between 1973 and 1996. Such documented cases are considered to be the tip of the iceberg (Leo, 2001a). No one knows the rate of false confessions per interrogation, but some studies in Iceland suggest that it might be less than 1% (Sigurdsson & Gudjonsson, 1994, 1996), with about half of the false confessions being induced by police.

As courts and the general public have come to recognize the potential accuracy of DNA evidence,[1] it is now universally accepted that some people falsely confess to some crimes some times. U.S. law is designed to reduce the occurrence of false confessions, and to increase the chance that false confessions will be identified as such. Psychologists can assist the courts in both of these tasks.

---

[1]   Of course, lab errors or lab fraud can occur with DNA analysis also. See, for example, Judging DNA work: More funds and cautious regulation are needed to solve problems of crime labs, *Omaha World Herald*, July 8, 2003, at p. 6b. Retrieved May 13, 2004, from http://www.law-forensic.com/cfr_reforms_12.htm

— PART I —

IMPLICATIONS OF FALSE CONFESSIONS

Part I of this book uses a framework presented by Ofshe and Leo (1997) and revisited by Leo (2001a) to assist in the explanation of causes and consequences of false confessions, as well as three policy solutions.

— 2 —

THE CAUSES OF
POLICE-INDUCED
FALSE CONFESSIONS

WHY DO SUSPECTS CONFESS?

As we set out to understand why some people confess to crimes they did not commit, we begin with the more general question of why anyone, guilty or innocent, confesses to crimes during police interrogation. Gudjonsson (2003) notes that self-incriminating admissions or confessions lead to serious negative consequences, commonly including adverse effects to self-esteem and integrity, loss of freedom and liberty, and possible financial penalties. Police interrogation can be construed as a process of at least temporarily overcoming whatever factors inhibit a suspect from confessing. As Gudjonsson (2003) notes, the following factors are expected to occur frequently: fear of legal sanctions, concern about one's reputation, not wanting to admit to oneself what one has done, not wanting one's family and friends to know about the crime, and fear of retaliation. Nevertheless, the percentage of suspects who confess during police interrogation is substantial, ranging from under 40% to over 70% in various studies (see Gudjonsson, 2003, p. 137).

Why do so many people confess during police interrogation? Gudjonsson (2003, Chapter 5) presents five different models (not mutually exclusive, not exhaustive), including a decision-making model, psychoanalytic models, an interaction process model, the Reid Model, and Gudjonsson's own Cognitive-Behavioral Model. The last two are of particular interest, as is Ofshe and Leo's (1997) Decision-Making Model.

The Reid Model

The Reid Model (Inbau et al., 2001; Jayne, 1986) is based on the "Nine Steps" of interrogation that are laid out in a series of police training manuals. These manuals predated *Miranda* (1966) and, with periodic revisions, have continued to be mainstays of American police work. New police interrogators learn to extract confessions from initially unwilling suspects by working alongside more experienced peers. The Reid training manuals document the process, and the Reid Model (Jayne, 1986) attempts to explain the psychological principles underlying the process. (Here, "Reid manuals" and "Nine Steps" refer to the how-to descriptions, and "Reid Model" refers to the why-it-works explanation.) Although written in an authoritative style, both the manuals and the model are based more on observation than scientific experimentation.

According to this model, "all criminal deception shares a common motivation," that of "distorting or denying the truth for the purpose of benefit to the individual. . . . Psychologically, interrogation can be thought of as the undoing of deception" (Jayne, 1986, p. 327). Criminals are seen as being motivated to avoid both the "real" consequences of confessing (loss of freedom, loss of income, etc.) and the "personal" consequences (decreased self-esteem and pride, embarrassment, etc.). Through the process of operant conditioning, a person learns from experience that *successful* deception is rewarded: the person gets away with it. Meanwhile, the person learns from moral training that it is always best to tell the truth. "Psychologically, the results of the inner conflict produced by lying are frustration and anxiety" (Jayne, 1986, p. 329). The conflict between these opposing forces – tell a lie to get away with it, tell the truth to avoid anxiety – sets the internal stage for the interrogator's performance.

Interrogators are encouraged to become astute observers of human behavior (or, arguably, to come to believe that they are astute observers, since their hunches are typically not formally tested). Although "there is no overt behavior or internal change occurring within an individual that is unique to deception, . . . deception can be inferred *with a degree of statistical accuracy* by not only observing the behavior of anxiety reduction, but also by paying close attention to the timing and consistency of the behavior" (Jayne, 1986, p. 331, emphasis added). (The "degree of statistical accuracy" is not stated because it is untested and unknown; it could, of course, be a low degree of accuracy.)

Suspects are seen as giving off both verbal and nonverbal clues about truthfulness. For example, when accused of theft, a suspect's verbal responses could take any of four forms which, in order of increasing anxiety and decreasing responsibility-taking are: truth, omission, evasion, and denial. The interrogator is encouraged to consider that an innocent suspect is more likely to directly deny guilt, whereas a guilty suspect is likely to avoid the question or evade the issue. Meanwhile, "nonverbal behavior reduces anxiety by displacement or distraction" (Jayne, 1986, p. 330). Fidgeting or adjusting one's clothes is considered to be indicative of anxiety and therefore a clue that the suspect is lying. The behavioral identification process is an integral part of the Reid method. Interrogators are encouraged to form opinions about a suspect's truthfulness on the basis of observations of his or her verbal and nonverbal behavior:

> The suspect who, after being accused, says, "No offense to you, sir, but I didn't do it," "I know you are just doing your job," or "I understand what you are saying" is evidencing his lying about the matter under investigation (Inbau, Reid, & Buckley, 1986, p. 47). . . . *Generally speaking, a suspect who does not make direct eye contact is probably being untruthful.* (p. 51, emphasis in original)

Kassin (1997, p. 222) rather generously notes that "Inbau et al. may well be correct in this diagnostic advice," but adds:

> It is important to realize, however, that there is currently no hard empirical support for their propositions. Research has consistently shown that people are poor intuitive judges of truth and deception. . . . In fact, even so-called experts who make such judgments for a living – police investigators; judges; psychiatrists; and polygraphers for the Central Intelligence Agency, the Federal Bureau of Investigation, and the military – are highly prone to error.

Recent research, particularly that of Ekman, O'Sullivan, and Frank (1999), shows that at least under some circumstances some professional lie catchers, including some federal law enforcement agents with special interest in deception, are able to quickly respond to behavioral clues to detect lying at rates above chance. The best agents correctly detected lies 80% of the time and correctly detected truths 66% of the time. Meanwhile, "most people cannot tell from demeanor when others are lying. Such poor performance is typical not only of lay people but also of most professionals concerned with lying" (Ekman et al., 1999, p. 263). Indeed, in this study the group of municipal, state, and federal law enforcement agents with no special interest in deception was only accurate 51% of the time.

Another study, which used videotapes of actual suspects in real interrogations, found that ordinary police officers in England were able to detect truth or lies, each at about 65% accuracy (where 50% accuracy would be a chance result; Mann, Vrij, & Bull, 2004). More experienced officers tended to have better success rates than those with less experience. Thus, there may be some potential for research-based training in behavioral lie detection to provide meaningful hunches, but there is no research basis for believing that the behavioral identification process in the Inbau et al. training is reliable. Indeed, in the Mann et al. (2004) study, the more officers relied on traditional cues (e.g., gaze, fidgeting) *a la* Inbau, the worse they became at distinguishing between truths and lies.

The pattern of law enforcement officers overdiagnosing lying is a consistent concern. After spending a year observing Baltimore homicide detectives, the journalist Simon (1991, p. 206) wrote:

> Nervousness, fear, confusion, hostility, a story that changes or contradicts itself – all are signs that the man in an interrogation room is lying, particularly in the eyes of someone as naturally suspicious as a detective. Unfortunately, these are also signs of a human being in a state of high stress, which is pretty much where people find themselves after being accused of a capital crime. [A detective sergeant] once mused that the best way to unsettle a suspect would be to post in [the] interrogation room a written list of those behavior patterns that indicate deception:
>
> Uncooperative.
> Too cooperative.
> Talks too much.
> Talks too little.
> Gets his story perfectly straight.
> F***s his story up.
> Blinks too much, avoids eye contact.
> Doesn't blink. Stares.

Although Inbau et al. (1986, p. 59) generally encourage interrogators to trust their hunches, they do acknowledge that behavioral signs can be misread:

> An example of how misleading behavior symptoms may surface is one in which a male friend of a female murder victim was interrogated about her death. He displayed a number of guilty symptoms, according to his initial interrogators. It was reported that he could not look them "straight in the eye," that he sighed a lot, that he had a disheveled appearance, and that he seemed to be going through a great deal of mental anguish. An investigator reported that "He looked guilty as hell!" During a subsequent interrogation, conducted by a professionally competent interrogator, however, it was ascertained that the suspect was emotionally upset because of the young woman's death and that he had been crying uncontrollably over it. . . . The investigators mistakenly confused his emotional behavior as indicative of guilt, and therefore, he became the prime suspect. Later developments in the case produced factual evidence that totally exonerated him from any part in the murder.

Nevertheless, interrogators are encouraged to use body language, and so on, to determine the likely guilt of a subject, and then use the "Nine Steps to Effectiveness" to extract a confession from a subject *whom they believe to be guilty*. Specific themes are recommended to manipulate a suspect into confessing. For example, "It is advisable, whenever possible, to point out the relative insignificance of the offense in terms of how much worse it could have been" (Inbau et al., 1986, p. 127). Psychologists analyzing confessions include this in the "soft sell" technique of *minimization*, "in which the detective tries to lull the suspect into a false sense of security" (Kassin, 1997, p. 223). In another approach, *maximization*,

> The interrogator uses "scare tactics" designed to intimidate a suspect believed to be guilty. . . . To summarize, maximization communicates an implicit threat of punishment, whereas minimization implies an offer of leniency. Yet, although trial judges exclude confessions elicited by *explicit* threats and promises, they often admit into evidence those prompted by *implicit* threats and promises. For all intents and purposes, these commonly used techniques circumvent laws designed to prohibit the use of coerced confessions. Indeed, Inbau et al. (1986, p. 320) were quick to reassure their readers that "although recent

Supreme Court opinions have contained derogatory statements about "trickery" and "deceit" as interrogation devices, no case has prohibited their usage. (Kassin, 1997, pp. 223-224)

So, according to the Reid Model, why does a person confess during police interrogation? Jayne (1986, p. 332) offers a detailed, untested theory:

An individual will confess (tell the truth) when he perceives the consequences of a confession as more desirable than the continued anxiety of deception. If, on the other hand, the consequences of the confession are perceived as less desirable than the anxiety associated with deception, the individual will continue to lie. The variables contained within these two conditions are perceived consequences and perceived anxiety; both of these variables can be affected psychologically during an interrogation. The goal of interrogation, therefore, is to decrease the suspect's perception of the consequences of confessing, while at the same time increasing the suspect's internal anxiety associated with his deception.

The model identifies four[1] basic concepts important in influencing behavior change, such as getting someone to confess to a crime, purchase a certain product, or vote for a particular political candidate:

The concept of *expectancy* refers to a want or goal perceived as desirable or inevitable. The deceptive[2] suspect's expectancy at the onset of the interrogation is that if he confesses, the consequences (as he perceives them at that time) are inevitable, and that the most desirable goal would be not to confess.
The concept of *persuasion* is a form of communication wherein the listener's attitudes, beliefs, or perceptions are changed. Expectancies are changed through persuasion. If one person can change what another person believes to be desirable or inevitable, a change of expectancy will result.
The concept of *belief* is the vehicle of persuasion; beliefs are not facts and therefore are subject to interpretation and external influences. (Jayne, 1986, p. 333)

---

[1] Three of the four are italicized in the quote that follows. The fourth concept is the behavior change itself.

[2] Is this qualifier needed? Wouldn't a truthful, innocent suspect have the same expectancy?

Jayne stresses the distinction between internal and external reality. It would be illegal for an interrogator to directly add anxiety by physically beating a suspect or threatening to do so. It would also be illegal for an interrogator to make a direct but false promise that a suspect would not be punished for a crime or would receive a reduced sentence if he or she confessed. Interrogators are trained, though, that they "can legally change the suspect's perception of the consequences of confessing or the suspect's perception of the anxiety associated with deception through influencing the suspect's beliefs" (Jayne, 1986, p. 333). Thus, interrogators are taught that (a) torture, physical brutality, and certain types of false promises are illegal, but (b) interrogators can get the same results – getting someone who does not want to confess, to confess – by using more subtle, psychological techniques.

In later sections of this book, we will consider how the law distinguishes between direct and implied promises and threats, and how subtle psychological persuasive techniques should be considered in the "totality of the circumstances" regarding a particular interrogation and confession. For now, note that police interrogators are taught how to change a suspect's perception of reality, at least temporarily, in order to get the subject to change his or her behavior. As Gudjonsson (2003, p. 120)[3] notes,

> According to the [Reid Model], it seems that the success of the interrogation depends on the extent to which the interrogator is successful in identifying psychological vulnerabilities, exploiting them to alter the suspect's belief system and perceptions of the consequences of making self-incriminating admissions, and persuading him to accept the interrogator's version of the "truth." This represents a potentially very powerful way of breaking down resistance during interrogation.

Next we turn to Gudjonsson's model.

Gudjonsson's Cognitive-Behavioral Model

Born in Iceland, Gisli Gudjonsson is a former police officer who now practices psychology in England. One of the most prolific

---

[3] From *The Psychology of Interrogations and Confessions: A Handbook* by G. H. Gudjonsson. Copyright © 2003 by John Wiley and Sons Limited. Quotes from this book are reproduced with permission.

researchers and writers in the field of interrogations and confessions, he states that both true and false confessions "are best construed as arising through the existence of a particular relationship between the suspect, the environment, and significant others [notably police interrogators] in that environment" (2003, p. 124). His analysis embodies a social learning framework, viewing behavior in terms of antecedents and consequences construed as *social, emotional, cognitive, situational, and physiological* events.

Social antecedents include isolating the subject and using interrogation procedures such as the Reid method. The immediate social consequences of admissions include social reinforcement by the police interrogators. Emotional antecedents include anxiety, distress, uncertainty, fear, and guilt. The immediate emotional consequence of confession may include a sense of relief from talking and from the cessation of police pressure.

Cognitive factors include the suspect's thoughts, interpretations, assumptions, and strategies. Gudjonsson (2003, p. 127) notes that "the suspects' behavior during the interrogation is likely to be more influenced by their perceptions, interpretations, and assumptions about what is happening than by the actual behavior of the police. When the suspect perceives the evidence against him as being strong he is more likely to confess, believing that there is no point in denying the offense." Situational factors include the circumstances of the arrest, perhaps being confined for several hours or days before the interrogation, and prior experiences with law enforcement. Expected physiological antecedents embody heightened arousal, including increased heart rate, blood pressure, rate and irregularity of respiration, and perspiration, all of which are expected to recede following confession.

An advantage of Gudjonsson's model is that, if enough information is available, an evaluator can attempt to reconstruct a time line that encompasses both external and internal events. When the interrogation has been recorded, observable antecedents and consequences (including the interrogators' tactics and the suspect's responses) can be mapped, and the suspect-cum-defendant can offer an ongoing reconstruction of his or her thoughts, feelings, and so forth.

Ofshe and Leo's Decision Model

Social psychologist Richard Ofshe and sociologist Richard Leo have longstanding interests in interrogations and confessions. Their decision model is based on observational studies such as that described in Leo's 1992 article. To appreciate Ofshe and Leo's model, it is useful to consider a decision faced by criminal defendants at a later stage in the judicial process: whether to plead out or go to trial. In making that decision, the defendant typically has guidance from his or her attorney, as well as from friends and family, along with the luxury of time to weigh the options. The defendant has considerable opportunity to gain accurate information about the strength of the case against him or her, often including detailed depositions of prospective witnesses and authentication of any physical evidence. The prosecutor has an ethical responsibility to provide exculpatory as well as inculpatory evidence to the defense. If the defendant chooses to enter a plea of guilty or no contest, the judge will engage him or her in a colloquy to ensure that the defendant understands the rights he or she is forgoing (e.g., the right to confront witnesses, the right to be tried by a jury of peers), and to ensure that he or she is competent to waive these rights and enter a plea. If there is doubt about the defendant's competence to proceed, that must be explored, which typically involves, at minimum, one psychological or psychiatric evaluation relevant to his or her decision-making ability and understanding about the charges (cf. *Pate v. Robinson*, 1966).

It is estimated that over 90% of criminal convictions are obtained via plea (bargaining) rather than trial (Melton et al., 1997). In at least some jurisdictions, a defendant has the right to enter a "best interests" plea, saying that, although not admitting guilt, the defendant believes it is in his or her best interests to plead out to the case and accept the consequences that would accrue to a person guilty of the crime (*North Carolina v. Alford*, 1970). Thus, it is formally recognized that under some circumstances an innocent person might choose to do the functional equivalent of pleading guilty.

Now, compare the foregoing to the situation of a suspect who agrees to talk to the police – which the majority of suspects do (Gudjonsson, 2003). There are some obvious similarities in the decisions to be made, and, superficially, both involve a rational decision about whether or not to say that one committed a crime: an interrogation suspect decides whether or not to make admissions, and a criminal defendant decides whether or not to plead guilty. However, the difference in the processes and in the safeguards afforded is monumental.

The safeguards afforded a criminal defendant are designed to ensure that he or she is both capable of, and actually performing, a rational act when pleading guilty (or no contest). In contrast, interrogation procedures are designed to encourage rational people to make decisions that no rational person would make[4] outside the context of the influence of modern police interrogation. "All approaches to the analysis of human behavior that presume rationality would, if applied superficially, classify confession as an irrational act – whether the person is innocent or guilty of the crime. . . . Psychological methods of interrogation have evolved for the purpose of influencing a rational person who knows he is guilty to alter his initial decision to deny culpability and decide instead to confess" (Ofshe & Leo, 1997, p. 194).[5]

During the shift from denial to admission, police use one set of tactics to alter the suspect's perception of his or her immediate situation, and another set of tactics to communicate information to the subject about incentives to confess and disincentives for continued denial. Routinely, police interrogators exert great control over the suspect's environment and distort or fabricate information to temporarily alter the suspect's subjective reality.

"The process of interrogation produces confession because it results in the suspect being convinced either that he has been caught (if he is guilty) or that his situation is hopeless (if he is innocent), that further denial is pointless, and that it is in his self-interest to confess. For both innocent and guilty suspects, confessing is something neither would have chosen to do prior to the start of the interrogation and something

---

[4] Here, "rational" refers to social psychologists' analysis of the decision maker. Unlike the economist's hypothetical, rational, fully informed decision maker, where the decision maker chooses among all the possible alternatives, the social psychologist notes which possible alternatives the decision maker considered. To be rational is to select the best of the alternatives under consideration. In a typical situation in which a suspect originally denies guilt, and then through the process of interrogation makes admissions, the decision to confess would likely be irrational in a social psychological sense, but not irrational in a clinical psychological sense. From the social psychological perspective, confessing leads to less desirable outcomes than not confessing, and is therefore not a rational choice. From the clinical psychological perspective, confessing is rational because it makes sense based on the person's perceptions and beliefs at the time he or she confesses (see Ofshe & Leo, 1997, p. 241). Interrogators' tactics are designed to get a clinical-psychologically rational person to make a social-psychologically irrational choice.

[5] Reprinted from *Studies in Law, Politics, and Society,* Vol. 16, by R. Ofshe and R. Leo, "The Social Psychology of Police Interrogation: The Theory and Classification of True and False Confessions," pages 189-251, Copyright © 1997, with permission from Elsevier.

each would have predicted he would have resisted to his last breath" (Ofshe & Leo, 1997, p. 194).

HOW INTERROGATORS
GET SUSPECTS TO CONFESS

This section tracks Ofshe and Leo (1997):

> Although contemporary interrogation methods are intended to produce true confessions from the guilty, they can, unfortunately, also produce false confessions from the innocent. Interrogations are, by design, relentless in their focus on moving the suspect to confess and are insensitive to denials or protestations of innocence. . . . The unanticipated and unappreciated fact about psychological methods of interrogation is that they are so influential that if allowed to go forward without restraint or if directed at the exceptionally vulnerable they will have devastating consequences. These methods produce false confessions because they convince innocent suspects that their situations are hopeless just as surely as they convince the guilty that they are caught. (pp. 194-195)

Accusatory interrogation proceeds systematically with one goal: to obtain a confession from whomever has been selected as a suspect. When there is solid evidence linking the suspect to the crime, the interrogator will use that evidence, often along with additional, fabricated evidence, during the interrogation stage when he or she is persuading the suspect that there is an airtight case. When solid evidence is lacking, the interrogator relies entirely on deception and interpersonal dominance to gain a confession. During this stage, innocent suspects may recognize the inaccuracies in the interrogator's claims, but denials are expected initially and are likely to fall on deaf ears.

Ofshe and Leo (1997) describe two phases of interrogation. First is the *pre-admission phase*, which is designed to alter the suspect's decision to deny responsibility and to elicit the statement, "I did it." The second phase is designed to elicit a *post-admission narrative* of the crime that proves the suspect's guilt. Consulting psychologists should note that "The voluntariness of a confession is determined by the tactics and incentives police use to shift the suspect from denial to admission. The truth of the suspect's admission ("I did it") is established by the accuracy of the information elicited during the post-admission narrative phase of interrogation" (Ofshe & Leo, 1997, p. 198).

Pre-Admission Phase

Ofshe and Leo (1997) identify three steps in the pre-admission phase. First is *the decision to allow questioning*. Next is *shifting the suspect from confident to despairing*. The third step in the pre-admission phase is *eliciting the confession*.

What influences the *decision to allow questioning*? Suspects do not have to talk to the police, but most do (Gudjonsson, 2003). "Both innocent and guilty suspects waive their rights because they perceive themselves as better off by permitting questioning to proceed than by terminating the process. . . . A guilty suspect may be thought of as engaging in a game with the interrogator in which each has as his goal manipulating and deceiving his opponent" (Ofshe & Leo, 1997, p. 199). The guilty suspect is motivated to mislead the interrogator, learn what evidence the police have against him or her, and try to convince the police that he or she is innocent.

The innocent suspect may perceive the Miranda warnings as an unimportant formality, and may believe that speaking to the police carries little risk. He or she may begin talking to help the police with their investigation,[6] and then continue to speak with the police in an attempt to clear up apparent misunderstandings.

"Neither the guilty nor the innocent suspect is likely to appreciate that the methods of accusatory interrogations are designed to initially encourage the belief that questioning is relatively risk free. The opening procedures are intended to allow the guilty suspect to entertain the idea that he can start the questioning, mislead the interrogator and emerge in a more secure position by having allowed police to question him. Refusal, he is likely to believe, would cause the investigator to single him out for more rigorous investigation" (Ofshe & Leo, 1997, p. 200).

Once the suspect has agreed to talk and the Miranda warnings have been completed, the next step of the pre-admission phase entails *shifting the suspect from confident to despairing*. Both innocent and guilty people are assumed to consent to police interrogation because they expect to emerge unscathed from the questioning. During the process, though, the interrogator systematically strives to convince the suspect that "all his future holds is arrest, trial, conviction, and punishment" (Ofshe & Leo, 1997, p. 200).

---

[6] Note that some police questioning is properly categorized as investigation. The concern here is with interrogation of suspects, where the goal is to elicit a confession from the person suspected of committing the crime.

The process is insidious. Using a nonthreatening guise of gathering information, the interrogator typically begins by obtaining background information, such as the suspect's relationship with the victim and an account of the suspect's actions at the time of the crime. After obtaining the suspect's baseline account, the interrogator shifts his or her style, pointing out contradictions and confronting the suspect with flaws in the story. A skilled interrogator "will carefully conserve his supply of real evidence, [initially] revealing only enough to make confrontation appear reasonable. The interrogator's strategy is to return to this storehouse of evidence to neutralize each objection in the long series of roadblocks he anticipates that the suspect will erect. The tactic of introducing something new in response to each objection helps create the impression that the interrogator's supply of information is endless" (Ofshe & Leo, 1997, p. 201).

When there is considerable evidence linking the suspect to the crime, the combination of actual, exaggerated, and fabricated evidence creates the impression of an airtight case. A guilty suspect recognizes the truth in some of the interrogator's claims and may accept the interrogator's bluffs, all of which are delivered with a practiced air of confidence and certainty.

What effect does the process have for an innocent suspect? Knowing he or she is innocent, the suspect is likely to react to erroneous or fabricated evidence by saying that a mistake has been made and offering reasons why the interrogator's reported evidence is wrong. Interrogators are trained to encourage explanations, because even a suspect's denials might help build the case. (Alibis may be proven false. Partial admissions, such as admitting to being at the scene after previously denying it, may be damning). "The interrogator will reject the innocent suspect's denial just as he would if it were made by a guilty suspect – by expressing great confidence in the reliability of the evidence, assuring the suspect that no mistake is possible, and perhaps emphasizing that the suspect's reaction is further evidence of his guilt (e.g., 'You know you did it, I can see it in the expression on your face')" (Ofshe & Leo, 1997, p. 201).

In the face of increasingly relentless interpersonal pressure, the suspect is pushed to account for the purported evidence. By training, the interrogator interrupts any denial or introduction of exculpatory evidence offered by the suspect (e.g., I wasn't there, I was at my brother's house), and insists that the suspect explain the "facts" (e.g., your fingerprints were on the gun). As the list of inculpatory "evidence" grows, wrongly accused suspects develop some theory of what is going on. Some guess that someone has set them up by planting evidence. Others opine that they are being railroaded by the police – that the police have deliberately decided to fake evidence to produce a false conviction. Both types of theory are based on the suspect's partial acceptance of the interrogator's version of the facts: that the evidence, though false, does exist.

Once innocent suspects begin to try to explain the purported "evidence," they fall into a tangled web. "Some innocent suspects report that they eventually give up trying to understand what is happening, accept that they will be unable to convince the interrogator of their innocence and decide to try to find a way to tell the interrogator what he demands to hear without admitting guilt – in other words, they try to explain away false inculpatory facts because the pressures of the interrogation have overwhelmed them. They continue to maintain their innocence, but defend themselves in terms of the interrogator's invented evidence. They find themselves trying to craft a story that offers an explanation for the fabricated evidence that does not involve them in a crime" (Ofshe & Leo, 1997, p. 241). For both innocent and guilty suspects, the dominant fact is the interrogator's message that the case is airtight and arrest is inevitable.

The third and final step in the pre-admission phase, *eliciting the admission*, occurs if and when the interrogator believes two things: The suspect is guilty, and the suspect knows he or she is caught. Timing is essential here. (Earlier, as the interrogation commenced, the interrogator couched the interaction in terms that suggested that the suspect was likely to survive the experience without being arrested. After the suspect gave a version of events, the interrogator pointed out discrepancies, asked for clarification, presented some combination of true, exaggerated, and fabricated "facts" for which the suspect should account, and increasingly attacked the suspect's explanations.) The interrogator watches for the perfect psychological moment. When the interrogator perceives that the suspect has reached a point of hopelessness, accepting that his or her future is certain and undesirable, it is time to shift the focus of the interrogation. Interrogators are taught to expect that when the suspect knows that he or she is guilty and is caught, and knows that the police can prove it, subjectively there is little to lose by admitting what is already obvious and known. At that point even a fairly minor incentive may be enough to tip the balance and bring about the decision to confess.

Again, the same psychological pressure that is designed to cause guilty suspects to give up hope can induce despair in innocent suspects, especially when the pressure is great and/or the suspect is vulnerable. For both innocent and guilty suspects, from the perspective of objective reality, there may be no advantage to confessing. In time, as the suspect becomes a defendant and is represented by an attorney, the attorney is likely to see a confession as a major obstacle to efforts toward a finding of innocence, a reduction in charges, or a more lenient sentence. At the crucial psychological moment created by the interrogator, though, it appears to the suspect that there is little or nothing to lose by confessing, and something to gain.

Interpersonally, there is the expectation that the pressure of interrogation will cease. Although the suspect has been advised that he or she does not have to talk to the police and can cease talking at any time, the process of interrogation is designed to create the expectation that the only way out of the mess is to cooperate with the police by talking things out until things are straightened out. Some suspects report that during interrogation they came to a point where their only wish was to go home, and they came to expect that the only way they could do so was to admit to the crime.

When a police interrogator perceives a suspect as being ready to crack, he or she offers reasons why an admission would be to the suspect's advantage. In choosing what to offer a given suspect, the interrogator relies on background knowledge of the suspect from pre-interrogation investigation, clues about the suspect from the interrogation itself, and experience and training about what has worked with other suspects in the past. At the same time, the interrogator must be mindful of what courts do and do not allow, lest a confession be suppressed. As a general rule, an interrogator who believes a suspect is guilty will use whatever techniques – at this point, whatever incentives – will both work and be allowed by the courts. Examples include reducing feelings of guilt; doing the right thing; showing empathy for the victim or the victim's family; maintaining the good will of the police; showing remorse to look good for the prosecutor, judge, or jury; or avoiding a harsh sentence such as a lengthy prison sentence or death.[7]

---

[7] Note that in plea bargaining, the prosecutor makes a blatant offer of reduced charges or leniency to get the defendant to plead guilty. In interrogation, the police are not allowed to make blatant offers, but they may be allowed to imply threats or promises of leniency.

As the interrogator shifts the focus from inducing despair to eliciting a confession, he or she may introduce one or more themes that allow the suspect to account for some of the "facts" without accepting much, if any, responsibility. "The shift to a principle focus on eliciting the admission . . . is sometimes signaled by an interrogator's announcement that he is no longer interested in wasting time debating whether or not the suspect committed the crime. He may summarize the evidence supporting his position yet again and say that, 'all I'm really interested in is why you did it,' or 'all I'm interested in knowing is whether you planned to do this or whether it was an accident' " (Ofshe & Leo, 1997, pp. 204, 206).

The latter statement is used to introduce the ever-popular accident technique:

> As the technique is used, the interrogator suggests a version of the facts that drastically lowers the charge appropriate for the confessed crime in comparison with the charge appropriate for the actual crime. . . . This technique elicits a decision to confess because it communicates the understanding that the suspect will receive a reduced level of punishment if he admits to the lesser crime. The accident technique lies at the heart of the Reid method of interrogation. Even Inbau, Reid, and Buckley (1986) grant both that the accident technique elicits a confession that everyone (interrogator and suspect, whether guilty or innocent) knows is a false confession and that the false confession is to a lesser crime. Inbau, Reid, and Buckley fail to explain to their readers that the technique works by means that are coercive. The suspect is motivated to act by a threat of harm (a more serious charge) or a desire for a benefit (a lesser or no criminal charge). The accident scenario theme functions to systematically persuade a suspect that the beneficial consequences of confessing outweigh the harmful consequences. (Ofshe & Leo, 1997, p. 206; some references omitted)

The issue of coercive techniques will be discussed in subsequent sections. For now, the reader should recognize that (a) some social scientists see some common interrogation techniques as being inherently coercive and (b) the same techniques that facilitate confessions from guilty suspects can contribute to false confessions from innocent suspects.

Post-Admission Narrative

Social scientists who have analyzed interrogations report that there are no reliable, observable differences between interrogations yielding true or false confessions until after the "I did it" statement (Gudjonsson, 2003; Leo & Ofshe, 1998; Ofshe & Leo, 1997). Therefore, police interrogation should never end at the point when the police believe the suspect has made admissions allowing him or her to be charged with the most serious offense possible. In the next phase, the *post-admission narrative*, interrogators elicit detailed descriptions of events. If the suspect provides accurate information showing special knowledge of the details of the crime, then the confession can be judged as reliable. If the suspect's post-admission narrative does not match the facts of the case, the reliability of the confession is in doubt.

Gudjonsson (2003, pp. 179-180) provides the following summary of Leo and Ofshe's (1997) analysis:

> There are at least three ways to determine the reliability of the confession:
>
> 1. Does the confession statement lead to the discovery of evidence that is unknown to the police (e.g., a location of a missing murder weapon, or stolen property)?
> 2. Does it include highly unusual features of the crime that have not been made public (e.g., special mutilation of the body, unusual method of killing or sexual act)?
> 3. Does the suspect provide accurate descriptions of the mundane crime scene detail, which have not been made public (e.g., the type of clothing the victim was wearing, presence of certain pieces of furniture at the crime scene)?
>
> If one or more of the three criteria are met then this lends support for the view that the confession is reliable. . . . [However,] special knowledge about a crime scene can be obtained and contaminated through a variety of sources, including the following:
>
> 1. The media.
> 2. The police.
> 3. Crime scene visits.
> 4. Crime scene material, such as photographs.
> 5. A third party (i.e., being told about it by the real perpetrator).

... Once the police are in possession of that special knowledge, the possibility of it being communicated to the suspect during custodial confinement and interrogation may be difficult to rule out. Audio or video recording of all interrogations can be important to rule out such contamination, although even this procedure may not be foolproof.

Every police interrogator in every case should obtain a detailed post-admission narrative. Immediate analysis of the post-admission narrative and follow-up investigation of details can guide the police in deciding whether to focus their investigation on this suspect or to keep looking for the truly guilty party. If the suspect is charged, preservation of the post-admission narrative facilitates fair prosecution and defense of the case. Therefore, the post-admission narrative should always be video- or audio-recorded.

SOME PROVOCATIVE
LABORATORY RESEARCH

Communicating Threats and Promises Indirectly

Saul Kassin and his colleagues have analyzed what goes on in police interrogations and have conducted some laboratory experiments to test the impact of certain interrogation techniques. Some of their work is summarized in a pair of articles in the *American Psychologist* (Kassin, 1997, 1998). Kassin (1997, p. 221) summarizes the findings this way:

a) The police routinely use deception, trickery, and psychologically coercive methods of interrogation.
b) These methods may, at times, cause innocent people to confess to crimes they did not commit.
c) When coerced self-incriminating statements are presented in the courtroom, juries do not sufficiently discount the evidence in reaching a verdict.

Recall (from page 13) that police use the techniques of maximization and minimization to manipulate suspects during interrogations. Police use *maximization* techniques to intimidate a suspect by overstating the seriousness of the offense and the magnitude of the charges and/or by making false or exaggerated claims about the evidence. They use *minimization* techniques to lull the suspect into a false sense of security by offering excuses, justifications, sympathy, and tolerance; by blaming the victim or someone else; and/or by underplaying the seriousness or magnitude of the charges (Kassin, 1997; Kassin & McNall, 1991). Kassin (1997) cites research showing that these techniques are used routinely by police and that courts generally do not exclude confessions elicited via these techniques as long as the police do not use overt threats or promises.

Kassin and McNall (1991) conducted a laboratory study to test whether imbedded or implied threats or promises were functionally equivalent to blatant ones. They used variations of a transcript of an actual interrogation in which the detective made an explicit promise of leniency, threatened the suspect with a harsh sentence, used minimization by blaming the victim, used maximization by claiming to have found fingerprints, or used none of the above. Kassin (1997, p. 224) summarizes the key results: "(a) The use of maximization raised sentencing expectations, leading participants to expect a harsh sentence, as in the explicit threat group, and (b) minimization lowered sentencing expectations, which led participants to anticipate leniency, as in the explicit promise group."

Such research supports the understanding that police routinely circumvent the law, without drawing judicial ire, by using psychologically sophisticated techniques that have similar effects to direct threats or promises. Another study by Kassin and McNall (1991) shows how mock juries may discount a confession if they know that an explicit threat of punishment was used to elicit it, but may not similarly discount a confession obtained via promises or minimization. Thus, subtle interrogation techniques are more likely to pass judicial muster and are less likely to raise jurors' concerns about a false confession, while being functionally equivalent to techniques that are blatantly illegal. The wily techniques that police routinely employ to surreptitiously communicate threats and promises have been aptly described as a confidence game (Leo, 1996b).

In reviewing the preceding research, Gudjonsson (2003, p. 21) concludes: "The experiments of Kassin and McNall are important because they show that the techniques advocated by Inbau and his colleagues [e.g., Inbau et al., 2001] are inherently coercive in that they communicate implicit threats and promises to suspects. Taken as a whole, these experiments raise serious concerns about the use of 'maximization' and 'minimization' as methods of interrogation and the confessions they produce should be used cautiously as evidence in court."

Eliciting False Confessions in the Laboratory

Could experimenters use common police interrogation techniques to get subjects to confess to a "crime" they did not commit, believe that they actually did commit the "crime," and confabulate (make up) details consistent with that belief? Research by Kassin and Kiechel (1996; summarized in Kassin, 1997) suggests that the answer to all three questions is yes.

The crucial technique used was *false incriminating evidence.* Seventy-five college students participated in a study that ostensibly assessed reaction time. They typed letters read to them – at either a slow or a fast pace (43 or 67 letters per minute) – after being warned not to hit the ALT key near the space bar lest the computer malfunction.[8] Although all the students were actually innocent, in each case the computer supposedly crashed after 60 seconds and a frantic experimenter accused the participant of hitting the ALT key. All participants initially denied guilt. For half of the participants, a confederate (actually one of the researchers, posing as another student participant) said that she saw the participant hit the hidden key. To elicit compliance, the experimenter wrote out a standardized confession and encouraged the participant to sign it. To check for internalization of belief, participants were approached outside the original room by a second confederate who asked what the commotion was about. Some participants accepted blame (e.g., "I hit a key I wasn't supposed to and ruined the program"). Finally, the experimenter brought the participants back into the original room and asked if they could reconstruct how and when they hit the ALT key.

The results are intriguing.

> Overall, 69% of the participants signed the confession, 28% internalized guilt, and 9% confabulated details to support their false beliefs. More important, however, was the joint effect of the two independent variables. In the slow pace – no witness group, 35% of participants signed the note, but not a single one exhibited internalization or confabulated a memory. Yet, out of 17 participants

---

[8] Presenting the letters at different speeds provided a way of distinguishing the participants' vulnerability by affecting their level of certainty regarding their own actions.

in the fast pace – witness group, all signed the confession, 65% came to believe they were guilty, and 35% confabulated details to fit the newly created belief. The results of this study support the provocative hypothesis that people can be induced to internalize guilt for an outcome they did not produce and that the risk is increased by the presentation of false evidence – a trick often used by the police and sanctioned by the U.S. Supreme Court (e.g., *Frazier v. Cupp*, 1969). (Kassin, 1997, pp. 227-228)

— 3 —

THE CONSEQUENCES OF
POLICE-INDUCED
FALSE CONFESSIONS

TYPES OF CONFESSIONS

Kassin and Wrightsman

Social scientists have found it useful to distinguish between different types of false confessions. Kassin and Wrightsman (1985) categorize three types of false confessions: voluntary, coerced-compliant, and coerced-internalized. They define *voluntary false confessions* as "those purposely offered in the absence of elicitation" (Wrightsman & Kassin, 1993, p. 86). As an example, they mention the famous Lindbergh baby kidnapping, to which more than 200 people confessed. They offer several reasons why people sometimes voluntarily go to the police and confess to crimes they did not commit.

Wrightsman and Kassin (1993, p. 88, citation omitted) contrast voluntary false confessions with two types of coerced confessions, coerced-compliant and coerced-internalized:

> Psychologists have long recognized the importance of two conceptually different responses to social control attempts: compliance and internalization. Compliance is an overt, public acquiescence to a social influence attempt in order to achieve some immediate instrumental gain, whereas internalization is a personal acceptance of the values or beliefs espoused in that attempt.

When making a *coerced-compliant false confession*, "the suspect publicly professes guilt in response to extreme methods of interrogation, despite knowing privately that he or she is truly innocent" (Wrightsman & Kassin, 1993, pp. 88-89). A *coerced-internalized false confession* is made "when the suspect – through the fatigue, pressures, and suggestiveness of the interrogation process – actually comes to believe that he or she committed the offense (Wrightsman & Kassin, 1993, p. 92).

Ofshe and Leo

Ofshe and Leo (1997) acknowledge that Kassin and Wrightsman's classification scheme provided a useful framework for studying false confessions, generated a series of research questions, and was relied upon by scholars. In response to research, Ofshe and Leo came to consider Kassin and Wrightsman's classification scheme as being inadequate in some ways and as being based, in part, on erroneous assumptions. They note three weaknesses in the Kassin-and-Wrightsman scheme:

> First, it presents a different explanation for true and false confessions when both are driven by the same underlying logic and arise from interrogations that are to a considerable degree similar. Second, their classification scheme fails to encompass the entire range of police-induced false confessions that are not coerced. . . . Third, their classification scheme misapplies the concept of internalization to the phenomenon of false confessions. (Ofshe & Leo, 1997, p. 209)

Ofshe and Leo (1997, p. 209) continue:

> Internalized values and beliefs, as Kassin and Wrightsman correctly note, . . . persist over time and across a variety of situations. No reported [false-confession] case nor any case known to these authors has produced this type of relatively stable belief. . . . The case literature suggests that police-induced belief change during interrogation is temporary, inherently unstable, and situationally adaptive; it has never been observed to endure long after the influences and pressures of interrogation have been withdrawn. Individuals who falsely confess because they come to believe that they committed the crime do not demonstrate internalization of a belief in their guilt in any meaningful way. Rather, they confess falsely because they have been *temporarily persuaded* by the tactics of the interrogation to accept responsibility for a crime they have no actual knowledge of having committed. The

> person who has been persuaded to falsely confess is, at the moment of confession, only more certain than not that he committed the crime. . . . His inability to retrieve actual memories of the crime explains his inability to achieve complete certainty of his guilt. The tactic of claiming overwhelming evidence of culpability prevents him from remaining certain of his innocence. (emphasis in original)

Ofshe and Leo (1997, p. 210) present a classification scheme of five different types of confessions that they consider "useful for classifying and explaining the decision to make a true or false statement in response to interrogation." In addition to voluntary confessions, they distinguish two types of compliant confessions – stress-compliant and coerced-compliant – and two types of persuaded (replacing internalized) confessions – non-coerced-persuaded and coerced-persuaded.

Ofshe and Leo (1997, p. 241) note that a person may choose to confess in order to escape the aversive experience of interrogation, even in the absence of "classical forms of coercion (e.g., threats and promises)." In contrast, a coerced-compliant confession is defined as "a statement elicited by the use of classically coercive interrogation techniques, and is given knowingly in order to receive leniency or escape the harshest possible punishment. Coerced-compliant confessions thus differ from stress-compliant confessions in two fundamental ways. First, they are caused by the classically coercive influence techniques (e.g., threats and promises). Second, they are the result of the suspect's *conscious* decision to gain a benefit or to avoid an anticipated harsh punishment" (Ofshe & Leo, 1997, p. 214).

A voluntary confession, a stress-compliant confession, and a coerced-compliant confession can each be either true or false. In other words, similar social and psychological factors might cause either an innocent or a guilty person to voluntarily confess, to confess in order to escape a stressful situation, or to confess in response to threats or promises. As Ofshe and Leo define persuaded confessions, all persuaded confessions are false.

Ofshe and Leo (1997, p. 215) write:

> When a suspect confesses because he comes to believe that he is probably guilty of the offense, the necessary underlying social psychological process is persuasion. Persuaded belief change that is generated by interrogation does not necessarily persist over time or across situations; rather, it is temporary, unstable, situationally

adaptive and endures only as long as the suspect accepts the interrogator's definition of the situation. As soon as the suspect successfully challenges the interrogator's framing of reality and critically analyzes the facts on which his new position rests, the persuasive effects of interrogation are likely to disappear. There are two types of persuaded confessions: those produced solely through manipulation and those in which classical coercion plays a significant role as well. As the term is defined, a non-coerced-persuaded confession is elicited in response to the influence tactics and techniques of modern, psychologically sophisticated accusatorial interrogation, and given by a suspect who has temporarily come to believe that it is more likely than not that he committed the offense despite no memory of having done so.

Ofshe and Leo (1997, p. 219) write that coerced-persuaded confessions "follow the same structure, sequence, and logic as non-coerced-persuaded confessions. The only difference is that whereas the latter are elicited solely in response to the influence tactics of accusatorial interrogation, an interrogation that produces a coerced-persuaded false confession also incorporates threat, promise, or other classically coercive interrogation techniques."

Gudjonsson

Gudjonsson (2003) finds pros and cons to both the Kassin-and-Wrightsman and the Ofshe-and-Leo classification schemes. In Gudjonsson's (2003, p. 211) classification scheme, he replaces the word "coerced" with "pressured." He lists voluntary, pressured-internalized, and pressured-compliant false confessions. Gudjonsson's classification scheme also includes the source of pressure that led to the false confession. For voluntary confessions, the source of pressure is always "internal." For the two types of pressured confessions, the source of pressure could be "custodial" or "noncustodial."

Custodial pressure implies being interrogated by the police. Other governmental agencies also have powers of arrest and detention and interrogate people, including customs and immigration officials and the security services. Non-custodial pressure includes persons other than the police pressuring or coercing a confession from an innocent person (e.g., a peer, a spouse, a cellmate in prison, and undercover police officers). (Gudjonsson, 2003, p. 212)

Me, Too

Any of the three classification schemes described previously can be useful for classifying confessions that are known to be true or false and for which the underlying psychological motivation has been identified. Kassin and Wrightsman's classification scheme has been in existence longer and is perhaps more widely known at this point, but the more recent schemes were both developed on the basis of perceived deficiencies in the original scheme. At present, I recommend that psychologists who consult on confession cases be familiar with all three models.

Now imagine that you are on the witness stand and you are testifying about a statement made by a defendant who is the subject of the legal proceeding and whose guilt or innocence has not been established. Which of these schemes, if any, would you use? If you were to say that the statement is a coerced-compliant false confession (*a la* Kassin and Wrightsman), you would likely be considered to be usurping the roles of the judge and jury by declaring that the police had acted improperly, the defendant's will had been overborne, and the defendant was not guilty of the crime. If you were to say that the statement is a voluntary-unreliable[1] confession (*a la* Ofshe and Leo), you would be declaring that the police had not acted improperly, the defendant's will was not overborne, and the defendant is not guilty. If you were to say that the statement is a pressured-compliant custodial false confession (*a la* Gudjonsson), you would be saying that the defendant was in police custody (therefore Miranda warnings were required), the defendant confessed because of pressure applied by the police, and he or she is not guilty. Courts do not look to expert witnesses – or any witnesses – to make such statements. Those issues are decided by the judge and the jury.

Are there meaningful distinctions between different types of confessions that do not incorporate legal conclusions (guilty or not guilty, coerced or voluntary, custodial or noncustodial, etc.)? If so, then psychologists who testify in confession cases should welcome a classification scheme that does not incorporate legal conclusions. I propose a simple scheme that recognizes three distinct types of confessions: self-initiated, first-response, and police-induced.

---

[1] Ofshe and Leo (1997, p. 210) equate "reliable" with "true" and they equate "unreliable" with "false."

Self-initiated confessions occur when a person initiates contact with a law enforcement officer or other person in authority and declares that he or she is guilty of a crime. There is no police pressure. An example is the case of *Colorado v. Connelly* (1986), which is discussed in Chapter 6. I prefer "self-initiated" rather than "voluntary" as a label for these types of confessions because it introduces fewer legal connotations.[2]

First-response confessions occur when the police approach a person and initiate questioning, and the person's first response is "I did it."

Police-induced confessions occur when the police approach a person and initiate questioning, the person's first response is something other than "I did it" (e.g., "I didn't do it"), the police engage in further conversation with the person, and the person subsequently says, "I did it."

By design, this classification scheme avoids legally charged words, and it is not necessary to delve into the minds of the confessor or the police in order to classify a confession. Nevertheless, the scheme provides nontrivial distinctions that aid in considering the reliability of a confession, as well as whether it was given voluntarily. This classification scheme should be useful for psychologists testifying in court.

THE CONSEQUENCES OF
POLICE-INDUCED FALSE CONFESSIONS

In the 1966 *Miranda* decision, the U.S. Supreme Court referred to a confession as "the most compelling possible evidence of guilt" (p. 466). In the 1986 decision in *Colorado v. Connelly*, the Court wrote: "Triers of fact accord confessions such heavy weight in their determinations that 'the introduction of a confession makes the other aspects of a trial in court superfluous, and the real trial, for all practical purposes, occurs when the confession is obtained' " (p. 182). Note that these statements were made prior to the use of DNA fingerprinting. What does research show about the impact of a confession?

There are three ways that researchers have considered how important a confession is to the outcome of a case. The first, summarized by Gudjonsson (2003) simply looks at how important confessions were to

---

[2] Also, at least theoretically a self-initiated confession might not be fully voluntary in a psychological sense if the confessor were responding to a threat from the true perpetrator. ("If you don't confess to this crime and take the rap, I'll shoot your dog.")

a group of cases. The second, exemplified by Kassin and Neumann (1997), uses experimental methods in mock juries. The third, utilized by Leo and Ofshe (1998, 2001), looks specifically at known cases of false confessions and considers how important the confession was to the outcome of those cases.

Gudjonsson (2003) notes that the importance of a confession in a given case depends in part on the strength of the other evidence for or against the suspect. He summarizes research that shows confessions provided the single most important evidence against the suspect, were crucial to the prosecution in about 30% of the cases (Baldwin & McConville, 1980), and were the sole real prosecution evidence in about 8% of the cases (McConville, 1993). Wald et al. (1967) found confession evidence necessary in about 17% of the cases. This type of analysis is useful if one wants to imagine the potential impact of creating laws that would further restrict police officers' efforts to extract confessions from suspects.

Kassin and Neumann (1997) conducted a series of experiments to test the majority view in *Arizona v. Fulminante* (1991) that confessions should, in some cases, be considered harmless error, even though "a defendant's confession is like no other evidence. It is probably the most probative and damaging evidence that can be admitted against him, and, if it is a full confession, a jury may be tempted to rely on it alone in reaching its decision" (p. 280). Kassin and Neumann (1997) write, "Taken together, our findings demonstrate that confession evidence has a greater impact *on* jurors – and is seen as having a greater impact *by* jurors – than other potent types of evidence" (p. 481, italics in original). Their findings support widespread beliefs that confessions are "uniquely potent" (p. 482) and "devastating to the defendant" (p. 481). This is in line with the U.S. Supreme Court's majority in *Chapman v. California* (1967) that the erroneous admission of a coerced confession should never be treated as harmless, and with the minority in *Fulminante*, that coerced confessions are fundamentally different from other types of erroneously admitted evidence. The findings conflict with the *Fulminante* majority finding, that an erroneously admitted confession may, in principle, constitute harmless error.

Leo and Ofshe (1998, 2001), using a quite different research approach, reach findings that are comparable to those of Kassin and Neumann (1997). Leo and Ofshe desired to estimate how much influence a true or false confession exerts on investigators, prosecutors, and judges. Their research had two specific goals:

(1) To examine the fate in the criminal justice system of a group of persons who had in common only that police interrogators coerced from them false confessions to major felonies (typically murder); and

(2) To extend one component of Bedau and Radelet's study of miscarriages of justice forward into the era of psychological interrogation by documenting 60 cases of police-induced false confession in the last third of the twentieth century. . . .

The research design sought to identify essentially pure false confession cases so that we could assess whether the knowledge that a suspect had given an utterly uncorroborated confession could overcome even strong affirmative evidence of innocence and lead to the conclusion that the defendant was guilty. (Leo & Ofshe, 2001, pp. 198, 200)

Their research "empirically demonstrated that false confessions have a substantial prejudicial effect on a defendant at every stage in the process from arrest to imprisonment to execution" (p. 201).

Similarly, Leo (1996a) found that

suspects who incriminated themselves during interrogation were 20% more likely to be charged by prosecutors, 24% less likely to have their case dismissed, 25% more likely to have their cases resolved by plea bargaining, and 26% more likely to be found guilty and convicted. In addition, those who had confessed received heavier sentences following conviction. (quoted from Gudjonsson, 2003, p. 133)

Recall that the importance of a confession in a given case depends in part on the strength of the other evidence for or against the suspect. While the proportion of cases in which a confession is crucial appears to be below 50%, *in those cases involving a false confession and a false conviction, the confession is typically crucial to the outcome of the case.* With hindsight, we know that the subject is innocent, so it is not surprising that in such cases

no physical or other significant and credible evidence indicated the suspect's guilt; the state's evidence consisted of little or nothing more than the suspect's statement "I did it"; and the suspect's factual innocence was supported by a variable amount of evidence – often substantial and compelling – including exculpatory evidence from the suspect's post-admission narrative of the crime. (Leo & Ofshe, 2001, p. 300)

Of course, investigators, prosecutors, judges, and juries proceed without hindsight. Each step of the way, their consideration of other case evidence is colored by knowledge that the suspect said "I did it." A suspect's confession trumps all other evidence: "To obtain a written confession from a suspect is tantamount to securing his conviction in court" (Baldwin & McConville, 1980, p. 19). This held true in the cases analyzed by Leo and Ofshe (2001, p. 300) even though "Fairly analyzed, the defendant's confession constituted evidence of innocence rather than guilt."

As we will soon see, fair analysis of confession evidence is a recommended safeguard for decreasing the frequency of wrongful convictions.

— 4 —

POLICY RECOMMENDATIONS FOR POLICE-INDUCED FALSE CONFESSIONS

As we have seen in previous chapters, the same techniques that police use to elicit confessions from guilty subjects can and do lead some innocent subjects to confess. Once a subject has confessed, his or her admission overshadows any evidence pointing toward innocence, even when the confession itself (in particular, the post-admission narrative) points to his or her innocence. Ofshe and Leo (1997, p. 238) therefore recommend "three procedural safeguards . . . to protect innocent defendants against the admission of false confession evidence into trial proceedings and the subsequent likelihood of wrongful conviction":

1. Courts should adopt mandatory tape recording requirements in felony cases.
2. The admissibility of confession evidence should be allowed only when the accused subject's guilt is corroborated by independent evidence.
3. All confessions should meet a reasonable standard of reliability before being admitted.

 Courts should adopt mandatory tape recording requirements in felony cases.

I agree that this is necessary. Expert law enforcement officers recognize that interrogators can inadvertently contaminate confessions by asking questions that contain crime scene data and investigative results (Napier & Adams, 2002). Unless the entire interrogation is audio- or video-recorded, it is impossible to know which details, if any, were imbedded in the interrogators' questions.

In a recent case on which I consulted, for example, the suspect's confession contained numerous details that would presumably only be known by someone knowledgeable of the crime scene (e.g., the perpetrator). Careful analysis of the videotaped interrogation revealed that all of the correct details of the crime that were mentioned by the suspect had been previously provided to the suspect during the course of the interrogation. There was no reason to believe that the interrogators were intentionally planting crime details in the suspect's mind, but without the videotape of the interrogation it might have appeared improbable that so many details were conveyed in the course of the interrogation.

Inbau et al. (2001) note that videotaping the entire interrogation can benefit the prosecution by showing that no illegal coercive tactics were used and that the confession was not contaminated. They consider the possibility of "wider sweeping court rulings or standards that could eventually require the videotaping of the entire interrogation along with the subsequent confession for each and every suspect interrogated. In the final analysis, would this be good for the criminal justice system?" (p. 396). Although their question may have been posed rhetorically, Gudjonsson (2003, p. 22) replies: "My answer is definitely yes. The electronic recording of all police interviews and interrogations would be in the interests of justice, and it will come. . . . There is no doubt that tape-recording, or video-recording, of police interviews protects the police against false allegations as well as protecting the suspect against police impropriety."

Gudjonsson (2003) writes that laws implementing mandatory recording of statements were implemented in England and Wales beginning in 1986, and since 1991 there has been mandatory tape-recording of interviews of persons suspected of indictable offenses. He cites studies (see pp. 22-24) showing that tape-recording does not interfere unduly with standard interrogation practices. "The use of electronic recording of interrogations, whether audio or video recorded, is one of the best protections against wrongful convictions. However, it is not foolproof" (p. 23). Gudjonsson specifically derides the common American practice of only making an electronic recording of the part of the interrogation that favors the prosecution (i.e., after the suspect has been broken down to confess and provides a post-confession statement). The danger here is that the recording will not give the whole picture of the interrogation process and may seriously mislead the court. It is essential that all interviews are properly recorded so that the court will have the best record possible of what took place during the interrogation. . . . Indeed, without a complete record, allegations of police impropriety (e.g., threats, inducements, feeding suspects with pertinent case details) are difficult to prove or disprove. (pp. 23-24)

Ofshe and Leo (1997) note that electronic recording of certain interrogations is mandatory in Alaska (*Stephan v. State,* 1985) and Minnesota (*State v. Scales,* 1994). This is standard policy for some law enforcement agencies, including Broward County, Florida,[1] and is being considered by other states and municipalities, including Illinois and Chicago.[2] Meanwhile, developing research addresses how to avoid bias in videotaping interrogations, including the need to focus the camera on both the suspect and the interrogator equally (Lassiter & Geers, 2004).

In summary, I am convinced that police officers should be required to electronically record entire interrogations because:

1. The same techniques that police use to elicit confessions from guilty suspects can cause some innocent people to confess some times.
2. It is very likely that police do not intend to create false confessions, nor do they recognize when they do so.
3. There is no scientific, objective, reliable way of distinguishing between true and false confessions, up to and including the point of "I did it."
4. Careful analysis can often distinguish between true and false confessions via a properly conducted post-admission narrative. For example, a guilty subject can give accurate details that would only be known by people who had intimate knowledge of the crime scene (e.g., by perpetrating the crime). (Of course, the ultimate question about the truth is the province of the trier of fact – the judge or jury.)

---

[1] Judy Couwels, personal communication, June 7, 2003.
[2] James E. Rollins, personal communication, June 11, 2003.

5. In the process of interrogation, police officers typically confront the suspect with a combination of true and fabricated evidence, building the impression that the suspect is caught and there is nothing to be lost by confessing.
6. Just by human nature, people, including the police, do not accurately recall the form and content of their own questions, focusing instead on the other person's answers.
7. Police interrogators contaminate the confession to varying degrees as they provide details of the crime to the suspect.
8. Only by recording the entire interrogation is it possible to show whether the suspect is providing details that come from guilty knowledge or is merely spitting back what was fed to him or her along the way.

As Gudjonsson (2003) notes, even when a recorded interrogation shows that the suspect described details of the crime that were not provided to him or her by the police, that does not guarantee that the confession is reliable. The suspect could have gotten details from nonpolice sources such as the media, or by being told about it by the true perpetrator.

Requiring that interrogations be recorded is not to imply that police are liars or cheats. It has been clearly shown (e.g., by DNA evidence) that some people falsely confess some times, and it appears that when this occurs in the context of police interrogation, it is often because the police are just trying to do their jobs (not "railroading"). The best reason for requiring that interrogations be recorded, in my opinion, is so that one can see whether the post-admission narrative includes details that were never supplied by the police to the suspect.

 The admissibility of confession evidence should be allowed only when the accused subject's guilt is corroborated by independent evidence.

Ofshe and Leo (1997, p. 239) argue that this is necessary because

Research demonstrates that police interrogators all too frequently come to believe that a suspect is providing them with key details of the crime that only the perpetrator could know when, in fact, an innocent suspect is merely regurgitating information that police fed to him in the first place, inferring what the interrogators suggested through leading questions, or making guesses that will later be proven wrong.

They write that a true confession that is taken properly will include information that confirms the confession's trustworthiness and leads to new corroborating evidence, but a false confession will not. They recommend that police officers should be trained to seek clear-cut corroboration for every confession, and to consider a suspect's failure to provide accurate, corroborating details as a red flag that he or she may be innocent.

In describing the need for this procedural safeguard, Ofshe and Leo (1997, p. 239) write:

> Police will not be in a position to be self-monitoring and self-critical until they are given adequate training about how and why interrogation works. Only awareness that false confessions happen and reliance on objective standards for evaluating a confession statement will allow police to stop themselves from making the all too frequent mistake of arresting an innocent suspect.

Of the three procedural safeguards recommended by Ofshe and Leo, this is the one that has caused me some concern. What if a guilty person confessed to a crime and was willing to provide corroborating details, but it was impossible to do so because there was no evidence to confirm or disconfirm his or her guilt, or even that a crime had been committed? I imagine that this would be a rare, but not impossible, event. Let us look at how courts have considered cases where (a) there is no corroborating evidence that a crime has been committed, or (b) there is evidence that a crime was committed, but there is no evidence to corroborate the person's confession that he or she is the guilty party.

If a person confesses to a crime, but there is no other evidence that the crime has been committed, courts generally do not allow the person to be prosecuted or convicted. An example comes from *Gonzalez v. State* (1998, p. 412, citations omitted):

> A defendant's extrajudicial confession alone is not sufficient to support a conviction. There must be other evidence independent of the confession that tends to prove the *corpus delicti.* The independent evidence of the *corpus delicti* does not need to connect the defendant

to the crime, be sufficient by itself to prove the crime nor be a great quantum of evidence; it only needs to be some evidence which renders the *corpus delicti* more probable than it would be without the evidence.

Note that this Texas rule allows for a person to be convicted if there is independent evidence suggesting that the crime was committed, even if there is no evidence – other than his or her confession – connecting the person to the crime for which he or she is confessing. Presumably, a rule such as this would have allowed prosecution and conviction of any of the 200 people who confessed to kidnapping the Lindbergh baby (Wrightsman & Kassin, 1993).

In *Smith v. United States* (1954, pp. 153-154, citations omitted),[3] the U.S. Supreme Court briefly traced the history of the rule requiring corroboration, then considered whether it should apply to *Smith,* a case involving alleged tax evasion:

> The corroboration rule, at its inception, served an extremely limited function. In order to convict of serious crimes of violence, then capital offenses, independent proof was required that someone had indeed inflicted the violence, the so-called *corpus delicti.* Once the existence of the crime was established, however, the guilt of the accused could be based on his own otherwise uncorroborated confession. But in a crime such as tax evasion there is no tangible injury which can be isolated as a *corpus delicti.* As to this crime, it cannot be shown that the crime has been committed without identifying the accused. Thus we are faced with the choice either of applying the corroboration rule to this offense and according the accused even greater protection than the rule affords to a defendant in a homicide prosecution, or of finding the rule wholly inapplicable because of the nature of the offense, stripping the accused of this guarantee altogether. We choose to apply the rule, with its broader guarantee, to crimes in which there is no tangible *corpus delicti,* where the corroborative evidence must implicate the accused in order to show that a crime has been committed.

Thus courts currently require some corroboration that a crime occurred, even when that necessarily entails corroboration that the confessing person committed the crime. Ofshe and Leo's (1997)

---

[3] This case is discussed further in Chapter 6. See also the following cases, also discussed in Chapter 6: *Opper v. United States* (1954); *Wong Sun v. United States* (1963).

recommendation would take the rule one step further, to require in all cases corroboration that the confessing person committed the crime. I believe that this is not too onerous a requirement, especially when one considers how much – or indeed how little – independent evidence is needed. The U.S. Supreme Court addressed "the quantum of corroboration necessary to substantiate the existence of the crime charged" in the same case just cited:

> It is agreed that the corroborative evidence does not have to prove the offense beyond a reasonable doubt, or even by a preponderance, as long as there is substantial independent evidence that the offense has been committed, and the evidence as a whole proves beyond a reasonable doubt that defendant is guilty. . . . All elements of the offense must be established by independent evidence or corroborated admissions, but one available mode of corroboration is for the independent evidence to bolster the confession itself and thereby prove the offense through the statements of the accused. (*Smith v. United States,* p. 156, citations omitted)

I assume that if Ofshe and Leo's recommended procedural safeguard, to require corroboration of the subject's guilt by independent evidence, were to be implemented, the required amount of independent evidence pointing to the subject's guilt would be no greater than the amount of independent evidence currently required to prove that a crime had been committed. Simply put, there would have to be *something* other than the person's confession that tied him or her to the crime. Although there might be rare cases for which that would be impossible, I concur with Ofshe and Leo that the risk of convicting an innocent person on the basis of a false confession is significant enough to counterbalance that risk, and I support this recommendation.

 All confessions should meet a reasonable standard of reliability before being admitted.

I concur with this third and final recommended safeguard, at least as I interpret it. Ofshe and Leo (1997, p. 239) write:

> The decision to admit a confession should be based not only on voluntariness but also on the fit between a defendant's post-admission narrative and the facts of the crime. A confession that cannot withstand

objective evaluation and reach a minimum standard of accuracy should be excluded because its prejudicial impact greatly outweighs its probative value.

As I read this recommendation, a judge would rule on a case-by-case basis whether a defendant's confession was sufficiently reliable that it should be allowed to be presented to a jury.

One way to indicate that the confession is reliable is to show that the entire interrogation was recorded and the defendant made admissions that included details that were not provided to him or her by the police. I agree with Ofshe and Leo that this may be the best way to show that a confession is reliable.

 Summary.

I recommend that all three of Ofshe and Leo's policy recommendations be implemented, which would require recording of the entire interrogation. When the defense challenges the reliability of a confession at a suppression hearing, the state would be required to make the recorded interrogation available and would be required to show something more than the defendant's "I did it" statement. The judge would decide on a case-by-case basis whether the confession is sufficiently reliable to be considered by the jury.

This chapter, a brief excursion into legal reform, has focused on recommended policy changes to reduce the number of miscarriages of justice via false confession. Why this excursion? The Preamble to the current Ethical Principles of Psychologists and Code of Conduct (American Psychological Association, 2002, p. 1062) includes:

> Psychologists are committed to increasing scientific and professional knowledge of behavior and people's understanding of themselves and others and to the use of such knowledge to improve the condition of individuals, organizations, and society. Psychologists respect and protect civil and human rights and the central importance of freedom of inquiry and expression in research, teaching, and publication. They strive to help the public in developing informed judgments and choices concerning human behavior. In doing so, they perform many roles, such as researcher, educator, diagnostician, therapist, supervisor, consultant, administrator, social interventionist, and expert witness.

In this chapter I have played the role of social interventionist. In reading about false confessions, I have formed opinions (largely guided by Ofshe and Leo) about how social policies could be improved, and I have stated my opinions. While social interventionist is a useful role, consistent with psychologists' ethical principles, it is essential that psychologists recognize that this role is incompatible with the roles of consultant, diagnostician, and expert witness. Woe be unto the consulting psychologist who attempts to use the witness stand as a soapbox for exhorting to the court about how social policies should be changed. It wouldn't be prudent.

— PART II —

FOUNDATION

Practicing forensic psychologists can assist the courts by applying a model that attempts to "reflect, not reform" the law relevant to interrogations and confessions (Grisso, 2003, p. 20). That is the subject of the next three chapters of this book. First, Chapter 5 presents a model for forensic psychological assessment and consultation. Next, Chapter 6 summarizes the legal context for psychological assessment and consultation in this area. Then Chapter 7 identifies the legally relevant forensic assessment issues.

— 5 —

A MODEL FOR FORENSIC PSYCHOLOGICAL ASSESSMENT/CONSULTATION

Grisso's (1986, 2003) model is the standard for psychological assessment of legal competencies. The model is briefly presented here as a review. Readers thoroughly familiar with the model may prefer to skim this chapter. Readers new to the model are advised to also read Chapters 1, 2, 3, and 5 in Grisso (2003).[1]

In developing a conceptual model to guide the development and implementation of methods for assessing legal competencies, Grisso (2003, p. 2) identified commonalities across different legal competencies:

- Legal competencies are concerned with the rights of individuals to make decisions and control their own lives.
- Some individuals may not have the capacities to make important decisions in their lives. Their incapacities could jeopardize their welfare or that of others who would be influenced by their decisions.
- Legal concepts of competence provide a legal mechanism for identifying people for whom the relevant incapacities may exist.
- Government intervention may be allowed, obligated, or justified when legal incompetence is determined. That intervention may be needed to protect the welfare of the person declared

---

[1] The other chapters are also recommended, but not for the purpose of this book.

incompetent, which may curtail the person's rights in an attempt to promote the best interests of the person and/or society.

Grisso (2003, p. 23) described a common structure across legal competencies, with five components: (a) functional, (b) causal, (c) interactive, (d) judgmental, and (e) dispositional. We will continue to follow Grisso (2003) as we explore these components.

FUNCTIONAL COMPONENT

Legal competencies are concerned with a person's functional abilities, behaviors, or capacities: what the person understands, knows, believes, or can do that is directly related to the competence construct. This is distinct from psychodiagnosis. The examiner should perform the assessment in such a way that he or she will be prepared for a question such as this one:

> We understand that the defendant is schizophrenic and has severe delusions, Doctor. But that is not entirely the point. What can he do and what is he not able to do that is relevant to the question before this court? (Grisso, 2003, p. 25)

The assessment should link observed symptoms to the actual behaviors that are related to the law's concerns.[2] The measurement of functional abilities is at the core of an assessment for legal competence. In deciding whether a particular functional ability is relevant for a particular legal competence construct, psychologists should be guided by legal definitions, theory, and research.

CAUSAL COMPONENT

When deficiencies related to a legal competence are identified, the evaluator should attempt to ascribe the likely causes of those deficits. One reason is to consider the possibility that the individual may be exaggerating or feigning deficits. Another reason is that rules and laws may specify that different causes for the same deficit may have different consequences. For example, an impaired driver in a fatal accident is

---

[2] Similar links to legal concerns should be provided for other data such as psychological test results and input from collateral sources.

likely to face different legal repercussions if the impairment was due to acute psychosis than if the impairment was due to voluntary intoxication.

How do psychologists make clinical decisions about the likely cause of legal deficits? Psychologists use a variety of assessment techniques, including interview, assessment instruments, collateral contacts, and records review, to gather relevant data. Psychologists use their knowledge, training, and experience, including their knowledge of theories and empirical research results, to guide the collection and interpretation of data.

Rogers and Shuman (2000) present two models of clinical decision making: a *hypothesis-testing model* and a *linear best-fit model*. Forensic examiners who use a hypothesis-testing model formulate a hypothesis about the person's behavior and diagnosis near the beginning of the evaluation, and then gather data to confirm or disconfirm the hypothesis. If the hypothesis is disconfirmed, a new hypothesis is formed and tested. Borum, Otto, and Golding (1993) address potential problems with this approach and recommend that experts always test alternative hypotheses.

Although they believe that the hypothesis-testing model is the one most used by forensic experts,[3] Rogers and Shuman (2000) advocate the use of a linear best-fit model, in which the examiner conducts the assessment in two phases. First, in the data-collection phase, the examiner amasses comprehensive and relevant data, undistorted by bias and preconceptions. Second, in the decision phase, the examiner considers the relative merits of competing hypotheses, and, where possible, forms opinions and conclusions. The linear best-fit model has the advantage of avoiding such biases as primacy bias, confirmatory bias, over-reliance on unique data, and premature closure. The disadvantage is that by seeking to comprehensively collect all relevant data, the linear best-fit model will typically take longer than the hypothesis-testing model.[4]

Either a hypothesis-testing model or a linear best-fit model can lead to results that will assist the court, provided that the psychologist

---

[3] At least for insanity evaluations, the context of Rogers and Shuman's book.

[4] The time difference is likely to be less for clinicians who follow Rogers and Shuman's (2000) guidance regarding incremental validity and psychological testing. Rather than using a test battery of multiple measures of the same construct, clinicians would use the single, best-validated instrument for measuring the relevant issue (e.g., symptom or diagnosis) and only use additional instruments for which there is evidence of incremental validity (improved accuracy by adding the less-validated instrument).

gathers sufficient information to test multiple hypotheses (DeClue, 2002). When more than one cause for a deficit is plausible, the psychologist should state that, and, where possible and permissible, offer data and reasoning about which explanation(s) is/are more plausible.

INTERACTIVE COMPONENT

Legal competency does not inhere to an individual; it is an interaction between the person and the situation. Grisso (2003, pp. 32-33) writes that a decision about legal competence addresses the congruency or incongruency between the person's functional abilities and the performance demands of the person's legal case. From this perspective, legal competence decisions should be based on an understanding of the interaction between individual abilities and situational demands, not solely on the basis of the person's abilities. Although the law labels a person as competent or incompetent, it would be more accurate to say that the legal decision is a conclusion about a person-context incongruency or mismatch.

In some types of cases, the forensic referral question involves the demands of the past (or future) situation and an estimate of the person's past (or future) functioning. Forensic examiners need to collect information about the specific environmental and social context in which the examinee functioned (or will function). Examples where the evaluation issue concerns the past include insanity and other mental-state-at-the-time-of-the-offense defenses, and confession cases. Examples where the evaluation issue concerns the future include child custody and guardianship.

JUDGMENTAL AND
DISPOSITIONAL COMPONENTS

We have just considered the *interactive* component, which addresses functional abilities, situational demands, and any discrepancies between the two. The *judgmental* component addresses the ultimate question of whether the incongruency in the particular case is enough to warrant a finding of incompetence. If the incongruence is great enough, the person can be declared incompetent, which may give the government authority to act in specific ways toward the person.

Grisso sees the experts' tasks in the judgmental and dispositional components as informing and assisting judicial decision making, but he encourages experts not to offer judgments about the ultimate legal issue or to recommend legal dispositions. As Randy Otto has pointed out in numerous workshops, the same judge who invites an expert to opine whether a defendant is incompetent to proceed is likely to scold the expert if he or she offers an opinion about whether a confession was coerced. Whatever the reason for this difference in judicial preferences, an expert preparing a report or testimony should know whether ultimate opinion testimony about a particular legal issue in a particular jurisdiction before a particular judge is legally permissible and judicially palatable.

— 6 —

LEGAL CONTEXT

For psychologists interested in working on confession cases, it is helpful to have some knowledge of the legal context. I recommend reading all available U.S. Supreme Court cases that have dealt with custodial confession issues. Most are available online via services such as FindLaw.[1] It is important to remember that if, like me, you are not an attorney, then, like me, you will not understand what you read – that is, you will not understand it as lawyers do. Just as people who watch doctor shows on television start imagining that they have the symptoms of the disease of the week, you may start seeing illegalities in your professional or personal life. It is even possible that you will occasionally be right. But remember, if you are not an attorney, you are not an attorney, and do not try to act like one.

So why read Supreme Court cases? In the written opinions, some of our brightest minds grapple with the most compelling issues of the day. There is conflict and turmoil and siblinghood (formerly known as brotherhood) and divisiveness. The next case you read is likely to be more interesting than what is on television tonight.

In this spirit, we open the present chapter. We will explore how the U.S. Supreme Court has dealt with confessions over the years. We will consider some of the circumstances that courts have found to be coercive, some of the personal characteristics that have been considered to make people more vulnerable to police coercion, and some of the person-situation interactions that have been deemed coercive. We will see some of the techniques police have used to try to induce people to confess to

---

[1]   http://www.findlaw.com/casecode/supreme.html

crimes, and we will selectively reflect on the Court's evolving criteria for determining whether a confession should be considered involuntary. The intent is to give some historical context, not to answer legal questions. The chapter is divided into three sections: Pre-*Miranda*, *Miranda*, and Post-*Miranda*.

PRE-*MIRANDA*

In *Hopt v. Territory of Utah* (1884), the U.S. Supreme Court held that

> A confession, if freely and voluntarily made, is evidence of the most satisfactory character. Such a confession is deserving of the highest credit, because it is presumed to flow from the strongest sense of guilt, and therefore it is admitted as proof of the crime to which it refers. . . . But the presumption upon which weight is given to such evidence, namely, that one who is innocent will not imperil his safety or prejudice his interests by an untrue statement, ceases when the confession appears to have been made [in response to] inducements, threats, or promises. (pp. 584-585, citation omitted)

In *Sparf v. United States* (1895), the Court wrote:

> Counsel for the accused insist that there cannot be a voluntary statement, a free, open confession, while a defendant is confined and in irons, under an accusation of having committed a capital offense. We have not been referred to any authority in support of that position. It is true that the fact of a prisoner being in custody at the time he makes a confession is a circumstance not to be overlooked, because it bears upon the inquiry whether the confession was voluntarily made, or was extorted by threats or violence, or made under the influence of fear. But confinement or imprisonment is not in itself sufficient to justify the exclusion of a confession, if it appears to have been voluntary and was not obtained by putting the prisoner in fear or by promises. (p. 55)

This was reiterated in *Pierce v. United States* (1896).

In *Bram v. United States* (1897), the Court distinguished the English and American accusatorial system from the inquisitorial system that had been used in Europe's monarchies. The Court held that the Self Incrimination Clause of the Fifth Amendment barred the introduction in federal cases of involuntary confessions made in response to custodial interrogation. This early case is frequently cited by later cases, and it presents the most comprehensive presentation of the Court's early views regarding confessions.

In *Hardy v. United States* (1902), the Court found a confession to be free of "coercion or threat or promise" (p. 229), and therefore voluntary.

In *Kent v. Porto Rico* (1907), the Court ruled that it was proper for the trial court to allow the jury to consider the voluntariness of "a certain letter claimed to constitute a confession of guilt and written by the accused to a private person before this prosecution was commenced" (p. 117).

The case of *United States ex rel. Bilokumsky v. Tod* (1923) involved a mute alien accused of advocating the overthrow of the government of the United States by force or violence. Prior to the application for a warrant for his arrest, he was questioned, and he admitted that he was an alien. At trial he stood mute, and later appealed on grounds that his admission of being an alien should not be admitted in court. The Court ruled that because citizenship is not an element of the crime of sedition, and because deportation hearings are civil rather than criminal, both his silence in the deportation hearing and his previous admission could be admitted as evidence tending to prove that he was an alien.

Ziang Sun Wan v. United States (1924) involved the interrogation of a physically ill man who was held incommunicado for 9 days and underwent an "excruciating" interrogation during which "Every supposed fact ascertained by the detectives in the course of their investigation was related to him" (p. 12). His statements were ruled involuntary.

In *Brown v. Mississippi* (1936), the undisputed facts of the case showed that the local sheriff, accompanied by some other men, took one of the defendants to the house of a recently deceased man, and there

> began to accuse the defendant of the crime. Upon his denial they seized him, and with the participation of the deputy they hanged him by a rope to the limb of a tree, and, having let him down, they hung him again, and when he was let down the second time, and he still protested his innocence, he was tied to a tree and whipped, and, still declining to accede to the demands that he confess, he was finally released, and he returned with some difficulty to his home, suffering intense pain and agony. The record of the testimony shows that the

signs of the rope on his neck were plainly visible during the so-called trial. (p. 281)

The U.S. Supreme Court in *Brown* ruled that confessions elicited via physical brutality and violence by the police could not be used as evidence. The Court noted that the suspects were "all ignorant negroes" (p. 281) who would be particularly vulnerable to police manipulation. In *Chambers v. Florida* (1940), the facts and findings included:

> For five days petitioners were subjected to interrogations culminating in Saturday's (May 20th) all night examination. Over a period of five days they steadily refused to confess and disclaimed any guilt. The very circumstances surrounding their confinement and their questioning without any formal charges having been brought, were such as to fill petitioners with terror and frightful misgivings. . . . The haunting fear of mob violence was around them in an atmosphere charged with excitement and public indignation. . . . To permit human lives to be forfeited upon confessions thus obtained would make of the constitutional requirement of due process of law a meaningless symbol. (pp. 239-240)

The Court in *Chambers* noted that "They who have suffered most from secret and dictatorial proceedings have almost always been the poor, the ignorant, the numerically weak, the friendless, and the powerless" (p. 238), and in this case the suspects were "ignorant young colored tenant farmers" (p. 238).

White v. Texas (1940) was the case of an illiterate farmhand who was held in custody for 6 or 7 days and taken nightly "up in the woods somewhere" for interrogation (p. 532). Although White said he was whipped in the woods by Texas Rangers, the Rangers denied the whippings, but not the trips to the woods. He was then interrogated in a locked elevator for 4 hours until he broke down, cried, and signed a confession. Considering only the undisputed facts, the Court ruled that White's confession was involuntary.

In *Lisenba v. California* (1941), the Court summarized the reasons for finding confessions to have been involuntary in some previous cases as follows:

- Mob violence. *Moore v. Dempsey* (1923).
- Fraud, collusion, trickery, and subornation of perjury on the part of those representing the state. *Mooney v. Holohan* (1935).

- A suspect is induced to confess by threats or promises. *Chambers v. Florida* (1940).

In *Ward v. Texas* (1942), the police actions included:

moving an ignorant negro by night and day to strange towns, telling him of threats of mob violence, and questioning him continuously. . . . This Court has set aside convictions based upon confessions extorted from ignorant persons who have been subjected to persistent and protracted questioning, or who have been threatened with mob violence, or who have been unlawfully held incommunicado without advice of friends or counsel, or who have been taken at night to lonely and isolated places for questioning. Any one of these grounds would be sufficient cause for reversal. All of them are to be found in this case. (p. 555)

McNabb v. United States (1943) involved members of a clan of Tennessee mountaineers who were in the business of selling whiskey on which federal taxes had not been paid, shots fired in the dark, and a federal agent who died in the McNabb Settlement's cemetery. The interrogation involved confinement in a "barren cell. . . . For two days they were subjected to unremitting questioning by numerous officers. Benjamin's confession was secured by detaining him unlawfully and questioning him continuously for five or six hours. The McNabbs had to submit to all this without the aid of friends or the benefit of counsel" (p. 345). Three of the clan confessed. The voluntariness of their confessions was questionable on grounds that it was "secured by protracted and repeated questioning of ignorant and untutored persons in whose minds the power of officers was greatly magnified or who have been unlawfully held incommunicado without advice of friends or counsel" (p. 340). Instead, the confessions were excluded because the federal officers had not promptly taken them to a judicial officer for a hearing, a remedy available to the Court because it was a federal case. The *McNabb* Court explained the need as follows:

A democratic society, in which respect for the dignity of all men is central, naturally guards against the misuse of the law enforcement process. Zeal in tracking down crime is not in itself an assurance of soberness of judgment. Disinterestedness in law enforcement does not alone prevent disregard of cherished liberties. Experience has therefore counseled that safeguards must be provided against the dangers of the overzealous as well as the despotic. The awful instruments of the criminal law cannot be entrusted to a single functionary. The complicated process of criminal justice is therefore divided into different parts, responsibility for which is separately vested in the various participants upon whom the criminal law relies for its vindication. Legislation such as this, requiring that the police must with reasonable promptness show legal cause for detaining arrested persons, constitutes an important safeguard – not only in assuring protection for the innocent but also in securing conviction of the guilty by methods that commend themselves to a progressive and self-confident society. For this procedural requirement checks resort to those reprehensible practices known as the "third degree" which, though universally rejected as indefensible, still find their way into use. It aims to avoid all the evil implications of secret interrogation of persons accused of crime. It reflects not a sentimental but a sturdy view of law enforcement. It outlaws easy but self-defeating ways in which brutality is substituted for brains as an instrument of crime detection. (pp. 343-344)

United States v. Mitchell (1944) had some similarities to *McNabb v. United States* (1943). Mitchell was held for 8 days before being arraigned, and he confessed to some burglaries while he was held. The Court found that he was held illegally. Following *McNabb* the confessions would be excluded, but in this case the police claimed Mitchell made the confession not at the end of the 8 days of illegal confinement, but "within a few minutes of his arrival at the police station" (p. 69). The Court considered that claim to be undisputed: "Mitchell, it must be emphasized, merely denied that he made these statements and so did not contest the time of making them" (p. 71). So, if Mitchell really did confess within minutes of his arrival at the police station, why did the police wait 8 days before arraignment? "The police explanation of this illegality is that Mitchell was kept in such custody without protest through a desire to aid the police in clearing up thirty housebreakings, the booty from which was found in his home" (p. 70). The Court therefore ruled that his confession was admissible, since the illegal confinement was deemed to have occurred after he had already confessed.[2]

In *Ashcraft v. Tennessee* (1944), a suspect had been questioned for 36 hours by a team of interrogators. The interrogators had to work in

---

[2] It is easy to see how electronic recording of the interrogation in a case like this could resolve lingering questions about what really happened during the interrogation.

shifts, taking breaks due to their exhaustion, but the pressure on the suspect was unrelenting. The Court noted that there were

> disputed questions of fact relating to the details of what transpired within the confession chamber of the jail or whether Ashcraft actually did confess. Such disputes, we may say, are an inescapable consequence of secret inquisitorial practices. And always evidence concerning the inner details of secret inquisitions is weighted against an accused, particularly where, as here, he is charged with a brutal crime, or where, as in many other cases, his supposed offense bears relation to an unpopular economic, political, or religious cause. . . .We think a situation such as that here shown by uncontradicted evidence is so inherently coercive that its very existence is irreconcilable with the possession of mental freedom by a lone suspect against whom its full coercive force is brought to bear. (pp. 152-153)

The dissent in *Ashcraft* noted that it was a first for the Court to rely on a *circumstance* of the interrogation to decide whether the confession was admissible:

> Different courts have used different terms to express the test by which to judge the inadmissibility of a confession, such as "forced," "coerced," "involuntary," "extorted," "loss of freedom of will." But always where we have professed to speak with the voice of the due process clause, the test, in whatever words stated, has been applied to the particular confessor at the time of confession. (pp. 159-160)

In the absence of actual or threatened violence, when

> we consider a confession obtained by questioning, even if persistent and prolonged, we are in a different field. . . . Even a "voluntary confession" is not likely to be the product of the same motives with which one may volunteer information that does not incriminate or concern him. The term "voluntary" confession does not mean voluntary in the sense of a confession to a priest merely to rid one's soul of a sense of guilt. "Voluntary confessions" in criminal law are the product of calculations of a different order, and usually proceed from a belief that further denial is useless and perhaps prejudicial. To speak of any confessions of crime made after arrest as being "voluntary" or "uncoerced" is somewhat inaccurate, although traditional. A confession is wholly and incontestably voluntary only if a guilty person gives himself up to the law and becomes his own accuser. The Court bases its decision on the premise that custody

and examination of a prisoner for thirty-six hours is "inherently coercive." Of course it is. And so is custody and examination for one hour. Arrest itself is inherently coercive, and so is detention. When not justified, infliction of such indignities upon the person is actionable as a tort. Of course such acts put pressure upon the prisoner to answer questions, to answer them truthfully, and to confess if guilty. (pp. 160-161)

The dissent in *Ashcraft* noted:

Always heretofore the ultimate question has been whether the confessor was in possession of his own will and self-control at the time of confession. . . . Instead of finding as a fact that Ashcraft's freedom of will was impaired, it substitutes the doctrine that the situation was "inherently coercive." (p. 162)

Thus, *Ashcraft* constitutes a shift in the focus of an analysis of voluntariness from the mind of the suspect to the actions of the police. The suspect's mental state is relevant to a consideration of voluntariness, but it is not the sole focus.

The shift to focusing on objectively identifiable circumstances of interrogations rather than subjective mental states has the advantage of potentially decreasing the amount of guesswork involved in the analysis. As we catalog the various circumstances that courts have found to be coercive, we should keep in mind that both person and situation variables are to be considered.

What if a suspect makes two separate confessions in 1 day, and the first one is ruled involuntary? Does that automatically mean the second was involuntary? No. In *Lyons v. Oklahoma* (1944), the Court described the test as follows:

The question of whether those confessions subsequently given are themselves voluntary depends on the inferences as to the continuing effect of the coercive practices which may fairly be drawn from the surrounding circumstances. The voluntary or involuntary character of a confession is determined by a conclusion as to whether the accused, at the time he confesses, is in possession of "mental freedom" to confess to or deny a suspected participation in a crime. (p. 602, citations omitted)

The Court allowed Lyons' second confession to stand.

Psychological techniques, including the humiliation of leaving the defendant partially undressed for hours and the induced fear that he would be beaten by the police, contributed to a finding that a confession was coerced in *Malinski v. New York* (1945).

In *United States v. Bayer* (1947), a case involving military justice, the defendant had given a confession that was considered to have been coerced, and then gave a second confession. Could the second confession be considered voluntary?

> Of course, after an accused has once let the cat out of the bag by confessing, no matter what the inducement, he is never thereafter free of the psychological and practical disadvantages of having confessed. He can never get the cat back in the bag. The secret is out for good. In such a sense, a later confession always may be looked upon as fruit of the first. But this Court has never gone so far as to hold that making a confession under circumstances which preclude its use, perpetually disables the confessor from making a usable one after those conditions have been removed. . . . The second confession in this case was made six months after the first. The only restraint under which Radovich labored was that he could not leave the base limits without permission. Certainly such a limitation on the freedom of one in the Army and subject to military discipline is not enough to make a confession voluntarily given after fair warning invalid as evidence against him. We hold the admission of the confession was not error. (pp. 540-541)

In a case involving a 15-year-old boy (*Haley v. Ohio,* 1948), the Court noted:

> Age 15 is a tender and difficult age for a boy of any race. He cannot be judged by the more exacting standards of maturity. That which would leave a man cold and unimpressed can overawe and overwhelm a lad in his early teens. This is the period of great instability which the crisis of adolescence produces. (p. 599)

The Court held:

> The age [maturity] of petitioner, the hours when he was grilled [overnight], the duration of his quizzing [five hours], the fact that he had no friend [such as a parent] or counsel to advise him, the callous attitude of the police towards his rights combine to convince us that this was a confession wrung from a child by means which the law should not sanction. (pp. 600-601)

A Mississippi court held that a defendant who denied that he made a confession was therefore barred from challenging that the disputed confession was coerced. In *Lee v. Mississippi* (1948), the U.S. Supreme Court held:

> The due process clause of the Fourteenth Amendment invalidates a state court conviction grounded in whole or in part upon a confession which is the product of other than reasoned and voluntary choice. A conviction resulting from such use of a coerced confession, however, is no less void because the accused testified at some point in the proceeding that he had never in fact confessed, voluntarily or involuntarily. Testimony of that nature can hardly regalize a procedure which conflicts with the accepted principles of due process. And since our constitutional system permits a conviction to be sanctioned only if in conformity with those principles, inconsistent testimony as to the confession should not and cannot preclude the accused from raising the due process issue in an appropriate manner. (p. 745)

Upshaw v. United States (1948) contains rich discussions of the rule applied in *McNabb v. United States* (1943) and *United States v. Mitchell* (1944) regarding federal cases in which confessions were obtained during illegal detention. Rather than take Upshaw for arraignment as the law required, the police held him for 30 hours. The purpose for the illegal detention "as stated by the officers themselves, was only to furnish an opportunity for further interrogation" (p. 412). In a 5-4 decision, the majority in *Upshaw* held that "a confession is inadmissible if made during illegal detention due to failure promptly to carry a prisoner before a committing magistrate, whether or not the confession is the result of torture, physical or psychological" (p. 413, citation omitted). Thus, in 1948 this was a controversial, 5-4 decision: Federal courts cannot admit confessions that were obtained illegally.

In *Watts v. Indiana* (1949), the Court ruled involuntary a confession that followed 6 nights of relentless interrogation. The Court reasoned:

> To turn the detention of an accused into a process of wrenching from him evidence which could not be extorted in open court with all its safeguards, is so grave an abuse of the power of arrest as to offend the procedural standards of due process. . . . This is so because it violates the underlying principle in our enforcement of the criminal law. Ours is the accusatorial as opposed to the inquisitorial system. Such has been the characteristic of Anglo-American criminal justice

since it freed itself from practices borrowed by the Star Chamber from the Continent whereby an accused was interrogated in secret for hours on end. Under our system society carries the burden of proving its charge against the accused not out of his own mouth. It must establish its case, not by interrogation of the accused even under judicial safeguards, but by evidence independently secured through skillful investigation. (p. 54, citations omitted)

As in *Watts,* the cases of *Turner v. Pennsylvania* (1949) and *Harris v. South Carolina* (1949) involved prolonged questioning over several days. The resulting confessions were considered to have been illegally coerced.

In *United States v. Carignan* (1951), the Court declined to extend the rule from *McNabb v. United States* (1943). Justice Douglas' concurring opinion in *Carignan* (one that does not set precedence) included:

There are time-honored police methods for obtaining confessions from an accused. One is detention without arraignment, the problem we dealt with in *McNabb v. United States,* 318 U.S. 332. Then the accused is under the exclusive control of the police, subject to their mercy, and beyond the reach of counsel or of friends. What happens behind doors that are opened and closed at the sole discretion of the police is a black chapter in every country – the free as well as the despotic, the modern as well as the ancient. In the *McNabb* case we tried to rid the federal system of those breeding grounds for coerced confessions. Another time-honored police method for obtaining confessions is to arrest a man on one charge (often a minor one) and use his detention for investigating a wholly different crime. This is an easy short cut for the police. How convenient it is to make detention the vehicle of investigation! Then the police can have access to the prisoner day and night. Arraignment for one crime gives some protection. But when it is a pretense or used as the device for breaking the will of the prisoner on long, relentless, or repeated questionings, it is abhorrent. We should free the federal system of that disreputable practice which has honeycombed the municipal police system in this country. We should make illegal such a perversion of a "legal" detention. (pp. 45-46, citation omitted)

Although the majority did not follow Douglas' lead, the Court held that Carignan could pursue an appeal regarding whether his confession (which was extracted after conversations with a priest) was coerced.

The defendant in *Gallegos v. Nebraska* (1951) was a Mexican farm hand who could neither speak nor write English. The facts (taken from the dissent) include:

> While working in a field in El Paso County, Texas, on September 19, 1949, the petitioner was arrested by a local deputy sheriff without a warrant. The excuse given for the arrest was that immigration officers had requested it. No charge was ever filed against petitioner in any Texas state court nor was any warrant sworn out against him during the eight days he was kept in the Texas jail. His detention was incommunicado except for repeated questioning by the deputies. Part of the time petitioner was kept in an 8' x 8' cell with no windows, a cell which a Texas deputy testifying in this case referred to as the "dark room" or the "punishment room," although petitioner was a "docile prisoner" and did all he was told to do by the officers. It was during this incarceration of eight days that the petitioner gave a confession used to convict him in this case. As is usual in this type of case the deputies say that the confession was wholly "voluntary"; petitioner says that it was due to fear engendered by his incarceration and the actions of the deputies. (p. 74)

The interrogator, the Chief Deputy Sheriff, said he used no violence, threat of violence, or promises. The Court considered only undisputed evidence, and ruled the confession voluntary:

> We have carefully weighed the circumstances of the petitioner's lack of education and familiarity with our law, his experience and condition in life, his need for advice of counsel as to the law of homicide and the probable effect on such a man of interrogation during confinement. We have also taken into consideration Gallegos' uncontradicted testimony about his accommodations, his limited amounts of food and certain threats made by a Texas assistant sheriff not present at the trial. The uncertain character of this uncontradicted testimony, its lack of definiteness, and the action of the trial judge and jury lead us to place little weight upon it. (pp. 67-68)

The case of *Stroble v. California* (1952) presents several interesting issues. Stroble gave two confessions. The Supreme Court of California assumed the first to be coerced and considered the second to be voluntary. The U.S. Supreme Court held that if any coerced confession was submitted to the jury, then the conviction could not stand. The

Court then considered the record, decided that both confessions were voluntary, and allowed the conviction. Two justices dissented:

> The fact that the later confessions may have been lawfully obtained or used is immaterial. For once an illegal confession infects the trial, the verdict of guilty must be set aside no matter how free of taint the other evidence may be. Moreover, the fact that the accused started talking shortly after he was arrested and prior to the time he was taken before the District Attorney does not save the case. That talk was accompanied or preceded by blows and kicks of the police; and the Supreme Court of California assumed that it was part and parcel of the first confession obtained through "physical abuse or psychological torture or a combination of the two." (p. 204, citation omitted)

The following excerpt from *Stroble* provides an early example of how taping of an interrogation (not just a confession) can provide an accurate record, implicitly shows how prior influences (the earlier blows and kicks by the police) are omitted from incomplete tapes, and explicitly illustrates the fact that psychologists who choose to work on disputed confession cases will sometimes be faced with heinous acts:

> The entire proceeding was recorded on a recording machine which had been set in operation before petitioner's arrival. Petitioner stated that on the afternoon of November 14, his victim came to the home of petitioner's daughter, where petitioner was visiting; he took his victim into the bedroom and made advances upon her; when she began to scream, he became frightened, got hold of her throat, and squeezed it until she became quiet; she started to squirm again, so he took a necktie from the dresser and tied it around her neck; when she continued to move, he took her off the bed, wrapped her in a blanket, and hit her on the temple with a hammer which he had obtained from the kitchen drawer; he then dragged her across the back yard to the incinerator, returned to the kitchen to get an ice pick, and pushed the pick into her three times in an effort to reach her heart; next he got an axe from the garage and hit her on the head and backbone; finally he got a knife from the kitchen and stabbed her in the back of the neck, covered her body with boxes, and left for Ocean Park, a beach resort within the city of Los Angeles, where he remained for the three nights before his apprehension. Towards the end of the recording petitioner stated that the officers had not threatened or abused him in any way, either in the park foreman's office or the District Attorney's office.

The recording disclosed no mistreatment at the time of the making of the confession. (pp. 186-187)

In *Brown v. Allen* (1953), an illiterate man was held without counsel for 5 days before being charged, and for 18 days before his initial arraignment. A confession was extracted during that time, but there was no record about how the confession was extracted. The Court held: "Mere detention and police examination in private of one in official state custody do not render involuntary the statements or confessions made by the person so detained" (p. 476).

In *Stein v. New York* (1953), three men confessed to participation in a murder related to the hijacking of a *Reader's Digest* truck near Pleasantville. The three were examined by a prison physician on the morning of June 9, after they had been in custody for 2 to 4 days.

Wissner had a broken rib and various bruises and abrasions on the side, legs, stomach and buttocks; Cooper had bruises on the chest, stomach, right arm, and both buttocks; Stein had a bruise on his right arm. Counsel for the petitioners, who examined them on the 9th and 10th of June, testified that the injuries sustained by each were more extensive than those described in the doctor's testimony. (pp. 169-170)

In preparation for trial, they were faced with a difficult choice. If they testified that their confessions had been coerced, they would be subject to cross-examination that could reveal their prior criminal records. They did not testify at trial. Therefore, on appeal the Court saw no basis to consider that their injuries were the results of police action. In considering whether *psychological* coercion had been applied, the Court identified the proper test as this:

The limits in any case depend upon a weighing of the circumstances of pressure against the power of resistance of the person confessing. What would be overpowering to the weak of will or mind might be utterly ineffective against an experienced criminal. (p. 185)

The Court allowed their confessions to stand.

In *Leyra v. Denno* (1954), a suspect complained of pain and asked for a doctor to treat him for a medical condition. In response to his request, he was introduced to a state-appointed psychiatrist with considerable knowledge of hypnosis.

Instead of giving petitioner the medical advice and treatment he expected, the psychiatrist by subtle and suggestive questions simply continued the police effort of the past days and nights to induce petitioner to admit his guilt. For an hour and a half or more the techniques of a highly trained psychiatrist were used to break petitioner's will in order to get him to say he had murdered his parents. Time and time and time again the psychiatrist told petitioner how much he wanted to and could help him, how bad it would be for petitioner if he did not confess, and how much better he would feel, and how much lighter and easier it would be on him if he would just unbosom himself to the doctor. Yet the doctor was at that very time the paid representative of the state whose prosecuting officials were listening in on every threat made and every promise of leniency given. (pp. 559-560)

The Court ruled that Leyra's statements to the psychiatrist and his subsequent statements (within about 5 hours) to police and to a business associate, should all be considered involuntary.

In *Opper v. United States* (1954), the Court noted that an uncorroborated confession is insufficient to convict someone because

the doubt persists that the zeal of the agencies of prosecution to protect the peace, the self-interest of the accomplice, the maliciousness of an enemy or the aberration or weakness of the accused under the strain of suspicion may tinge or warp the facts of the confession. (pp. 89-90)

The Court ruled:

The need for corroboration extends beyond complete and conscious admission of guilt – a strict confession. . . . Statements of the accused out of court that show essential elements of the crime . . . have the same possibilities for error as confessions. They, too, must be corroborated. (p. 91)

The Court extended this reasoning in *Smith v. United States* (1954):

The general rule that an accused may not be convicted on his own uncorroborated confession has previously been recognized by this Court and has been consistently applied in the lower federal courts and in the overwhelming majority of state courts. Its purpose is to prevent "errors in convictions based upon untrue confessions alone";

its foundation lies in a long history of judicial experience with confessions and in the realization that sound law enforcement requires police investigations which extend beyond the words of the accused. Confessions may be unreliable because they are coerced or induced, and although separate doctrines excluded involuntary confessions from consideration by the jury, further caution is warranted because the accused may be unable to establish the involuntary nature of his statements. Moreover, though a statement may not be "involuntary" within the meaning of this exclusionary rule, still its reliability may be suspect if it is extracted from one who is under the pressure of a police investigation – whose words may reflect the strain and confusion attending his predicament rather than a clear reflection of his past. Finally, the experience of the courts, the police and the medical profession recounts a number of false confessions voluntarily made. These are the considerations which justify a restriction on the power of the jury to convict, for this experience with confessions is not shared by the average juror. (pp. 152-153, citations omitted)

The *Smith* court considered how much corroboration is enough.

There has been considerable debate concerning the quantum of corroboration necessary to substantiate the existence of the crime charged. It is agreed that the corroborative evidence does not have to prove the offense beyond a reasonable doubt, or even by a preponderance, as long as there is substantial independent evidence that the offense has been committed, and the evidence as a whole proves beyond a reasonable doubt that defendant is guilty. In addition to differing views on the substantiality of specific independent evidence, the debate has centered largely about two questions: (1) whether corroboration is necessary for all elements of the offense established by admissions alone, and (2) whether it is sufficient if the corroboration merely fortifies the truth of the confession, without independently establishing the crime charged. We answer both in the affirmative. All elements of the offense must be established by independent evidence or corroborated admissions, but one available mode of corroboration is for the independent evidence to bolster the confession itself and thereby prove the offense "through" the statements of the accused. (p. 156)

Fikes v. Alabama (1957) introduces considerations of mental illness. Fikes was an uneducated Negro of low mentality or mentally ill . . . who started school at age eight and left at 16 while still in the third grade. There was testimony by three psychiatrists at the trial, in connection with a pleaded defense of insanity, to the effect that petitioner is a schizophrenic and highly suggestible. His mother testified that he had always been "thick-headed." (pp. 191, 193)

He was questioned over a period of 5 days for several hours at a time, without being able to see a lawyer or his father, then gave the first of two confessions. He "responded chiefly in yes-or-no answers to his questions, some of which were quite leading or suggestive" (p. 195). His confession was deemed involuntary.

Lest one think that the Supreme Court was overly profligate in finding confessions involuntary, consider the case of *Thomas v. Arizona* (1958). Thomas, an itinerate Negro laborer suspected of murder, was accosted in the bushes by 12 to 15 members of a sheriff's posse. The State's version of events included:

A local rancher on horseback, who had no official connection with the Sheriff's posse, lassoed petitioner around the neck and jerked him a few steps in the general direction of both the Sheriff's car and the nearest trees, some 200 yards away. The Sheriff quickly intervened, removed the rope, and admonished, "Stop that. We will have none of that." There was no talk of lynching among the other members of the posse. (p. 395)

Thomas was roped again, as was another Negro suspect, and was dragged to his knees. The ropes were removed, he was transported for questioning, and 20 hours later he made a confession before a Justice of the Peace. He signed two subsequent written confessions, which

were found "procured by threat of lynch" and declared involuntary by the trial judge after his preliminary inquiry. Although the oral confession before the Justice of the Peace was made between the time of the ropings and the written confessions, the trial judge made an initial determination that it was voluntary. He justified this seeming incongruity on the basis of the different circumstances under which the oral statement was made, namely, the judicial surroundings and the presence of the Sheriff with only one other deputy, the Sheriff being "the very man who had protected [petitioner]." (p. 400)

In *Thomas* the Supreme Court held:

> Deplorable as these ropings are to the spirit of a civilized administration of justice, the undisputed facts before us do not show that petitioner's oral statement was a product of fear engendered by them. . . . Coercion here is posited solely upon the roping incidents. There is no claim and no evidence of physical beating, of continuous relay questioning, of incommunicado detention, or of psychiatric inducement. Petitioner is neither of tender age nor of subnormal intelligence. Nor, in view of his extensive criminal record, can he be thought an impressionable stranger to the processes of law. . . . Nothing *in the undisputed record* seriously substantiates the contention that a fear engendered by the ropings overbore petitioner's free will at the time he appeared in the Justice Court. His statement appears to be the spontaneous exclamation of a guilty conscience. (pp. 401-402, citations omitted, emphasis added)

If one considers the *disputed record* in *Thomas,* his statement might not appear to be "the spontaneous exclamation of a guilty conscience." In the U.S. Court of Appeals different facts of the case were emphasized:

> It is apparent that the trial judge believed the testimony of a State Highway patrolman that the county sheriff not only stood by while petitioner and another prisoner in his custody were roped about the neck and dragged by mounted members of a mob, but that he even said to petitioner "Will you tell the truth, or I will let them go ahead and do this," or "I will go ahead and let them use this." (p. 402)

That Highway patrolman's chief had forbidden him to talk to the Defense prior to trial, so when the trial judge permitted the confession to be presented to the jury, he did not know that there was evidence that the sheriff had participated in the lynching activities. At trial, it was left to the jury to decide whether or not the confession was voluntary. In applying the Fourteenth Amendment to any disputed confession case, the Supreme Court does not consider "disputed evidence" of coercive tactics, but only what the police admit/acknowledge that they did. In this case, there was dispute among various law enforcement officers about what transpired, and the Supreme Court took the facts as they most favored the State's case. It is not that the Supreme Court believes the prosecution more than the defense. The Supreme Court does not attempt to re-try the facts of the case to determine what happened.

Instead, the Court accepts the determination of fact made by the trial court and then considers whether the law was applied properly. Four justices dissented in *Thomas,* but I could find no record of a written dissenting opinion.

In *Payne v. Arkansas* (1958)

> the undisputed evidence in this case shows that petitioner, a mentally dull 19-year-old youth, (1) was arrested without a warrant, (2) was denied a hearing before a magistrate at which he would have been advised of his right to remain silent and of his right to counsel, as required by Arkansas statutes, (3) was not advised of his right to remain silent or of his right to counsel, (4) was held incommunicado for three days, without counsel, advisor or friend, and though members of his family tried to see him they were turned away, and he was refused permission to make even one telephone call, (5) was denied food for long periods, and, finally, (6) was told by the chief of police "that there would be 30 or 40 people there in a few minutes that wanted to get him," which statement created such fear in petitioner as immediately produced the "confession." It seems obvious from the totality of this course of conduct, and particularly the culminating threat of mob violence, that the confession was coerced and did not constitute an "expression of free choice," and that its use before the jury, over petitioner's objection, deprived him of "that fundamental fairness essential to the very concept of justice," and, hence, denied him due process of law, guaranteed by the Fourteenth Amendment. (p. 567)

The Court ruled that

> even though there may have been sufficient evidence, apart from the coerced confession, to support a judgment of conviction, the admission in evidence, over objection, of the coerced confession vitiates the judgment because it violates the Due Process Clause of the Fourteenth Amendment. (p. 568)

Ashdown v. Utah (1958) involved the case of a widow questioned on the day of her husband's funeral (the sheriff approached her at the cemetery, just after the internment). The dissenting justices wrote:

> The uncle and the father of petitioner appeared at the sheriff's office shortly after petitioner was arrested. The uncle testified that he said, "I don't think she has got a right to be questioned without her father's

presence or some attorney." The father testified that he said, "I made the remark that it didn't look to me like a fair, square deal, to railroad that girl into that sheriff's office without counsel or friends of any description." The uncle and the father were denied admission. They were calmed by the assurance that the accused had a lawyer at her side to aid her under the questioning of the police – which was not true. (pp. 431-432)

The majority emphasized other aspects of the case:

A study of the record as a whole convinces us that the interview with petitioner was temperate and courteous. The sheriff proceeded cautiously and acted with consideration for the feelings of petition-er . . . Petitioner's emotional distress during the interview may be attributed to her remorse, rather than to any coercive conduct of the officers. There is nothing in the record which indicates that the sheriff chose to question petitioner immediately after her husband's funeral in order to capitalize on her feelings. Rather, he appears to have taken the first opportunity to talk with her after it had been established that her husband's death was caused by poisoning. The questioning was done by officers whom petitioner knew. She was not questioned in relays or made to repeat a story over and over while the interrogators searched for an inconsistency or flaw. She was allowed to talk without interruption about such matters as she chose. In sum, we find ample support in this record for a finding that the officers did not intend to take advantage of petitioner and that nothing they did had the effect of overbearing her will. (pp. 430-431)

The confession was ruled voluntary.

In *Crooker v. California* (1958), by a 5-4 vote, the Court allowed a confession to be admitted even though the defendant had asked over and over to have his attorney present, and was denied. On the same day, the Court considered similar facts in *Cicenia v. Lagay* (1958) and reached a similar decision.

Spano v. New York (1959) provides a good example of the Court's consideration of a person-situation interaction. The Court described its role in disputed confession cases: "We are forced to resolve a conflict between two fundamental interests of society; its interest in prompt and efficient law enforcement, and its interest in preventing the rights of its individual members from being abridged by unconstitutional methods of law enforcement" (p. 315). Relevant facts about Spano included:

He had suffered a cerebral concussion in 1955. He was described by a private physician in 1951 as "an extremely nervous tense individual who is emotionally unstable and maladjusted," and was found unacceptable for military service in 1951, primarily because of "Psychiatric disorder." He failed the Army's AFQT-1 intelligence test. (p. 324)

The truthfulness of Spano's confession was not in question, but the methods used to extract it were. After Spano was beaten and robbed by an ex-pugilist, he went home, got a gun, and found and killed his assailant. A childhood friend of Spano's, who was in training to become a police officer, participated in the subsequent interrogation. The court cited a couplet from John Gay:

> *An open foe may prove a curse*
> *But a pretended friend is worse.*

Also considered by the Court in *Spano* were the following:

Petitioner was a foreign-born young man of 25 with no past history of law violation or of subjection to official interrogation, at least insofar as the record shows. He had progressed only one-half year into high school and the record indicates that he had a history of emotional instability. He did not make a narrative statement, but was subject to the leading questions of a skillful prosecutor in a question and answer confession. He was subjected to questioning not by a few men, but by many . . . and the effect of such massive official interrogation must have been felt. Petitioner was questioned for virtually eight straight hours before he confessed. . . . Nor was the questioning conducted during normal business hours, but began in early evening, continued into the night, and did not bear fruition until the not-too-early morning. The drama was not played out, with the final admissions obtained, until almost sunrise. In such circumstances slowly mounting fatigue does, and is calculated to, play its part. The questioners persisted in the face of his repeated refusals to answer on the advice of his attorney, and they ignored his reasonable requests to contact the local attorney whom he had already retained and who had personally delivered him into the custody of these officers in obedience to the bench warrant. . . . We conclude that petitioner's will was overborne by official pressure, fatigue and sympathy falsely aroused, after considering all the facts in their post-indictment setting. Here a grand jury had already found sufficient cause to require petitioner to face trial on a charge of first-degree murder, and the police had an eyewitness to the shooting. The police were not therefore merely trying to solve a crime, or even to absolve a suspect. . . . They were rather concerned primarily with securing a statement from defendant on which they could convict him. The undeviating intent of the officers to extract a confession from petitioner is therefore patent. When such an intent is shown, this Court has held that the confession obtained must be examined with the most careful scrutiny. (321-324)

Blackburn v. Alabama (1960) is the case of "a 24-year-old Negro [who had] suffered a lengthy siege of mental illness" (p. 200), had been discharged from the military as permanently disabled by psychosis in 1944, and had been hospitalized for 4 years. He left the hospital on a 10-day leave in care of his sister in February 1948, did not return, and robbed a store in April 1948. He was arrested and a confession was elicited. He was treated for insanity for another 4 years, until 1952. (In the meantime, he escaped, committed a new crime, and was found incompetent and insane.) When his 1948 case went to trial, most, but not all of the psychiatric testimony suggested that he was mentally ill at the time that the confession was elicited in 1948. The Supreme Court wrote:

the evidence indisputably establishes the strongest probability[3] that Blackburn was insane and incompetent at the time he allegedly confessed. Surely in the present stage of our civilization a most basic sense of justice is affronted by the spectacle of incarcerating a human being upon the basis of a statement he made while insane; and this judgment can without difficulty be articulated in terms of the unreliability of the confession, the lack of rational choice of the accused, or simply a strong conviction that our system of law enforcement should not operate so as to take advantage of a person in this fashion. And when the other pertinent circumstances are considered – the eight- to nine-hour sustained interrogation in a tiny room which was upon occasion literally filled with police officers; the absence of Blackburn's friends, relatives, or legal counsel; the composition of the confession by the Deputy Sheriff rather than by Blackburn – the chances of the confession's having been the product of a rational intellect and a free will become even more remote and the denial of due process even more egregious. (pp. 207-208)

---

[3] Note the language: the *probability* is indisputable. Contrast with *Thomas v. Arizona* (1958), cited previously, where the *facts* of a lynching were not undisputed. Could the Court have used different language and decided each case differently?

In *Rogers v. Richmond* (1961), the Court ruled that it was a violation of the Fourteenth Amendment for a state court to consider whether a confession was *true* as an element of whether it was voluntary:

> Our decisions under that Amendment have made clear that convictions following the admission into evidence of confessions which are involuntary, i.e., the product of coercion, either physical or psychological, cannot stand. This is so not because such confessions are unlikely to be true but because the methods used to extract them offend an underlying principle in the enforcement of our criminal law: that ours is an accusatorial and not an inquisitorial system – a system in which the State must establish guilt by evidence independently and freely secured and may not by coercion prove its charge against an accused out of his own mouth. To be sure, confessions cruelly extorted may be and have been, to an unascertained extent, found to be untrustworthy. But the constitutional principle of excluding confessions that are not voluntary does not rest on this consideration. Indeed, in many of the cases in which the command of the Due Process Clause has compelled us to reverse state convictions involving the use of confessions obtained by impermissible methods, independent corroborating evidence left little doubt of the truth of what the defendant had confessed. Despite such verification, confessions were found to be the product of constitutionally impermissible methods in their inducement. Since a defendant had been subjected to pressures to which, under our accusatorial system, an accused should not be subjected, we were constrained to find that the procedures leading to his conviction had failed to afford him that due process of law which the Fourteenth Amendment guarantees. (pp. 540-541, citations omitted)

The case of *Reck v. Pate* (1961) involved a defendant who had been convicted of murder and sentenced to 199 years in prison. The Court wrote:

> At the time of his arrest Reck was a nineteen-year-old youth of subnormal intelligence. He had no prior criminal record or experience with the police. He was held nearly eight days without a judicial hearing. Four of those days preceded his first confession. During that period Reck was subjected each day to six- or seven-hour stretches of relentless and incessant interrogation. The questioning was conducted by groups of officers. For the first three days the interrogation ranged over a wide variety of crimes. On the night of the third day of his detention the interrogation turned to the crime for

which petitioner stands convicted. During this same four-day period he was shuttled back and forth between police stations and interrogation rooms. In addition, Reck was intermittently placed on public exhibition in "show-ups." On the night before his confession, petitioner became ill while on display in such a "show-up." He was taken to the hospital, returned to the police station and put back on public display. When he again became ill he was removed from the "show-up," but interrogation in the windowless "handball court" continued relentlessly until he grew faint and vomited blood on the floor. Once more he was taken to the hospital, where he spent the night under the influence of drugs. The next morning he was removed from the hospital in a wheel chair, and intensive interrogation was immediately resumed. Some eight hours later Reck signed his first confession. The next afternoon he signed a second. During the entire period preceding his confessions Reck was without adequate food, without counsel, and without the assistance of family or friends. He was, for all practical purposes, held incommunicado. He was physically weakened and in intense pain. We conclude that this total combination of circumstances is so inherently coercive that its very existence is irreconcilable with the possession of mental freedom by a lone suspect against whom its full coercive force is brought to bear. (pp. 441-442, citation omitted)

Perhaps the most detailed analysis of issues in confession cases prior to *Miranda* is found in *Culombe v. Connecticut* (1961). In his dissent, Chief Justice Warren noted that the opinion of the majority

attempts to resolve with finality many difficult problems [regarding cases of disputed confessions]. . . . The opinion was unquestionably written with the intention of clarifying these problems and of establishing a set of principles which could be easily applied in any coerced-confession situation. However, it is doubtful that such will be the result, for while three members of the Court agree to the general principles enunciated by the opinion, they construe those principles as requiring a result in this case exactly the opposite from that reached by the author of the opinion. This being true, it cannot be assumed that the lower courts and law enforcement agencies will receive better guidance from the treatise for which this case seems to have provided a vehicle. . . . In my view, the reasons which have compelled the Court to develop the law on a case-by-case approach, to declare legal principles only in the context of specific factual situations, and to avoid expounding more than is necessary for the decision of a given case are persuasive. (p. 636)

Within what Justice Rehnquist later termed an "interesting but somewhat mystical exegesis" (*Miller v. Fenton*, 1985, p. 119), the majority in *Culombe* wrote:

> This much seems certain: It is impossible for this Court, in enforcing the Fourteenth Amendment, to attempt precisely to delimit, or to surround with specific, all-inclusive restrictions, the power of interrogation allowed to state law enforcement officers in obtaining confessions. No single litmus-paper test for constitutionally impermissible interrogation has been evolved: neither extensive cross-questioning . . . nor undue delay in arraignment . . . nor failure to caution a prisoner . . . nor refusal to permit communication with friends and legal counsel at stages in the proceeding when the prisoner is still only a suspect. Each of these factors, in company with all of the surrounding circumstances – the duration and conditions of detention (if the confessor has been detained), the manifest attitude of the police toward him, his physical and mental state, the diverse pressures which sap or sustain his powers of resistance and self-control – is relevant. The ultimate test remains that which has been the only clearly established test in Anglo-American courts for two hundred years; the test of voluntariness. Is the confession the product of an essentially free and unconstrained choice by its maker? If it is, if he has willed to confess, it may be used against him. If it is not, if his will has been overborne and his capacity for self-determination critically impaired, the use of his confession offends due process. The line of distinction is that at which governing self-direction is lost and compulsion, of whatever nature or however infused, propels or helps to propel the confession. (pp. 601-602)

The *Culombe* Court identified a three-step process:

> The inquiry whether, in a particular case, a confession was voluntarily or involuntarily made involves, at the least, a three-phased process. First, there is the business of finding the crude historical facts, the external, "phenomenological" occurrences and events surrounding the confession. Second, because the concept of "voluntariness" is one which concerns a mental state, there is the imaginative recreation, largely inferential, of internal, "psychological" fact. Third, there is the application to this psychological fact of standards for judgment informed by the larger legal conceptions ordinarily characterized as rules of law but which, also, comprehend both induction from, and anticipation of, factual circumstances. (p. 603)

The *Culombe* Court wrote that the first step, determining the facts, is generally a matter for the trial court to determine. One might think that the second step, determining the psychological facts, would also generally be left to the trial court, but such is not the case:

> The second and third phases of the inquiry – determination of how the accused reacted to the external facts, and of the legal significance of how he reacted – although distinct as a matter of abstract analysis, become in practical operation inextricably interwoven. This is so, in part, because the concepts by which language expresses an otherwise unpresentable mental reality are themselves generalizations importing preconceptions about the reality to be expressed. It is so, also, because the apprehension of mental states is almost invariably a matter of induction, more or less imprecise, and the margin of error which is thus introduced into the finding of "fact" must be accounted for in the formulation and application of the "rule" designed to cope with such classes of facts. The notion of "voluntariness" is itself an amphibian. It purports at once to describe an internal psychic state and to characterize that state for legal purposes. Since the characterization is the very issue "to review which this Court sits," the matter of description, too, is necessarily open here. No more restricted scope of review would suffice adequately to protect federal constitutional rights. For the mental state of involuntariness upon which the due process question turns can never be affirmatively established other than circumstantially – that is, by inference; and it cannot be competent to the trier of fact to preclude our review simply by declining to draw inferences which the historical facts compel. . . . Where, on the uncontested external happenings, coercive forces set in motion by state law enforcement officials are unmistakably in action; where these forces, under all the prevailing states of stress, are powerful enough to draw forth a confession; where, in fact, the confession does come forth and is claimed by the defendant to have been extorted from him; and where he has acted as a man would act who is subjected to such an extracting process [the confession will be ruled involuntary]. (pp. 604-605, citations omitted)[4]

As the *Culombe* Court turned to the facts in the case under review, it wrote: "Since judgment as to legal voluntariness *vel non* under the Due Process Clause is drawn from the totality of the relevant circum-

---

[4] While this was written to explain why the Court did not leave it solely to the trial courts to determine psychological facts, it could also help to explain why some judges are hostile to psychologists offering ultimate opinion testimony regarding the voluntariness of confessions.

stances of a particular situation, a detailed account of them is unavoidable" (p. 606).

> Arthur Culombe was a thirty-three-year-old mental defective of the moron class with an intelligence quotient of sixty-four and a mental age of nine to nine and a half years. He was wholly illiterate. Expert witnesses for the State, whose appraisal of Culombe's mental condition was the most favorable adduced at trial, classified him as a "high moron" and "a rather high grade mentally defective" and testified that his reactions would not be the same as those of the chronological nine-year-old because his greater physical maturity and fuller background of experience gave him a perspective that the nine-year-old would not possess. Culombe was, however, "handicapped." Culombe had been in mental institutions for diagnosis and treatment. He had been in trouble with the law since he was an adolescent and had been in prison at least twice in Connecticut since his successful escape from a Massachusetts training school for mental defectives. A psychiatrist testifying for the State said that, although he was not a fearful man, Culombe was suggestible and could be intimidated. (pp. 620-621)

The *Culombe* Court compared the circumstances of Culombe's interrogation to those of previous cases (including many of those summarized earlier), noting similarities and differences, then wrote:

> What appears in this case, then, is this. Culombe was taken by the police and held in the carefully controlled environment of police custody for more than four days before he confessed. During that time he was questioned [daily] with the avowed intention, not merely to check his story to ascertain whether there was cause to charge him, but to obtain a confession if a confession was obtainable. All means found fit were employed to this end. Culombe was not told that he had a right to remain silent. Although he said that he wanted a lawyer, the police made no attempt to give him the help he needed to get one. [He was illiterate and could not use the phone book.] (p. 631)

He was not properly arraigned. The police used his family to manipulate him, and used other manipulative tactics in questioning him. In considering its determination, the Court wrote:

> Regardful as one must be of the problems of crime-detection confronting the States, one does not reach the result here as an easy decision. In the case of such unwitnessed crimes as the Kurp's killings,

the trails of detection challenge the most imaginative capacities of law enforcement officers. Often there is little else the police can do than interrogate suspects as an indispensable part of criminal investigation. But when interrogation of a prisoner is so long continued, with such a purpose, and under such circumstances, as to make the whole proceeding an effective instrument for extorting an unwilling admission of guilt, due process precludes the use of the confession thus obtained. Under our accusatorial system, such an exploitation of interrogation, whatever its usefulness, is not a permissible substitute for judicial trial. (p. 635)

In *Wong Sun v. United States* (1963), a case involving an alleged narcotics trafficker known as Sea Dog, the Court reiterated that "It is a settled principle of the administration of criminal justice in the federal courts that a conviction must rest upon firmer ground than the uncorroborated admission or confession of the accused" (pp. 488-489). The Court went on to consider whether a confession could be admitted if it came after an illegal arrest. It can, when the person's act in making the statements is "sufficiently an act of free will to purge the primary taint of the unlawful invasion" (p. 486).

The defendant in *Townsend v. Sain* (1963) was a 19-year-old "near mental defective . . . just above a moron" (p. 303) who was a heroin addict and who experienced withdrawal symptoms during police interrogation. He contended that the treatment purported to assist him with withdrawal symptoms contained a drug that acted as a truth serum. The Court held that "a crucial fact was not disclosed at the state-court hearing: that the substance injected into Townsend before he confessed has properties which may trigger statements in a legal sense involuntary" (p. 321), and remanded the case for an evidentiary hearing. *Townsend* held that the ultimate constitutional question of the admissibility of a confession was a mixed question of fact and law subject to plenary federal review.

In *Lynumn v. Illinois* (1963), a woman was accused of selling marijuana to Zeno. Her

oral confession was made only after the police had told her that state financial aid for her infant children would be cut off, and her children taken from her, if she did not "cooperate." These threats were made while she was encircled in her apartment by three police officers and a twice convicted felon who had purportedly "set her up." There was no friend or adviser to whom she might turn. She had had no previous experience with the criminal law, and had no reason not to believe that the police had ample power to carry out their threats. We think it clear that a confession made under such circumstances must be deemed not voluntary, but coerced. (p. 534)

In the dissent in *Haynes v. Washington* (1963), Lynumn is characterized as a "naïve and impressionable defendant" (p. 522).

The defendant in *Haynes v. Washington* (1963) gave two oral confessions and signed one confession that was written out for him to sign, but refused to sign another written confession.

Haynes was not taken before a magistrate and granted a preliminary hearing until he had acceded to demands that he give and sign the written statement. Nor is there any indication in the record that prior to signing the written confession, or even thereafter, Haynes was advised by authorities of his right to remain silent, warned that his answers might be used against him, or told of his rights respecting consultation with an attorney. In addition, there is no contradiction of Haynes' testimony that even after he submitted and supplied the written confession used at trial, the police nonetheless continued the incommunicado detention while persisting in efforts to secure still another signature on another statement. Upon being returned to the deputy prosecutor's office during the week following his arrest and while still being held incommunicado, the petitioner was again asked to sign the second statement which he had given there several days earlier. He refused to do so, he said, because, as he then told the deputy prosecutor, "all the promises of all the officers I had talked to had not been fulfilled and I had not been able to call my wife and I would sign nothing under any conditions until I was allowed to call my wife to see about legal counsel." The State offered no evidence to rebut this testimony. (pp. 510-511)

There was no doubt about the defendant's guilt, and there was no doubt that the earlier confessions were voluntary, but the 5-4 majority nevertheless concluded that the police actions were a violation of Haynes' Constitutional rights:

Confronted with the express threat of continued incommunicado detention and induced by the promise of communication with and access to family, Haynes understandably chose to make and sign the damning written statement; given the unfair and inherently coercive context in which made, that choice cannot be said to be the voluntary product of a free and unconstrained will, as required by the Fourteenth Amendment. (p. 514)

The *Haynes* Court commented:

> We cannot blind ourselves to what experience unmistakably teaches: that even apart from the express threat, the basic techniques present here – the secret and incommunicado detention and interrogation – are devices adapted and used to extort confessions from suspects. Of course, detection and solution of crime is, at best, a difficult and arduous task requiring determination and persistence on the part of all responsible officers charged with the duty of law enforcement. And, certainly, we do not mean to suggest that all interrogation of witnesses and suspects is impermissible. Such questioning is undoubtedly an essential tool in effective law enforcement. The line between proper and permissible police conduct and techniques and methods offensive to due process is, at best, a difficult one to draw, particularly in cases such as this where it is necessary to make fine judgments as to the effect of psychologically coercive pressures and inducements on the mind and will of an accused. (pp. 514-515)

In *Massiah v. United States* (1964), the Court ruled that it was illegal to conduct an "indirect and surreptitious interrogation" (p. 206) by secretly taping his conversations "after he had been indicted and in the absence of his counsel" (p. 206).

In *Jackson v. Denno* (1964), the Court noted:

> It is now axiomatic that a defendant in a criminal case is deprived of due process of law if his conviction is founded, in whole or in part, upon an involuntary confession, without regard for the truth or falsity of the confession, and even though there is ample evidence aside from the confession to support the conviction. Equally clear is the defendant's constitutional right at some stage in the proceedings to object to the use of the confession and to have a fair hearing and a reliable determination on the issue of voluntariness, a determination uninfluenced by the truth or falsity of the confession. (pp. 376-377)

In other words, the trial court must consider whether a disputed confession was voluntary before allowing it to be presented to the jury. This overruled *Stein v. New York* (1953).

The dissent in *Escobedo v. Illinois* (1964) characterized the majority decision as "another major step in the direction of the goal which the

Court seemingly has in mind – to bar from evidence all admissions obtained from an individual suspected of crime, whether involuntarily made or not" (p. 496). One year before, in *Gideon v. Wainwright* (1963), the Court had held that every person accused of a crime is entitled to a lawyer at trial. And now, with the *Escobedo* decision, a defendant was going to have a right to consult with an attorney prior to police questioning! The dissent:

> Under this new approach one might just as well argue that a potential defendant is constitutionally entitled to a lawyer before, not after, he commits a crime, since it is then that crucial incriminating evidence is put within the reach of the Government by the would-be accused. Until now there simply has been no right guaranteed by the Federal Constitution to be free from the use at trial of a voluntary admission made prior to indictment. (p. 497)

So what did the Court decree in *Escobedo?* First was a history lesson:

> We have learned the lesson of history, ancient and modern, that a system of criminal law enforcement which comes to depend on the "confession" will, in the long run, be less reliable and more subject to abuses than a system which depends on extrinsic evidence independently secured through skillful investigation. . . . We have also learned the companion lesson of history that no system of criminal justice can, or should, survive if it comes to depend for its continued effectiveness on the citizens' abdication through unawareness of their constitutional rights. No system worth preserving should have to fear that if an accused is permitted to consult with a lawyer, he will become aware of, and exercise, these rights. If the exercise of constitutional rights will thwart the effectiveness of a system of law enforcement, then there is something very wrong with that system. (pp. 488-489)

Then came the decision:

> We hold, therefore, that where, as here, the investigation is no longer a general inquiry into an unsolved crime but has begun to focus on a particular suspect, the suspect has been taken into police custody, the police carry out a process of interrogations that lends itself to eliciting incriminating statements, the suspect has requested and been denied an opportunity to consult with his lawyer, and the police have

not effectively warned him of his absolute constitutional right to remain silent, the accused has been denied the Assistance of Counsel in violation of the Sixth Amendment to the Constitution as made obligatory upon the States by the Fourteenth Amendment, and that no statement elicited by the police during the interrogation may be used against him at a criminal trial. (p. 491, citation omitted)

Finally, "We hold only that when the process shifts from investigatory to accusatory – when its focus is on the accused and its purpose is to elicit a confession – our adversary system begins to operate, and, under the circumstances here, the accused must be permitted to consult with his lawyer" (p. 492).

MIRANDA

Attorney General George Wickersham was appointed by President Herbert Hoover to head the National Commission on Law Observance and Law Enforcement in 1929. In 1931 the Commission issued the "Report on Lawlessness in Law Enforcement" as volume 11 of a 14-volume report on criminal justice in America. "Documenting various in-custody abuses, the Wickersham Commission concluded that police use of brute physical force, threats of harm, intimidation, and protracted, incommunicado detention during interrogation was widespread. In short, the 'third degree' flourished in most American police departments" (Leo, 1992, p. 38).

When the U.S. Supreme Court considered the issue of interrogations and confessions in the seminal case of *Miranda v. Arizona* (1966), they cited the Wickersham report. The Court noted that continuing to the time of the *Miranda* decision in the 1960s, in some cases police continued to use brute force in the form of "beating, hanging, whipping" and in a case decided the year before *Miranda,* the police "placed lighted cigarette butts on the back of a potential witness under interrogation for the purpose of securing a statement incriminating a third party" (p. 446). The Court considered such cases to be exceptions in the 1960s, but sufficiently widespread to be cause for concern.

The Court quoted Lord Sankey: "It is not admissible to do a great right by doing a little wrong. . . . It is not sufficient to do justice by obtaining a proper result by irregular or improper means" (p. 448). Use of the third degree involves flagrant violations of the law by law enforcement officers, increases the danger of false confessions, "brutalizes the police, hardens the prisoner against society, and lowers the esteem in which the administration of Justice is held by the public" (p. 448).

The Court noted that, "the modern practice of in-custody interrogation is psychologically, rather than physically, oriented" and "recognized that coercion can be mental as well as physical" (p. 448). The Court noted that "Interrogation still takes place in privacy. Privacy results in secrecy, and this, in turn, results in a gap in our knowledge as to what, in fact, goes on in the interrogation rooms" (p. 448). The Court quotes from police interrogation manuals about how officers are encouraged to obtain confessions,[5] and concludes:

> From these representative samples of interrogation techniques, the setting prescribed by the manuals and observed in practice becomes clear. In essence, it is this: to be alone with the subject is essential to prevent distraction and to deprive him of any outside support. The aura of confidence in his guilt undermines his will to resist. He merely confirms the preconceived story the police seek to have him describe. Patience and persistence, at times relentless questioning, are employed. To obtain a confession, the interrogator must "patiently maneuver himself or his quarry into a position from which the desired objective may be attained." When normal procedures fail to produce the needed result, the police may resort to deceptive stratagems such as giving false legal advice. It is important to keep the subject off balance, for example, by trading on his insecurity about himself or his surroundings. The police then persuade, trick, or cajole him out of exercising his constitutional rights. (p. 455)

> The current practice of incommunicado interrogation is at odds with one of our Nation's most cherished principles – that the individual may not be compelled to incriminate himself. Unless adequate protective devices are employed to dispel the compulsion inherent in custodial surroundings, no statement obtained from the defendant can truly be the product of his free choice. (pp. 457-458)

The privilege against self-incrimination was elevated to Constitutional status in 1886 and "has always been 'as broad as the mischief

---

[5] I encourage the reader to read the *Miranda* decision (available via several online sources and accessible via an Internet search engine) to see what police interrogators were being encouraged to do before the interrogation manual writers anticipated that their works would be read by the Supreme Court justices.

against which it seeks to guard' " (pp. 459-460). Various government policies point to one overriding thought:

> The constitutional foundation underlying the privilege is the respect a government – state or federal – must accord to the dignity and integrity of its citizens. To maintain a "fair state-individual balance," to require the government "to shoulder the entire load," to respect the inviolability of the human personality, our accusatory system of criminal justice demands that the government seeking to punish an individual produce the evidence against him by its own independent labors, rather than by the cruel, simple expedient of compelling it from his own mouth. In sum, the privilege is fulfilled only when the person is guaranteed the right "to remain silent unless he chooses to speak in the unfettered exercise of his own will." (p. 460, citations omitted)

The Court ruled that these rights must be afforded people in police custody, not just at court hearings and trials, because "As a practical matter, the compulsion to speak in the isolated setting of the police station may well be greater than in courts or other official investigations, where there are often impartial observers to guard against intimidation or trickery" (p. 461).

In considering four cases, the Court addressed

> questions which go to the roots of our concepts of American criminal jurisprudence: the restraints society must observe consistent with the Federal Constitution in prosecuting individuals for crime. More specifically, we deal with the admissibility of statements obtained from an individual who is subjected to custodial police interrogation and the necessity for procedures which assure that the individual is accorded his privilege under the Fifth Amendment to the Constitution not to be compelled to incriminate himself. (p. 439)

The Court recognized "precious rights [that] were fixed in our Constitution only after centuries of persecution and struggle" (p. 442): "that 'No person . . . shall be compelled in any criminal case to be a witness against himself,' and that 'the accused shall . . . have the Assistance of Counsel' " (p. 442). The Court held:

> The prosecution may not use statements, whether exculpatory or inculpatory, stemming from custodial interrogation of the defendant unless it demonstrates the use of procedural safeguards effective to

secure the privilege against self-incrimination. By custodial interrogation, we mean questioning initiated by law enforcement officers after a person has been taken into custody or otherwise deprived of his freedom of action in any significant way. As for the procedural safeguards to be employed, unless other fully effective means are devised to inform accused persons of their right of silence and to assure a continuous opportunity to exercise it, the following measures are required. Prior to any questioning, the person must be warned that he has a right to remain silent, that any statement he does make may be used as evidence against him, and that he has a right to the presence of an attorney, either retained or appointed. The defendant may waive effectuation of these rights, provided the waiver is made voluntarily, knowingly and intelligently. If, however, he indicates in any manner and at any stage of the process that he wishes to consult with an attorney before speaking, there can be no questioning. Likewise, if the individual is alone and indicates in any manner that he does not wish to be interrogated, the police may not question him. The mere fact that he may have answered some questions or volunteered some statements on his own does not deprive him of the right to refrain from answering any further inquiries until he has consulted with an attorney and thereafter consents to be questioned. (pp. 444-445)

Of particular note to consulting psychologists is the following:

If the interrogation continues without the presence of an attorney and a statement is taken, a heavy burden rests on the government to demonstrate that the defendant knowingly and intelligently waived his privilege against self-incrimination and his right to retained or appointed counsel. This Court has always set high standards of proof for the waiver of constitutional rights, and we reassert these standards as applied to in-custody interrogation. Since the State is responsible for establishing the isolated circumstances under which the inter-rogation takes place, and has the only means of making available corroborated evidence of warnings given during incommunicado interrogation, the burden is rightly on its shoulders. (p. 475, citations omitted)

Miranda in Context

In *Berkemer v. McCarty* (1984), the U.S. Supreme Court explained that the purposes of the safeguards prescribed by *Miranda* are threefold:

1. to ensure that police do not coerce or trick captive suspects into confessing;
2. to relieve the inherently compelling pressures generated by the custodial setting itself, which work to undermine the individual's will to resist; and
3. as much as possible to free courts from the task of scrutinizing individual cases to try to determine, after the fact, whether particular confessions were voluntary.

There has been much commentary about how well these goals have been met (e.g., Leo, 1992; Leo & Thomas, 1998). To summarize: The first two goals were met to some extent in the first decade after *Miranda,* but police have developed effective ways to get around *Miranda,* and courts have allowed it. The third goal has not been met. More importantly, because the first two goals have not been met, the third goal *should not be met.* To expand on these points, we will follow Leo's (2001b) law review article. He writes:

> Contrary to . . . dire predictions, . . . police have successfully adapted to *Miranda* in the last four decades. Following an initial adjustment period, police have learned how to comply with *Miranda,* or at least how to create the appearance of compliance with *Miranda,* and still successfully elicit a high percentage of incriminating statements, admissions, and confessions from criminal suspects. (p. 1016)

> *Miranda* has exercised a long term impact on police behavior, court cases, and popular consciousness in at least four ways. First, *Miranda* increased the professionalism of police detectives, removing the last entrenched vestiges of the third degree. Second, *Miranda* has transformed the culture of police detecting in America by fundamentally reframing how police talk and think about the process of custodial interrogation. Third, *Miranda* has increased public awareness of constitutional rights. And fourth, *Miranda* has inspired police to develop more specialized, more sophisticated, and seemingly more effective interrogation techniques with which to elicit inculpatory statements from custodial suspects. (p. 1026)

Although *Miranda* led to significant changes following its inception, Leo (2001b) does not see it as fulfilling its promise now or in the future:

> Contrary to the visions of its creators, *Miranda* does not meaningfully dispel compulsion inside the interrogation room. *Miranda* has not

changed the psychological interrogation process it excoriated, but has only motivated police to develop more subtle and sophisticated – and arguably more compelling – interrogation strategies. How police "work" *Miranda* in practice makes a mockery of the notion that a suspect is effectively apprised of his rights and has a continuous opportunity to exercise them. *Miranda* offers no protection against traditionally coercive interrogation techniques, but may have, instead, weakened existing legal safeguards in this area. And *Miranda* offers suspects little, if any, protection against the elicitation and admission into evidence of false confessions. As a safeguard, *Miranda* produces very few benefits. (p. 1027)

Psychologists who consult on cases involving disputed confessions should keep this in mind. Although *Miranda* has had significant effects on our society, in an individual case there is no reason to treat proper *Miranda* warnings as a proxy for a detailed analysis of whether the confession was made voluntarily. Prior to the decision in *Miranda*, "Under the due process approach, . . . courts look to the totality of circumstances to determine whether a confession was voluntary. Those potential circumstances include . . . the failure of police to advise the defendant of his rights to remain silent and to have counsel present during custodial interrogation" (*Withrow v. Williams*, 1993, pp. 693-694, citing *Haynes v. Washington*, 1963). Subsequent to *Miranda*, due process continues to require that courts consider the totality of the circumstances in deciding voluntariness (*Berkemer v. McCarty*, 1984, at p. 433, n. 20; *Dickerson v. United States*, 2000). Post-*Miranda*, advising a suspect of his rights is a necessary, but not a sufficient, factor in determining that a confession was made voluntarily.

POST-*MIRANDA*

In *Johnson v. New Jersey* (1966), the Court decided that *Escobedo* and *Miranda* would not apply retroactively to cases heard before that decision, lest it pose an unjustifiable burden on the administration of justice. The totality-of-the-circumstances approach to voluntariness would continue to apply. Then in *Jenkins v. Delaware* (1969), the Court decided that *Miranda's* standards for determining the admissibility of in-custody statements would not apply to cases that were first tried before *Miranda*, then retried after *Miranda*.

In one such case, *Davis v. North Carolina* (1966), the fact that the defendant had not been advised of the rights subsequently spelled out in *Miranda* was one factor contributing to the Court's finding that the confession was involuntary. The Court commented:

> As is almost invariably so in cases involving confessions obtained through unobserved police interrogation, there is a conflict in the testimony as to the events surrounding the interrogations. Davis alleged that he was beaten, threatened, and cursed by police and that he was told he would get a hot bath and something to eat as soon as he signed a statement. This was flatly denied by each officer who testified. Davis further stated that he had repeatedly asked for a lawyer and that police refused to allow him to obtain one. This was also denied. Davis' sister testified at the habeas corpus hearing that she twice came to the police station and asked to see him, but that each time police officers told her Davis was not having visitors. Police officers testified that, on the contrary, upon learning of Davis' desire to see his sister, they went to her home to tell her Davis wanted to see her, but she informed them she was busy with her children. These factual allegations were resolved against Davis by the District Court (p. 741) [and therefore were not subject to review by the Supreme Court]. Wholly apart from the disputed facts, a statement of the case from facts established in the record, in our view, leads plainly to the conclusion that the confessions were the product of a will overborne. Elmer Davis is an impoverished Negro with a third or fourth grade education (p. 742), [with low intelligence, whose mother murdered his father, and who began his first prison sentence at age 15 or 16. He was held incommunicado, with limited food, for 16 days, and was interrogated once or twice each day. He was taken on a 14-mile hike on the railroad tracks to dispute an alibi, and was taken to a cemetery which was the scene of the crime. The Court noted:] We have never sustained the use of a confession obtained after such a lengthy period of detention and interrogation as was involved in this case. . . . Davis' confessions were the involuntary end product of coercive influences and are thus constitutionally inadmissible in evidence. (p. 752)

Teamsters president Jimmy Hoffa was the defendant in *Hoffa v. United States* (1966). The Court ruled that, going back to the 1807 trial of Aaron Burr, the Justices "all have agreed that a necessary element of compulsory self-incrimination is some kind of compulsion" (p. 304). The Court ruled that a paid police informant need not identify himself in order to collect incriminating statements, and the fact that a police agent gathers information surreptitiously does not mean that the statements were compelled.

In *Sims v. Georgia* (1967), the Court cited *Jackson v. Denno* (1964) and clarified that the voluntariness of a confession must be decided by the trial judge prior to submitting the confession to the jury.

In *Clewis v. Texas* (1967), the Court found the defendant's confession to be coerced. Clewis, "a Negro, had only a fifth-grade education" (p. 712). He was not advised of his rights prior to questioning. Regarding the interrogation procedures, which produced three statements, the Court wrote:

> The first statement was secured following an initial taking-into-custody which was concededly not supported by probable cause, followed by 38 hours of intermittent interrogation – despite the Texas rule that an accused be taken before a magistrate "immediately." . . . This was followed by prolonged, if intermittent, interrogation by numerous officers, in several buildings, punctuated by a trip to the gravesite and a long trip to another town, and accompanied by several polygraph tests. The police testimony makes it clear that the interrogation was not intended merely to secure information, but was specifically designed to elicit a signed statement of "the truth" – and the police view of "the truth" was made clear to petitioner. The petitioner repudiated each of the first two confessions shortly after it was made, and denied the truth of the third one at his trial. The record inspires substantial concern as to the extent to which petitioner's faculties were impaired by inadequate sleep and food, sickness, and long subjection to police custody with little or no contact with anyone other than police. (pp. 712-713)

In *In re Gault* (1967), the Court noted that "This Court has emphasized that admissions and confessions of juveniles require special caution" (p. 45) and "with respect to juveniles, both common observation and expert opinion emphasize that the 'distrust of confessions made in certain situations' . . . is imperative in the case of children from an early age through adolescence" (p. 48). The Court held:

> We conclude that the constitutional privilege against self-incrimination is applicable in the case of juveniles as it is with respect to adults. We appreciate that special problems may arise with respect to waiver of the privilege by or on behalf of children, and that there may well be some differences in technique, but not in principle, depending upon the age of the child and the presence and competence of parents. The participation of counsel will, of course, assist the police, Juvenile Courts and appellate tribunals in administering the

privilege. If counsel was not present for some permissible reason
when an admission was obtained, the greatest care must be taken to
assure that the admission was voluntary, in the sense not only that it
was not coerced or suggested, but also that it was not the product of
ignorance of rights or of adolescent fantasy, fright or despair. (p. 55)

The facts in *Beecher v. Alabama* (1967) and *Beecher v. Alabama*
(1972) were so severe that the Supreme Court unanimously ruled
Beecher's confessions involuntary – twice. The 1972 Court cited its
earlier ruling:

The uncontradicted facts of record are these. Tennessee police officers
saw the petitioner as he fled into an open field and fired a bullet into
his right leg. He fell, and the local Chief of Police pressed a loaded
gun to his face while another officer pointed a rifle against the side
of his head. The Police Chief asked him whether he had raped and
killed a white woman. When he said that he had not, the Chief called
him a liar and said, "If you don't tell the truth I am going to kill you."
The other officer then fired his rifle next to the petitioner's ear, and
the petitioner immediately confessed. Later the same day he received
an injection to ease the pain in his leg. He signed something the
Chief of Police described as "extradition papers" after the officers
told him that "it would be best ... to sign the papers before the gang
of people came there and killed" him. He was then taken by ambulance
from Tennessee to Kilby Prison in Montgomery, Alabama. By June
22, the petitioner's right leg, which was later amputated, had become
so swollen and his wound so painful that he required an injection of
morphine every four hours. Less than an hour after one of these
injections, two Alabama investigators visited him in the prison
hospital. The medical assistant in charge told the petitioner to
"cooperate" and, in the petitioner's presence, he asked the
investigators to inform him if the petitioner did not "tell them what
they wanted to know." The medical assistant then left the petitioner
alone with the State's investigators. In the course of a 90-minute
"conversation," the investigators prepared two detailed statements
similar to the confession the petitioner had given five days earlier at
gunpoint in Tennessee. Still in a "kind of slumber" from his last
morphine injection, feverish, and in intense pain, the petitioner signed
the written confessions thus prepared for him. (pp. 234-235)

The Court ruled that from when he,

already wounded by the police, was ordered at gunpoint to speak
his guilt or be killed . . . until he was directed five days later to tell

Alabama investigators "what they wanted to know," there was no break in the stream of events. For he was then still in pain, under the influence of drugs, and at the complete mercy of the prison hospital authorities. (p. 236)

Therefore any statements made during that time were considered to have been coerced.

Greenwald v. Wisconsin (1968) was the case of a nearly-30-year-old man with a ninth grade education. The Court considered that the following facts were

relevant to the claim that the statements were involuntary: the lack of counsel, especially in view of the accused's statement that he desires counsel; the lack of food, sleep, and medication; the lack or inadequacy of warnings as to constitutional rights. Considering the totality of these circumstances, we do not think it credible that petitioner's statements were the product of his free and rational choice. (p. 521, citations omitted)

In *Mathis v. United States* (1968), the Court held that Miranda warnings must be given prior to questioning an inmate in state prison about his taxes in a way that could lead to criminal charges. And in *Orozco v. Texas* (1969), the Court ruled that a person in his bedroom surrounded by four police officers and told he was under arrest was in custody, and therefore Miranda warnings were required prior to questioning.

Darwin v. Connecticut (1968) arose before the decisions in *Escobedo* and *Miranda,* so those decisions do not apply. Darwin was held incommunicado for 30 to 48 hours, was subjected to a device used to induce hypnosis, and was refused the use of a telephone. Police did not allow his lawyer to see him, and when his lawyer came to the police barracks, the officer in charge "took petitioner from the barracks and drove him around, apparently to protect him from what the officer thought were newspapermen" (p. 347). The Court deemed Darwin's eventual confession to be involuntary.

In *Harrison v. United States* (1968), the trial court admitted (over the defendant's objection) three in-custody confessions that were later deemed to have been coerced. But by then, the defendant had testified in an attempt to counteract the impact of the confessions. After a successful appeal, he was granted a new trial, but (over his objection) his testimony from the first trial was admitted. The Court ruled that the second trial court erred in admitting his earlier testimony because it was the fruit of the illegally obtained confessions.

The Court accepted as voluntary two of the defendant's three confessions in *Boulden v. Holman* (1969). As the dissent points out, the Court did not consider the voluntariness of the first confession, or its possible impact on subsequent interrogations. The defendant was "a slight, sickly youth, with an IQ of 83" (p. 488). His description, partially disputed by law enforcement officers, was that he

> was apprehended by law enforcement officers near the scene of the crime. According to petitioner, an officer of the Highway Patrol approached him and asked his name. "I told him; then he told me to run because he had been wanting to kill him a nigger a long time. . . . He told me to run, and then he throwed the rifle up like he was getting ready to shoot there." Petitioner was taken to the scene of the crime, where he was placed, in handcuffs, in a police car alone with Highway Patrol Captain Williams. He was not given any of the *Miranda* warnings. As petitioner related: "Captain Williams asked me what had happened, and I started to tell him; he cussed me and told me it wasn't. . . . I told Captain Williams I didn't do it, and he told me that I did . . . and he told me I was lying again. And he got mad and start cussing. . . . Well, he called me a little bastard and few more names. . . . Then he told me about if I didn't confess, that the officers that was wanting to kill me, he wasn't going to stop them. . . . I told him if he would get me out of there and wouldn't let them bother me, I would confess." Later, two other officers got into the back of the car. One of them "asked me how old I was, and I told him, and he told me I was old enough to die." There were about 15 or 20 officers at the scene, some of whom were armed with rifles and shotguns. Captain Williams testified that a "pretty good size crowd" was gathering – "I would say, in my best judgment, twenty-five or thirty cars . . . and people milling around out in the road." It was under these circumstances that petitioner first admitted to Captain Williams that he had committed the crime. (p. 487)

In *Frazier v. Cupp* (1969), the Court considered some trips and traps of interrogation. While interrogating Frazier regarding a murder, police falsely told him that his co-defendant had already confessed, and introduced a scenario that the deceased may have made homosexual advances prior to the attack. The Court held that police deception does not render a confession involuntary *per se*. Frazier's confession was deemed voluntary.

In *Procunier v. Atchley* (1971), the Court ruled that a person could utilize *habeas corpus* to seek a new hearing on voluntariness if he could show that his version of the events, if true, would require the conclusion that the statement was involuntary.

In *Harris v. New York* (1971), the Court ruled that any statements obtained during custodial interrogation conducted in violation of the *Miranda* rules may not be admitted against the accused, at least during the State's case in chief, but may, if its trustworthiness satisfies legal standards, be used for impeachment purposes to attack the credibility of a defendant's trial testimony.

In *Lego v. Twomey* (1972), the Court considered what standard of proof the trial judge should use when making a voluntariness determination as required by *Jackson v. Denno* (1964). The Court ruled: "the prosecution must prove at least by a preponderance of the evidence that the confession was voluntary. Of course, the States are free, pursuant to their own law, to adopt a higher standard" (p. 489).

In *Swenson v. Stidham* (1972), the Court held that at least in some cases an appeal based on *Jackson v. Denno* (1964) could be resolved in an appeals court without the necessity of a new trial.

In *LaValle v. Delle Rose* (1973), the Court was faced with a question about whether the trial court had properly considered the voluntariness of the defendant's two confessions. As with most (if not all) cases involving disputed confessions, there was dispute about what occurred in the process of interrogation. The trial court in this case had ruled Delle Rose's confessions voluntary, but had not articulated the factual basis for that decision. The District Court therefore conducted a hearing, and considered both confessions to be involuntary. Then the U.S. Supreme Court remanded the case, finding that the trial court's finding of voluntariness should have been allowed to stand.

The dissent in *LaValle v. Delle Rose* makes it clear that the crucial issue was what really happened during the interrogation: if what Delle Rose said about the interrogation procedures was true, including a "macabre" trip to the morgue and the forcing of his hands into his dead wife's blood, the confession was involuntary. If none of what Delle Rose said was true, then the confession would be considered voluntary. But, the Court wondered, what if some of what he said was true and some was not? This case exemplifies the potential utility of requiring that all interrogations be electronically recorded, and the frequent futility of trying to resolve disputes via swearing contests (with the defendant swearing that things happened one way and the interrogators swearing that they happened another way).

Although the case of *Schneckloth v. Bustamonte* (1973) involved the question of whether a *search* was voluntary, the Court provided a valuable review of the concept of voluntariness as it reflected on its decisions in *confession* cases:

> Those cases yield no talismanic definition of "voluntariness," mechanically applicable to the host of situations where the question has arisen. . . . It is thus evident that neither linguistics nor epistemology will provide a ready definition of the meaning of "voluntariness." Rather, "voluntariness" has reflected an accommodation of the complex of values implicated in police questioning of a suspect. At one end of the spectrum is the acknowledged need for police questioning as a tool for the effective enforcement of criminal laws. Without such investigation, those who were innocent might be falsely accused, those who were guilty might wholly escape prosecution, and many crimes would go unsolved. In short, the security of all would be diminished. At the other end of the spectrum is the set of values reflecting society's deeply felt belief that the criminal law cannot be used as an instrument of unfairness, and that the possibility of unfair and even brutal police tactics poses a real and serious threat to civilized notions of justice. In cases involving involuntary confessions, this Court enforces the strongly felt attitude of our society that important human values are sacrificed where an agency of the government, in the course of securing a conviction, wrings a confession out of an accused against his will. This Court's decisions reflect a frank recognition that the Constitution requires the sacrifice of neither security nor liberty. The Due Process Clause does not mandate that the police forgo all questioning, or that they be given carte blanche to extract what they can from a suspect. . . . In determining whether a defendant's will was overborne in a particular case, the Court has assessed the totality of all the surrounding circumstances – both the characteristics of the accused and the details of the interrogation. Some of the factors taken into account have included the youth of the accused, his lack of education, or his low intelligence, the lack of any advice to the accused of his constitutional rights, the length of detention, the repeated and prolonged nature of the questioning, and the use of physical punishment such as the deprivation of food or sleep. *In all of these cases, the Court determined the factual circumstances surrounding the confession, assessed the psychological impact on the accused, and evaluated the legal significance of how the accused reacted.* The significant fact about

all of these decisions is that none of them turned on the presence or absence of a single controlling criterion; each reflected a careful scrutiny of all the surrounding circumstances. In none of them did the Court rule that the Due Process Clause required the prosecution to prove as part of its initial burden that the defendant knew he had a right to refuse to answer the questions that were put. While the state of the accused's mind, and the failure of the police to advise the accused of his rights, were certainly factors to be evaluated in assessing the "voluntariness"'of an accused's responses, they were not in and of themselves determinative. (pp. 224-227, citations omitted, emphasis added)

In *Michigan v. Tucker* (1974), the Court considered a case that was tried after *Miranda* was decided, but that included a confession taken before *Miranda* was decided. There was no evidence of coercion. Although the police warnings were not as inclusive as the warnings outlined in *Miranda,* the Court ruled that the confession was admissible.

In *Oregon v. Hass* (1975), the Court considered facts similar to those in *Harris v. New York* (1971), and reached similar conclusions. A statement that is inadmissible due to lack of or improper Miranda warnings can be used for impeachment if the defendant testifies at trial.

In *Brown v. Illinois* (1975), two Chicago police officers "broke into [Richard Brown's] apartment, searched it, and then arrested Brown when he arrived, all without probable cause and without any warrant. They later testified that they made the arrest for the purpose of questioning Brown as part of their investigation of [a] murder" (p. 592). Although the arrest was illegal, the Supreme Court of Illinois ruled that Brown's subsequent statements could be admitted because he had been advised of his Miranda rights. As the U.S. Supreme Court put it, the Illinois Supreme Court

appears to have held that the Miranda warnings in and of themselves broke the causal chain so that any subsequent statement, even one induced by the continuing effects of unconstitutional custody, was admissible so long as, in the traditional sense, it was voluntary and not coerced in violation of the Fifth and Fourteenth Amendments. (p. 597)

The U.S. Supreme Court ruled that "Miranda warnings, and the exclusion of a confession made without them, do not alone sufficiently deter a Fourth Amendment violation" (p. 601). The Court recognized that otherwise

> Arrests made without warrant or without probable cause, for questioning or "investigation" would be encouraged by the knowledge that evidence derived therefrom could well be made admissible at trial by the simple expedient of giving Miranda warnings. Any incentive to avoid Fourth Amendment violations would be eviscerated by making the warnings, in effect, a "cure-all," and the constitutional guarantee against unlawful searches and seizures could be said to be reduced to "a form of words." (pp. 602-603, citation omitted)

Instead, the Court ruled, the facts of each case must be considered:

> The Miranda warnings are an important factor, to be sure, in determining whether the confession is obtained by exploitation of an illegal arrest. But they are not the only factor to be considered. The temporal proximity of the arrest and the confession, the presence of intervening circumstances, and, particularly, the purpose and flagrancy of the official misconduct are all relevant. The voluntariness of the statement is a threshold requirement. And the burden of showing admissibility rests, of course, on the prosecution. (pp. 603-604, citations omitted)

Similar analysis led to exclusion of confessions in *Dunaway v. New York* (1979), and *Taylor v. Alabama* (1982).

Quick Quiz: If a suspect exercises his or her right to remain silent, police may not question him or her further until

(a) after he or she is arraigned before a judicial officer (e.g., a judge), or
(b) after he or she has met with defense counsel, or
(c) after a couple of hours.

In *Michigan v. Mosley* (1975), the correct answer was "c." Richard Bert Mosley was arrested in connection to robberies at the Blue Goose Bar and the White Tower restaurant. After he declined to answer questions about those robberies, he was taken to a cellblock. Then a couple of hours later, a different detective had him brought to a different interrogation room, and he was advised of his Miranda rights regarding an unrelated murder. That was good enough. The Court wrote: "We therefore conclude that the admissibility of statements obtained after the person in custody has decided to remain silent depends under *Miranda* on whether his right to cut off questioning was scrupulously honored" (p. 104).

In *Beckwith v. United States* (1976), the Court declined to extend the necessity for Miranda warnings to situations other than custodial police interrogations, specifically, a noncustodial encounter with tax officials.

This quiz is based on *Doyle v. Ohio* (1976), which resolved an issue that had been raised in *United States v. Hale* (1975). True or false? If you exercise your Miranda right to remain silent, that can be used against you in court. The answer is "false." The Court reasoned:

> Silence in the wake of these warnings may be nothing more than the arrestee's exercise of these Miranda rights. . . . It would be fundamentally unfair and a deprivation of due process to allow the arrested person's silence to be used to impeach an explanation subsequently offered at trial. (p. 618)

Quiz: Given the following facts from *Oregon v. Mathiason* (1977), will the confession be allowed?

> The respondent in this case was interrogated behind closed doors at police headquarters in connection with a burglary investigation. He had been named by the victim of the burglary as a suspect, and was told by the police that they believed he was involved. He was falsely informed that his fingerprints had been found at the scene, and in effect was advised that by cooperating with the police he could help himself. Not until after he had confessed was he given the warnings set forth in *Miranda.* (p. 496)

If you said no, you would be consistent with Justice Marshall, who dissented, but you would nevertheless be wrong. The majority ruled that Miranda warnings were not necessary because it was not a custodial interrogation:

> In the present case . . . there is no indication that the questioning took place in a context where respondent's freedom to depart was restricted in any way. He came voluntarily to the police station, where he was immediately informed that he was not under arrest. At the close of a 1/2-hour interview respondent did in fact leave the police station

without hindrance. It is clear from these facts that Mathiason was not in custody or otherwise deprived of his freedom of action in any significant way. (p. 495)

Can you spell loophole? Remember that, because there will be more quizzes.

Here is another quiz based on *Brewer v. Williams* (1977):

Respondent was arrested, arraigned, and committed to jail in Davenport, Iowa, for abducting a 10-year-old girl in Des Moines, Iowa. Both his Des Moines lawyer and his lawyer at the Davenport arraignment advised respondent not to make any statements until after consulting with the Des Moines lawyer upon being returned to Des Moines, and the police officers who were to accompany respondent on the automobile drive back to Des Moines agreed not to question him during the trip. During the trip respondent expressed no willingness to be interrogated in the absence of an attorney but instead stated several times that he would tell the whole story after seeing his Des Moines lawyer. However, one of the police officers, who knew that respondent was a former mental patient and was deeply religious, sought to obtain incriminating remarks from respondent by stating to him during the drive that he felt they should stop and locate the girl's body because her parents were entitled to a Christian burial for the girl, who was taken away from them on Christmas Eve. Respondent eventually made several incriminating statements in the course of the trip and finally directed the police to the girl's body. (p. 387)

Can those incriminating statements be used against him at trial? No, because "the right to counsel granted by the Sixth and Fourteenth Amendments means at least that a person is entitled to the help of a lawyer at or after the time that judicial proceedings have been initiated against him – whether by way of formal charge, preliminary hearing, indictment, information, or arraignment" (p. 398). The disagreements about limiting police interrogation involve actions prior to initiation of judicial proceedings; once a defendant is charged, the right to an attorney is uncontroversial.

In *United States v. Washington* (1977), the Court did not consider a grand jury to be a setting that compels witnesses to incriminate themselves. Therefore, they did not require the same type of warnings for a person testifying before a grand jury as would be required for a suspect to be interrogated in police custody.

In *Mincey v. Arizona* (1978), the Court considered whether a confession taken while the suspect was suffering in the hospital could be used to impeach his testimony at trial. The Court wrote:

It is hard to imagine a situation less conducive to the exercise of a rational intellect and a free will than Mincey's. He had been seriously wounded just a few hours earlier, and had arrived at the hospital "depressed almost to the point of coma," according to his attending physician. Although he had received some treatment, his condition at the time of Hust's interrogation was still sufficiently serious that he was in the intensive care unit. He complained to Hust that the pain in his leg was "unbearable." He was evidently confused and unable to think clearly about either the events of that afternoon or the circumstances of his interrogation, since some of his written answers were on their face not entirely coherent. Finally, while Mincey was being questioned he was lying on his back on a hospital bed, encumbered by tubes, needles, and breathing apparatus. He was, in short, at the complete mercy of Detective Hust, unable to escape or resist the thrust of Hust's interrogation. In this debilitated and helpless condition, Mincey clearly expressed his wish not to be interrogated. As soon as Hust's questions turned to the details of the afternoon's events, Mincey wrote: "This is all I can say without a lawyer." Hust nonetheless continued to question him, and a nurse who was present suggested it would be best if Mincey answered. Mincey gave unresponsive or uninformative answers to several more questions, and then said again that he did not want to talk without a lawyer. Hust ignored that request and another made immediately thereafter. Indeed, throughout the interrogation Mincey vainly asked Hust to desist. Moreover, he complained several times that he was confused or unable to think clearly, or that he could answer more accurately the next day. But despite Mincey's entreaties to be let alone, Hust ceased the interrogation only during intervals when Mincey lost consciousness or received medical treatment, and after each such interruption returned relentlessly to his task. The statements at issue were thus the result of virtually continuous questioning of a seriously and painfully wounded man on the edge of consciousness. . . . It is apparent from the record in this case that Mincey's statements were not the product of his free and rational choice. To the contrary, the undisputed evidence makes clear that Mincey wanted not to answer Detective Hust. But Mincey was weakened by pain and shock, isolated from family, friends, and legal counsel, and barely conscious, and his will was simply overborne. Due process of law requires that statements obtained as these were cannot be used in any way against a defendant at his trial. (pp. 398-402)

Quick quiz, based on *North Carolina v. Butler* (1979): North Carolina's "prophylactic rule requiring the police to obtain an express waiver of the right to counsel before proceeding with interrogation" (p. 379) is

(a) required by the U.S. Constitution, consistent with *Miranda,*
(b) forbidden by the U.S. Constitution, or
(c) allowed by the U.S. Constitution, but not required.

The correct answer is "b." The U.S. Supreme Court does not require an *express* waiver. Therefore, "By creating an inflexible rule that no implicit waiver can ever suffice, the North Carolina Supreme Court has gone beyond the requirements of federal organic law. It follows that its judgment cannot stand, since a state court can neither add to nor subtract from the mandates of the United States Constitution" (p. 375). Even though "the respondent had refused to waive in writing his right to have counsel present and . . . there had not been a specific oral waiver" (p. 372), one was not required.

> An express written or oral statement of waiver of the right to remain silent or of the right to counsel is usually strong proof of the validity of that waiver, but is not inevitably either necessary or sufficient to establish waiver. The question is not one of form, but rather whether the defendant in fact knowingly and voluntarily waived the rights delineated in the *Miranda* case. As was unequivocally said in *Miranda,* mere silence is not enough. That does not mean that the defendant's silence, coupled with an understanding of his rights and course of conduct indicating waiver, may never support a conclusion that a defendant has waived his rights. The courts must presume that a defendant did not waive his rights; the prosecution's burden is great; but in at least some cases waiver can be clearly inferred from the actions and words of the person interrogated. (p. 373)

> Our decision today . . . is merely that a court may find an intelligent and understanding rejection of counsel in situations where the defendant did not expressly state as much. (p. 374)

A clarification is needed. Although state courts are not allowed to interpret the U.S. Constitution contrary to the U.S. Supreme Court's interpretation, states are still allowed to adopt greater safeguards than the U.S. Constitution requires, as noted in Justice Brennan's dissent in *Michigan v. Mosley* (1975):

> In light of today's erosion of *Miranda* standards as a matter of federal constitutional law, it is appropriate to observe that no State is precluded by the decision from adhering to higher standards under state law. Each State has power to impose higher standards governing police practices under state law than is required by the Federal Constitution.... Understandably, state courts and legislatures are, as matters of state law, increasingly according protections once provided as federal rights but now increasingly depreciated by decisions of this Court. (p. 121)

In *Dunaway v. New York* (1979), the Court ruled that "Detention for custodial interrogation – regardless of its label – intrudes so severely on interests protected by the Fourth Amendment as necessarily to trigger the traditional safeguards against illegal arrest" (p. 216), as described in *Brown v. Illinois* (1975). As later described in the dissent in *Moran v. Burbine* (1986), the *Dunaway* Court "corrected the long-held but mistaken view of the police that they have some sort of right to take any suspect into custody for the purpose of questioning him even though they may not have probable cause to arrest" (pp. 458-459).

Fare v. Michael C. (1979) is an important case that deals with issues relevant to juvenile court cases. The 16½-year-old Michael C. requested his probation officer, but did not specifically request the services of an attorney. The dissent considered that "a juvenile's request for a probation officer may frequently be an attempt to secure protection from the coercive aspects of custodial questioning" (pp. 730-731) (which was denied), "it is fatuous to assume that a minor in custody will be in a position to call an attorney for assistance" (p. 730), and "a request for such adult assistance is surely inconsistent with a present desire to speak freely" (p. 730). Although the California Supreme Court considered a juvenile's request to speak to his probation officer to be a *per se* invocation of his Fifth Amendment rights comparable to an adult's request to speak to his or her attorney, the majority in the U.S. Supreme Court did not see it that way. The U.S. Supreme Court applied the totality-of-the-circumstances analysis and ruled that there was no indication that Michael C. did not understand his Miranda rights or that he was coerced into confessing, and ruled that the confession could stand.

True or False: The prosecution bears the burden of proving that a defendant knowingly and intelligently waived his Miranda rights. Answer: True. In *Tague v. Louisiana* (1980), the Court ruled that simply reading the defendant his rights was not enough.

Another quick quiz, this one from *Rhode Island v. Innis* (1980): A man who is placed under arrest and advised of his Miranda rights invokes those rights by saying that he wants to talk to an attorney before questioning. On the way to the police station, a police officer expresses concern that some handicapped student at the nearby school might find the shotgun that was used in the crime and hurt someone. The suspect responds by directing the police to the location of the shotgun. Can that information be used against him at trial? (Do not forget how to spell loophole.) This time a yes answer puts you in accord with Justices Marshall and Brennan who dissented, but the majority insists that you are wrong. Because the police officer directed the remark to another police officer rather than the suspect, it does not count:

> The case thus boils down to whether, in the context of a brief conversation, the officers should have known that the respondent would suddenly be moved to make a self-incriminating response. Given the fact that the entire conversation appears to have consisted of no more than a few offhand remarks, we cannot say that the officers should have known that it was reasonably likely that Innis would so respond. This is not a case where the police carried on a lengthy harangue in the presence of the suspect. Nor does the record support the respondent's contention that, under the circumstances, the officers' comments were particularly "evocative." It is our view, therefore, that the respondent was not subjected by the police to words or actions that the police should have known were reasonably likely to elicit an incriminating response from him. (p. 303)

If a suspect invokes his Miranda rights one day, can the police come back and ask him to waive them the next day? No. In *Edwards v. Arizona* (1981), the Court noted that "waivers of counsel must not only be voluntary, but must also constitute a knowing and intelligent relinquishment or abandonment of a known right or privilege, a matter which depends in each case upon the particular facts and circumstances surrounding that case, including the background, experience, and conduct of the accused" (p. 482, citations omitted).

Here . . . neither the trial court nor the Arizona Supreme Court undertook to focus on whether Edwards understood his right to counsel and intelligently and knowingly relinquished it. . . . Second, although we have held that after initially being advised of his Miranda rights, the accused may himself validly waive his rights and respond to interrogation, the Court has strongly indicated that additional safeguards are necessary when the accused asks for counsel; and we now hold that when an accused has invoked his right to have counsel present during custodial interrogation, a valid waiver of that right cannot be established by showing only that he responded to further police-initiated custodial interrogation even if he has been advised of his rights. We further hold that an accused, such as Edwards, having expressed his desire to deal with the police only through counsel, is not subject to further interrogation by the authorities until counsel has been made available to him, unless the accused himself initiates further communication, exchanges, or conversations with the police. (pp. 484-485, citation omitted)

In *California v. Prysock* (1981), the Court ruled that a suspect must be advised of his or her rights consistent with *Miranda,* but the warnings need not be delivered just like in *Miranda,* and they need not be presented in the same order.

In *Wyrick v. Fields* (1982), a soldier was charged with raping an 81-year-old woman. After consultation with a private attorney and with an attorney provided by the Army, Fields requested a polygraph examination. At issue before the court was the interrogation after the polygraph, which was initiated by the police and conducted without Fields' attorneys. The Court held that by requesting the polygraph Fields initiated further contact with police, which satisfied the requirement in *Edwards v. Arizona* (1981), so his confession was admissible.

The case of *Oregon v. Bradshaw* (1983) involved a traumatically injured and drowned boy, a suspect's request for an attorney followed shortly by his question "Well, what is going to happen to me now?", John-Paul Sartre[6] (p. 1055), and the mysterious phrase *"ex proprio vigore"*[7] (p. 1040). The decision in the case apparently hinged on what the meaning of "Well, what is going to happen to me now?" is. Was the suspect, who had allegedly gotten drunk and wrecked his pickup truck,

---

[6] For an interesting fictional discussion of existentialism in Botswana, see McCall Smith, A. (2001). *Morality for Beautiful Girls.* Edinburgh: Polygon (p. 76).

[7] An 1893 dictionary defines this as "by its own inherent force." See http://www.ecclesia.org/lawgiver/W.asp

initiating the kind of general discussion that Sartre would initiate before a class of philosophy students? Was he saying to the policeman who had stopped questioning him after his request for an attorney, "Please, sir, I want some more," or was he simply asking where the police were taking him?[8] The dissent noted that

> The Oregon Court of Appeals concluded that respondent's question was not "a waiver of his right to counsel, invoked only minutes before, or anything other than a normal reaction to being taken from the police station and placed in a police car, obviously for transport to some destination." (p. 1054)

The U.S. Supreme Court could not reach agreement one way or the other. They split 4-1-4, deciding that Bradshaw's confession was admissible, but not setting any precedent for future cases.

The Court clarified the loophole described in some of our quizzes in *California v. Behele* (1983). While Peggy Dean was selling hashish in the parking lot of a liquor store, Jerry Beheler and his stepbrother Danny Wilbanks tried to rob her. She resisted, and Wilbanks killed her. Beheler called the police, told them Wilbanks had killed Dean, and gave them information that helped them find the murder weapon. He then went to the police station and answered questions for less than 30 minutes, without being advised of his Miranda rights. Five days later he was arrested, and this time he was advised of his Miranda rights before questioning. In considering the totality of the circumstances, the California Court of Appeal reversed Beheler's conviction for aiding and abetting first-degree murder, finding that the initial questioning at the police station was custodial. The U.S. Supreme Court found that it was not, clarifying as follows:

> Although the circumstances of each case must certainly influence a determination of whether a suspect is "in custody" for purposes of receiving Miranda protection, the ultimate inquiry is simply whether there is a "formal arrest or restraint on freedom of movement" of the degree associated with a formal arrest. . . . We have explicitly recognized that Miranda warnings are not required simply because the questioning takes place in the station house, or because the questioned person is one whom the police suspect. (p. 1125, citation omitted)

---

[8] Bradshaw asked the question while in a police car that was to take him to jail.

Quiz: Which is true?

(a) If a suspect invokes his or her right to counsel, the police can continue to question the suspect if they want; it is up to the suspect whether or not to answer.

(b) Once a suspect has invoked his or her right to counsel, any subsequent discussion must be initiated by the suspect.

(c) Once a suspect has invoked his or her right to counsel, any subsequent discussion must be initiated by the suspect, unless that discussion began before May 18, 1981.

(d) Once a suspect has invoked his or her right to counsel, any subsequent discussion must be initiated by the suspect, unless that discussion began before May 18, 1981, *and* the case was *not* pending on direct appeal in a state court on May 18, 1981.

My reading of the relevant cases suggests the following. Choice "a" was correct until *Miranda* was decided in 1966. Choice "b" became correct in 1966, and was explicated in *Edwards v. Arizona* (1981).[9] Then in *Solem v. Stumes* (1984), the Court decided that the answer is "c" because it "would have a disruptive effect on the administration of justice" (p. 650) to apply the *Edwards* standards retroactively." Then in *Shea v. Louisiana* (1985), the Court added the additional qualifier in "d" because not to do so "would be a rule that confined the *Edwards* principle to prospective application unavailable even to Edwards himself" (p. 60).

A dissent in *New York v. Quarles* (1984) presents a nice summary of how the U.S. Supreme Court has addressed confession cases pre- and post-*Miranda,* which provides us with a useful review:

> *Miranda v. Arizona* was the culmination of a century-long inquiry into how this Court should deal with confessions made during custodial interrogations. Long before *Miranda,* the Court had recognized that the Federal Government was prohibited from introducing at criminal trials compelled confessions, including confessions compelled in the course of custodial interrogations. . . . Prosecutors in state courts were subject to similar constitutional restrictions. . . . When *Miranda* reached this Court, it was undisputed that both the States and the Federal Government were constitutionally

---

[9]   An alternate interpretation is that "a" remained true until *Edwards* was decided.

prohibited from prosecuting defendants with confessions coerced during custodial interrogations. As a theoretical matter, the law was clear. In practice, however, the courts found it exceedingly difficult to determine whether a given confession had been coerced. Difficulties of proof and subtleties of interrogation technique made it impossible in most cases for the judiciary to decide with confidence whether the defendant had voluntarily confessed his guilt or whether his testimony had been unconstitutionally compelled. Courts around the country were spending countless hours reviewing the facts of individual custodial interrogations. *Miranda* dealt with these practical problems. After a detailed examination of police practices and a review of its previous decisions in the area, the Court in *Miranda* determined that custodial interrogations are inherently coercive. The Court therefore created a constitutional presumption that statements made during custodial interrogations are compelled in violation of the Fifth Amendment and are thus inadmissible in criminal prosecutions. As a result of the Court's decision in *Miranda,* a statement made during a custodial interrogation may be introduced as proof of a defendant's guilt only if the prosecution demonstrates that the defendant knowingly and intelligently waived his constitutional rights before making the statement. The now-familiar Miranda warnings offer law enforcement authorities a clear, easily administered device for ensuring that criminal suspects understand their constitutional rights well enough to waive them and to engage in consensual custodial interrogation. (pp. 683-684)

Now for a quiz, based on *Quarles:* Quarles was suspected of committing rape and of illegally having a firearm. When he was caught late at night in the back of a near-empty supermarket, his hands were cuffed behind his back, he was frisked, and he was surrounded by four armed police officers. It was noted that he had an empty holster. Without administering the Miranda warnings, an arresting officer asked where the gun was. Quarles gestured and correctly told the police where the gun was. (a) Can that statement be used against him at trial? (b) Can the gun be presented as evidence? In considering these questions, the Court considered that the suspect was in custody and was questioned without Miranda warnings, which *until this case* would have required exclusion of both the statements and the gun. But the Court decided that both the statement and the gun could be admitted in evidence, creating a new exception to the Miranda rule: "We conclude that the need for answers to questions in a situation posing a threat to the public safety outweighs the need for the prophylactic rule protecting the Fifth Amendment's privilege against self-incrimination" (p. 657). (The aforementioned dissent provides [a] a convincing factual discussion that there was no real public safety risk in the *Quarles* case, and [b] a convincing legal argument that even when there might be a risk to public safety, it is neither necessary nor acceptable to violate a suspect's Constitutional rights in order to resolve such a safety issue.)

Berkemer v. McCarty (1984) was mentioned in the previous section dealing with *Miranda.* In *Berkemer,* the Court held that Miranda warnings are required for misdemeanor as well as felony arrests, but that a routine traffic stop does not constitute custodial interrogation for the purposes of the Miranda rule.

In *Smith v. Illinois* (1984), the Court clearly described the analysis relevant to the *Edwards v. Arizona* (1981) rule.

> An accused in custody, having expressed his desire to deal with the police only through counsel, is not subject to further interrogation by the authorities until counsel has been made available to him, unless he validly waives his earlier request for the assistance of counsel. This rigid prophylactic rule embodies two distinct inquiries. First, courts must determine whether the accused actually invoked his right to counsel. Second, if the accused invoked his right to counsel, courts may admit his responses to further questioning only on finding that he (a) initiated further discussions with the police, and (b) knowingly and intelligently waived the right he had invoked. (pp. 94-95, citations omitted)

In *Smith,* the Court rejected the notion that police could continue interrogation after an unambiguous request for counsel and then see if the suspect's subsequent responses would make the initial invocation seem ambiguous.

And now a quiz based on *Oregon v. Elstad* (1985): A defendant is interrogated in custody without Miranda warnings and admits involvement in the crime. That statement is inadmissible. If interrogators want to begin anew, give proper Miranda warnings, and get an admissible statement, the interrogators must

(a) advise the suspect that the earlier statement cannot be used against him or her, or

(b) advise the suspect that any earlier statement that was not preceded by Miranda warnings could not be used against him or her, or

(c) do nothing other than give ordinary proper Miranda warnings,
     since it would be mere speculation to imagine that a suspect
     would think that he or she would have nothing to lose by
     confessing to a crime to which he or she has already confessed.

Although two dissents eloquently and convincingly bemoaned the
continuing dilution of *Miranda,* the majority chose "c."

> This Court has never embraced the theory that a defendant's ignorance
> of the full consequences of his decisions vitiates their voluntari-
> ness. . . . We have not held that the *sine qua non* for a knowing and
> voluntary waiver of the right to remain silent is a full and complete
> appreciation of all of the consequences flowing from the nature and
> the quality of the evidence in the case. (pp. 316-317)

And,

> If errors are made by law enforcement officers in administering the
> prophylactic Miranda procedures, they should not breed the same
> irremediable consequences as police infringement of the Fifth
> Amendment itself. It is an unwarranted extension of *Miranda* to hold
> that a simple failure to administer the warnings, unaccompanied by
> any actual coercion or other circumstances calculated to undermine
> the suspect's ability to exercise his free will, so taints the investigatory
> process that a subsequent voluntary and informed waiver is ineffective
> for some indeterminate period. Though *Miranda* requires that the
> unwarned admission must be suppressed, the admissibility of any
> subsequent statement should turn in these circumstances solely on
> whether it is knowingly and voluntarily made. (p. 309)

The Court considered a case involving a loose heifer, a mutilated
human corpse, a disputed confession, and the question whether federal
courts should consider the voluntariness of a confession to be a factual
issue that, absent certain exceptions, should be left to the state courts.
In *Miller v. Fenton* (1985), the Court ignored the heifer and the mutilated
corpse, but ruled that the voluntariness of a confession would continue
to be considered to be a mixed question of fact and law, subject to
plenary federal review.

I take special interest in *Wainwright v. Greenfield* (1986) because it
arose from my home county of Sarasota, Florida (though the events
occurred slightly before I moved here). Greenfield, who was charged

with sexual battery, pled insanity. Despite the fact that Greenfield did not testify, the prosecution used his invocation of his Miranda rights as evidence that he was thinking clearly at the time of his arrest (which was two hours after the alleged assault). The Court disallowed this, noting that it violates "the implied assurance contained in the Miranda warnings that silence will carry no penalty" (p. 290).

Quiz: Is the following quote from the majority or the dissent in *Moran v. Burbine* (1986)?

> Police interference in the attorney-client relationship is the type of governmental misconduct on a matter of central importance to the administration of justice that the Due Process Clause prohibits. Just as the police cannot impliedly promise a suspect that his silence will not be used against him and then proceed to break that promise, so too police cannot tell a suspect's attorney that they will not question the suspect and then proceed to question him. Just as the government cannot conceal from a suspect material and exculpatory evidence, so too the government cannot conceal from a suspect the material fact of his attorney's communication. Police interference with communications between an attorney and his client violates the due process requirement of fundamental fairness. (pp. 467-468)

Answer: This quote is from the dissent. The majority ruled admissible a confession obtained from a suspect who was deprived of contact with his attorney by police deception, as long as the active deception (in this case, a lie) was perpetrated by the police against the attorney, not the suspect, and the deception of the suspect was by omission (not telling him that his attorney wanted to talk to him). The dissent wrote:

> This case turns on a proper appraisal of the role of the lawyer in our society. If a lawyer is seen as a nettlesome obstacle to the pursuit of wrongdoers – as in an inquisitorial society – then the Court's decision today makes a good deal of sense. If a lawyer is seen as an aid to the understanding and protection of constitutional rights – as in an accusatorial society – then today's decision makes no sense at all. Like the conduct of the police in the Cranston station on the evening of June 29, 1977, the Court's opinion today serves the goal of insuring that the perpetrator of a vile crime is punished. Like the police on that June night as well, however, the Court has trampled on well-

established legal principles and flouted the spirit of our accusatorial system of justice. (p. 467)

The dissent in *Burbine* documented the fact that "Police interference with communications between an attorney and his client is a recurrent problem. . . . Its recurrence suggests that it has roots in some condition fundamental and general to our criminal system" (p. 441, citation omitted).

The majority in *Burbine* wrote: "Quite understandably, the dissent is outraged by the very idea of police deception of a lawyer" (p. 434). The majority ruling was circumscribed as follows: "[We are not] prepared to adopt a rule requiring that the police inform a suspect of an attorney's efforts to reach him" (p. 425), but

> nothing we say today disables the States from adopting different requirements for the conduct of its employees and officials as a matter of state law. We hold only that the Court of Appeals erred in construing the Fifth Amendment to the Federal Constitution to require the exclusion of respondent's three confessions. (p. 428)

Indeed, the Court found the police action distasteful,[10] but they ruled that if it is to be prohibited, it should be prohibited on grounds other than the Fifth Amendment.

The majority in *Burbine* wrote that when a court is to decide whether a waiver was made voluntarily, knowingly, and intelligently,

> the inquiry has two distinct dimensions. First, the relinquishment of the right must have been voluntary in the sense that it was the product of a free and deliberate choice rather than intimidation, coercion, or deception. Second, the waiver must have been made with a full awareness of both the nature of the right being abandoned and the consequences of the decision to abandon it. Only if the totality of the circumstances surrounding the interrogation reveals both an uncoerced choice and the requisite level of comprehension may a court properly conclude that the Miranda rights have been waived. (p. 421, citations omitted)

In *Michigan v. Jackson* (1986), two "defendants had requested counsel during their arraignments, but were not afforded an opportunity

---

[10] So, arguably, it should be prohibited.

to consult with counsel before the police initiated further interrogations" (p. 626). The Court held that to be impermissible, and considered their confessions to be inadmissible.

For the next case, recall that in *Jackson v. Denno* (1964) and *Sims v. Georgia* (1967), the Court ruled that the voluntariness of a confession must be decided by the trial judge prior to submitting the confession to the jury. In *Crane v. Kentucky* (1986), the Court considered whether the jury must also be allowed to hear the same kind of evidence to consider the trustworthiness of a confession. In a decision that should be familiar to consulting psychologists, the Court unanimously decided that question in the affirmative:

> Prior to his trial for murder, petitioner moved to suppress his confession. The trial judge conducted a hearing, determined that the confession was voluntary, and denied the motion. At trial, petitioner sought to introduce testimony about the physical and psychological environment in which the confession was obtained. His objective in so doing was to suggest that the statement was unworthy of belief. The trial court ruled that the testimony pertained solely to the issue of voluntariness and was therefore inadmissible. The question presented is whether this ruling deprived petitioner of his rights under the Sixth and Fourteenth Amendments to the Federal Constitution. (p. 684)

At a suppression hearing (the defense had moved to suppress the confession), the defendant, a 16-year-old boy,

> testified that he had been detained in a windowless room for a protracted period of time, that he had been surrounded by as many as six police officers during the interrogation, that he had repeatedly requested and been denied permission to telephone his mother, and that he had been badgered into making a false confession. (p. 685)

The trial court denied the motion, and the jury was allowed to hear about the confession.

In her opening statement in *Crane,*

> defense counsel outlined what would prove to be the principal avenue of defense advanced at trial – that, for a number of reasons, the story petitioner had told the police should not be believed. The confession was rife with inconsistencies, counsel argued. For example, petitioner had told the police that the crime was committed during daylight

hours and that he had stolen a sum of money from the cash register. In fact, counsel told the jury, the evidence would show that the crime occurred at 10:40 p.m. and that no money at all was missing from the store. Beyond these inconsistencies, counsel suggested, "the very circumstances surrounding the giving of the [confession] are enough to cast doubt on its credibility." In particular, she continued, evidence bearing on the length of the interrogation and the manner in which it was conducted would show that the statement was unworthy of belief. (p. 685)

In response to the prosecution's objection, the trial court

expressly held that the defense could inquire into the inconsistencies contained in the confession, but would not be permitted to develop in front of the jury any evidence about the duration of the interrogation or the individuals who were in attendance. After registering a continuing objection, petitioner invoked a . . . procedure under which he was permitted to develop a record of the evidence he would have put before the jury were it not for the court's evidentiary ruling.[11] That evidence included testimony from two police officers about the size and other physical characteristics of the interrogation room, the length of the interview, and various other details about the taking of the confession. (p. 686)

The U.S. Supreme Court ruled in *Crane* that such evidence must be admitted:

The manner in which a statement was extracted is, of course, relevant to the purely legal question of its voluntariness, a question most, but not all, States assign to the trial judge alone to resolve. But the physical and psychological environment that yielded the confession can also be of substantial relevance to the ultimate factual issue of the defendant's guilt or innocence. Confessions, even those that have been found to be voluntary, are not conclusive of guilt. And, as with any other part of the prosecutor's case, a confession may be shown to be insufficiently corroborated or otherwise . . . unworthy of belief. Indeed, stripped of the power to describe to the jury the circumstances that prompted his confession, the defendant is effectively disabled from answering the one question every rational juror needs answered: If the defendant is innocent, why did he previously admit his guilt? Accordingly, regardless of whether the defendant marshaled the same

---

[11] This is called a "proffer."

evidence earlier in support of an unsuccessful motion to suppress, and entirely independent of any question of voluntariness, a defendant's case may stand or fall on his ability to convince the jury that the manner in which the confession was obtained casts doubt on its credibility. (pp. 688-689, citations omitted)

Colorado v. Connelly (1986) presented an extreme case. Recall that the dissent in *Ashcraft v. Tennessee* (1944) noted: "A confession is wholly and incontestably voluntary only if a guilty person gives himself up to the law and becomes his own accuser" (p. 161). Connelly did so, and the question of the voluntariness of his confession was related to command hallucinations telling him to confess, not to police officers encouraging him to do so. The Court ruled:

1. Coercive police activity is a necessary predicate to finding that a confession is not "voluntary" within the meaning of the Due Process Clause. Here, the taking of respondent's statements and their admission into evidence constituted no violation of that Clause. While a defendant's mental condition may be a "significant" factor in the "voluntariness" calculus, this does not justify a conclusion that his mental condition, by itself and apart from its relation to official coercion, should ever dispose of the inquiry into constitutional "voluntariness."
2. Whenever the State bears the burden of proof in a motion to suppress a statement allegedly obtained in violation of the Miranda doctrine, the State need prove waiver only by a preponderance of the evidence. . . . Thus, the Colorado Supreme Court erred in applying a "clear and convincing evidence" standard. That court also erred in its analysis of the question whether respondent had waived his Miranda rights. Notions of "free will" have no place in this area of constitutional law. Respondent's perception of coercion flowing from the "voice of God" is a matter to which the Federal Constitution does not speak. (pp. 157-158)

In *Connecticut v. Barrett* (1987), the Court considered a case in which a man, after being given the Miranda warnings, "was willing to talk about [the incident] verbally but he did not want to put anything in writing until his attorney came" (p. 526). The Connecticut Supreme Court considered his confession inadmissible because his express desire for counsel before making a written statement constituted an invocation of his right to counsel for all purposes. The U.S. Supreme Court ruled otherwise, stating that there had been a limited request for counsel, that Barrett himself had drawn a distinction between oral and written statements, and that the officers could therefore continue to question him.

Colorado v. Spring (1987) was not a case in which a state known for winter sports tried to judicially extend the skiing season. Rather, it was about how much interrogators need tell a suspect about the interrogation for the suspect to be able to knowingly waive Miranda rights. Federal agents questioned John Leroy Spring in Missouri, initially focusing on interstate transport of stolen firearms, but segueing into inquiry regarding a murder in Colorado. At the time Miranda warnings were given, there was no hint that his statement would be used in a murder investigation. Could his waiver be considered valid? It could. The Court ruled that an interrogator's silence about the possible or intended use of the suspect's statement could not be construed as misleading, and that interrogators were not required to tell a suspect what case or cases they were investigating.

Quiz, based on *Arizona v. Roberson* (1988): If a suspect remains confined after invoking the right to counsel for one police investigation, can he be approached for questioning by other police officers regarding a separate investigation? Answer: No.

The case of *Patterson v. Illinois* (1988) involved a rumble between the rival gangs Vice Lords and Black Mobsters, one dead Black Mobster lying face down in a puddle of water, and a post-indictment interrogation leading to a confession. The adversary process begins at indictment, and the Sixth Amendment guarantees the accused a right to counsel then, but there is typically a time gap "between the commencement of the adversary process and the time at which counsel is appointed for a defendant" (p. 301). Can police question a defendant (who is not just a suspect anymore) after indictment, without counsel, if the defendant is given the Miranda warnings and waives his right to counsel? Yes, said the Court, in a 5-4 decision.

Some police departments have employed variations of Miranda warnings that advise the suspect of the right to an attorney "if and when you go to court." The four justices who dissented in *Duckworth v. Eagan* (1989) wrote

> Under *Miranda,* a police warning must clearly inform a suspect taken into custody that if he cannot afford an attorney one will be appointed

for him prior to any questioning if he so desires. A warning qualified by an "if and when you go to court" caveat does nothing of the kind; instead, it leads the suspect to believe that a lawyer will not be provided until some indeterminate time in the future after questioning. (p. 214, citation omitted)

The dissent does not claim, but one might surmise, that when police add the "if and when you go to court" caveat, they do so purposefully, to mislead the suspect. The majority in *Duckworth v. Eagan* found the warning given to Eagan to be good enough because it "touched all of the bases required by Miranda" (p. 203) and could be understood[12] in a way consistent with the intent in *Miranda*.

Butler v. McKellar (1990) involved consideration of whether the decision in *Arizona v. Roberson* (1988) was a new rule or merely a clarification of the *Edwards v. Arizona* (1981) rule. A divided court held that it was a new rule that would therefore not be applied retroactively; therefore, Butler's confession was admissible.

The ploy used in *Illinois v. Perkins* (1990) is best described by Justice Brennan, who wrote an opinion concurring with the judgment:

The police devised a ruse to lure respondent into incriminating himself when he was in jail on an unrelated charge. A police agent, posing as a fellow inmate and proposing a sham escape plot, tricked respondent into confessing that he had once committed a murder, as a way of proving that he would be willing to do so again should the need arise during the escape. (p. 302)

It is not surprising that the undercover agent did not advise Perkins of his Miranda rights. The Court found that to be acceptable, and reminded us why Miranda warnings are necessary:

The warning mandated by *Miranda* was meant to preserve the privilege during incommunicado interrogation of individuals in a police-dominated atmosphere. That atmosphere is said to generate inherently compelling pressures which work to undermine the individual's will to resist and to compel him to speak where he would not otherwise do so freely. Fidelity to the doctrine announced in *Miranda* requires that it be enforced strictly, but only in those types of situations in which the concerns that powered the decision are implicated. Conversations between suspects and undercover agents

---

[12] The dissent considered that possibility to be insufficient, noting that *Miranda* requires a clear warning.

do not implicate the concerns underlying *Miranda*. The essential ingredients of a police-dominated atmosphere and compulsion are not present when an incarcerated person speaks freely to someone whom he believes to be a fellow inmate. Coercion is determined from the perspective of the suspect. When a suspect considers himself in the company of cellmates and not officers, the coercive atmosphere is lacking. There is no empirical basis for the assumption that a suspect speaking to those whom he assumes are not officers will feel compelled to speak by the fear of reprisal for remaining silent or in the hope of more lenient treatment should he confess. (pp. 296-297, citations omitted)

Perkins' statement was deemed admissible. (Justice Brennan notes that the lack of a Miranda warning might not be permissible if the person in custody had invoked his right to an attorney or had been formally charged on the case for which he was being questioned. Justice Brennan also notes that Perkins could pursue a separate appeal asserting that his statements were made involuntarily, due to deception.)

We now begin a new quiz: Name that Justice. The quote is from *Minnick v. Mississippi* (1990): "Today's extension of the *Edwards* prohibition is the latest stage of prophylaxis built upon prophylaxis, producing a veritable fairyland castle of imagined constitutional restriction upon law enforcement" (p. 166). *Answer:* Justice Antonin Scalia. Recall that in *Edwards v. Arizona* (1981) the Court held that once the accused invokes his right to counsel, the interrogation must cease until an attorney is present. But what happens after the attorney comes and eventually, inevitably, leaves? Are the police then allowed to re-initiate questioning, perhaps "badgering a defendant into waiving his previously asserted Miranda rights" (p. 150), without the advice or knowledge of the attorney? No. If the accused person does not initiate conversation or discussion with the police, the police cannot question him or her.

Quiz, based on *Michigan v. Harvey* (1990): A person has been arrested and charged with rape. He invokes his right to counsel and prepares for trial. After 2 months go by, with his trial due to begin in a few days, some police officers decide to question him, without the knowledge or consent of his attorney, to get further information that can be used against him at trial. Are they allowed to do that?

(a) Yes.
(b) No.

(c) Yes, but the defendant's statement cannot be used in the prosecution's case in chief; his or her statements can only be used to impeach his or her testimony if he or she testifies.

The dissent wrote: "Although the interview was conducted by a police officer rather than a lawyer, it was in many respects comparable to a pretrial deposition. The value of representation by counsel is evident" (pp. 367-368), so conducting such an interview without defense counsel is a "shabby practice" (p. 368). The dissent considered the majority's decision to mean that "a rule of law may be ignored, avoided, or manipulated" (p. 369). Nevertheless, the majority's opinion makes "c" the right answer.

The defendant in *Arizona v. Fulminante* (1991)[13] was suspected of murdering his 11-year-old stepdaughter. He confessed to a fellow prison inmate that he had driven her "to the desert on his motorcycle, where he choked her, sexually assaulted her, and made her beg for her life, before shooting her twice in the head" (p. 283). That fellow inmate was a police informant who offered to protect Fulminante from other inmates if Fulminante told him about the crime. The Court was faced with "three issues presented by the trial court's determination to admit Fulminante's first confession:[14] whether the confession was inadmissible because coerced; whether harmless-error analysis is appropriate; and if so whether any error was harmless here" (p. 313). Different justices answered those questions in different ways, and a majority was cobbled on each of the three questions: Fulminante's confession was coerced and therefore inadmissible, harmless-error analysis is appropriate, and this error was not harmless. Fulminante was to be retried. In the future when a trial court has admitted a coerced confession, appeals courts should consider case by case whether that error was harmless.

A majority in *Fulminante* acknowledged a weakening of the Court's standards regarding coerced confessions over the preceding century.

> Although the Court noted in *Bram* [*v. United States* (1897)] that a confession cannot be obtained by "any direct or implied promises, however slight, nor by the exertion of any improper influence," it is clear this passage from *Bram*, . . . under current precedent does not state the standard for determining the voluntariness of a confes-

---

[13] This case is mentioned in Chapter 3 of this book.

[14] He subsequently confessed the crime to his fiancé (who went ahead and married him after learning that).

sion. . . . A determination regarding the voluntariness of a confession . . . must be viewed in a totality of the circumstances. (pp. 285-286, citations omitted)

Thus, implied promises have gone from being a *per se* violation of a defendant's Constitutional rights to being one element that a court should consider, along with every other circumstance surrounding the interrogation and confession. To make this point even clearer, consider the paragraph in *Bram* from which the brief quote was taken:

But a confession, in order to be admissible, must be free and voluntary; that is, must not be extracted by any sort of threats or violence, nor obtained by any direct or implied promises, however slight, nor by the exertion of any improper influence. . . . A confession can never be received in evidence where the prisoner has been influenced by any threat or promise; for the law cannot measure the force of the influence used, or decide upon its effect upon the mind of the prisoner, and therefore excludes the declaration if any degree of influence has been exerted. (pp. 542-543, citation omitted)

In *McNeil v. Wisconsin* (1991), the Court addressed a question that had been posed to the Wisconsin Court of Appeals: "Does an accused's request for counsel at an initial appearance on a charged offense constitute an invocation of his fifth amendment right to counsel that precludes police interrogation on unrelated, uncharged offenses?" (p. 175). They answered: No. The Court distinguished the Sixth Amendment right to counsel from the right to an attorney during interrogation as follows:

The purpose of the Sixth Amendment counsel guarantee – and hence the purpose of invoking it – is to protect the unaided layman at critical confrontations with his expert adversary, the government, after the adverse positions of government and defendant have solidified with respect to a particular alleged crime. The purpose of the *Miranda-Edwards* guarantee, on the other hand – and hence the purpose of invoking it – is to protect a quite different interest: the suspect's desire to deal with the police only through counsel. (pp. 177-178, citations omitted)

The *McNeil* majority notes that the dissent sees it as showing "a preference for an inquisitorial system of justice. We cannot imagine what this means" (p. 182, citation omitted), and writes: "Our system of justice is, and has always been, an inquisitorial one at the investigatory stage (even the grand jury is an inquisitorial body), and no other disposition is conceivable" (p. 182). This seems disingenuous, given that numerous previous Supreme Court cases have distinguished inquisitorial from accusatorial systems of government and specifically considered the implications for custodial confessions. The interested reader can refer to the following cases (each discussed earlier): *Bram v. United States* (1897), *McNabb v. United States* (1943), *Ashcraft v. Tennessee* (1944), *Watts v. Indiana* (1949), *United States v. Carignan* (1951), *Culombe v. Connecticut* (1961), *Rogers v. Richmond* (1961), *Miranda v. Arizona* (1966), *Edwards v. Arizona* (1981), and *Moran v. Burbine* (1986). In brief, the *McNeil* dissent accuses the majority of preferring secret custodial inquisitions/interrogations of lone suspects as a way to determine guilt or innocence, rather than public trials of defendants represented by attorneys who can protect their rights.

In *Withrow v. Williams* (1993), the Court ruled that a person could continue to use *habeas corpus* in federal courts to appeal a state-court conviction, using either *Miranda* grounds or totality-of-the-circumstances consideration of voluntariness. The Court noted, as it had in *Bram v. United States* (1897), that the Self Incrimination Clause of the Fifth Amendment

> barred the introduction in federal cases of involuntary confessions made in response to custodial interrogation. We did not recognize the Clause's applicability to state cases until 1964, however, and, over the course of 30 years, beginning with the decision in *Brown* v. *Mississippi*, 297 U.S. 278 (1936), we analyzed the admissibility of confessions in such cases as a question of due process under the Fourteenth Amendment. Under this approach, we examined the totality of circumstances to determine whether a confession had been made freely, voluntarily and without compulsion or inducement of any sort. Indeed, we continue to employ the totality of circumstances approach when addressing a claim that the introduction of an involuntary confession has violated due process. (p. 689)

In *Stansbury v. California* (1994), the Court considered a question regarding whether a person was in custody for the purposes of *Miranda*. In that totality-of-the-circumstances analysis, how much weight should go to whether the police officer considers the person to be a suspect? How much weight should go to whether the person being interviewed considers himself or herself to be a suspect? The answer to both of these questions is: None. "The initial determination of custody depends on the objective circumstances of the interrogation, not on the subjective views harbored by either the interrogating officers or the person being questioned" (p. 322).

Quiz (based on *Davis v. United States,* 1994): During an inter-rogation, a suspect says, "Maybe I should talk to a lawyer." At that point, the police:

(a) must stop questioning because the suspect has invoked his or her Miranda rights.
(b) must stop questioning and get the suspect a lawyer.
(c) must stop questioning and clarify whether or not the suspect is requesting a lawyer.
(d) may ignore the suspect's ambiguous remark and continue the interrogation.
(e) may eschew Miranda warnings entirely if they can make the totality of the circumstances look like the suspect voluntarily confessed.

Four justices said "c," four justices said "d," and one justice said "e." Name that justice: Antonin Scalia. Justice Scalia also joined with the four justices who said "d," so "d" is all that the Constitution requires. The Court mentioned that it was "entirely proper" for police to stop to clarify whether the suspect wanted a lawyer or not (p. 461).

In what I read as an odd, gratuitous act, the *Davis* Court wrote that Miranda warnings are not required by the U.S. Constitution, but are nevertheless required by the U.S. Supreme Court:

> The Sixth Amendment right to counsel attaches only at the initiation of adversary criminal proceedings, and, before proceedings are initiated, a suspect in a criminal investigation has no constitutional right to the assistance of counsel. Nevertheless, we held in *Miranda v. Arizona,* 384 U.S. 436, 469-473 (1966), that a suspect subject to custodial interrogation has the right to consult with an attorney and to have counsel present during questioning, and that the police must explain this right to him before questioning begins. The right to counsel established in *Miranda* was one of a series of recommended procedural safeguards that were not themselves rights protected by the Constitution but were instead measures to insure that the right against compulsory self-incrimination was protected. (p. 455, citations omitted)

This issue resurfaced in *Dickerson v. United States* (2000, see below).

In *Thompson v. Keohane* (1995), the Court held that the question of whether a suspect was in custody at the time of interrogation (and therefore should be given Miranda warnings) is a mixed question of law and fact and therefore warrants independent review by the federal habeas court.

In *Dickerson v. United State* (2000), the Court was faced with the question of whether or not Miranda warnings are required by the U.S. Constitution. If not, then federal laws could provide some other mechanism for ensuring that an accused's Constitutional rights were upheld, for example, relying on a totality-of-the-circumstances analysis of voluntariness. The Court held that "*Miranda*, being a constitutional decision of this Court, may not be in effect overruled by an Act of Congress" (p. 530). Only the U.S. Supreme Court could overturn *Miranda*, and after consideration it decided not to do so.

The case of *Texas v. Cobb* (2001) involves burglary, murder by stabbing, another murder by burying a baby alive, and a question that followed the Court's decision in *McNeil v. Wisconsin* (1991). Recall that in *McNeil* it was decided that a suspect who requests counsel at a hearing for one charge can still be approached by police and interrogated regarding an unrelated charge. But what about a related charge? Fine, says the *Texas v. Cobb* court, even if the other charge is part of the same series of criminal acts, as long as it is not the exact same charge. In 1993 a house was burgled and two of the residents, a mother and daughter, were missing. In 1994 neighbor Raymond Levi Cobb confessed to the burglary, was charged with that offense, and had an attorney appointed to him. Cobb was twice questioned about the suspected murders, with the consent of his attorney, and both times he denied involvement. Then in 1995, without the knowledge or consent of his attorney, he was questioned again. A lower court held that once the right to counsel attaches to the offense charged, it also attaches to any other offense that is very closely related factually to the offense charged. The Supreme Court disagreed, allowing police to initiate interrogation of a charged defendant regarding any possible charge for which he or she has not yet been indicted.

Justice Stevens described the case of *Chavez v. Martinez* (2003), as follows:

> As a matter of fact, the interrogation of respondent was the functional equivalent of an attempt to obtain an involuntary confession from a

prisoner by torturous methods. As a matter of law, that type of brutal police conduct constitutes an immediate deprivation of the prisoner's constitutionally protected interest in liberty. (pp. 783-784)

During an altercation with police, Oliverio Martinez was shot several times, causing severe injuries that left him permanently blinded and paralyzed from the waist down. While Martinez was in the emergency room receiving treatment for his wounds, he was interrogated by police officer Ben Chavez. The question before the Supreme Court was not whether Martinez' statement was involuntary (it was),[15] but whether he could sue Chavez for violating his constitutional rights. The nine justices wrote six separate opinions. The entirety of what any five agreed on is the following: "Whether Martinez may pursue a claim of liability for a substantive due process violation is thus an issue that should be addressed on remand, along with the scope and merits of any such action that may be found open to him" (pp. 779-780).

That, such as it is, is the final word on U.S. Supreme Court confession cases as of this writing. More will follow, as the Court considers future cases.

RUMSFELDIAN AUTO-COLLOQUY

Have I summarized all the U.S. Supreme Court cases I found via Internet search engines? You bet I have. Have I inadvertently missed some cases? That wouldn't surprise me a bit. Have I provided the reader with an accurate understanding of the current legal standards in his or her jurisdiction? Absolutely not. Do I recommend that the reader treat this chapter as a legal text? Heavens, no. Do I expect that the reader will have gained a greater appreciation of the issues courts consider in confession cases? I surely do. Does this legal excursion lay the groundwork for lists of personal characteristics and interrogation tactics that are considered to increase the risk of a false confession and are listed as such in Chapter 10? Why, yes they do, and I thank me for asking that.

---

[15] The facts of the case are quite similar to those in *Mincey v. Arizona* (1978).

— 7 —

LEGAL ISSUES FOR WHICH
PSYCHOLOGICAL TESTIMONY
MAY BE RELEVANT

The foregoing discussion of U.S. Supreme Court cases sets the stage for the question posed in this chapter: In cases of disputed confessions, for what legal issues is psychological testimony relevant? We begin with a case example.

CASE EXAMPLE

In a 1992 Florida case on which I consulted,[1] the following issues were raised by the Defense in its Memorandum of Law in Support of Defendant's Motion to Suppress Statements, Admissions, or Confessions:

1. Was the Defendant in custody, thus requiring Miranda rights to be given, after conclusion of the polygraph test and before any admissions or confessions were obtained?
2. Were the police required to advise the Defendant of his Miranda rights, and obtain a knowing and intelligent waiver of those rights, after he was in custody?
3. Did the police fail to scrupulously honor the Defendant's right to remain silent at any time during the interrogation, so as to render any subsequent admissions or confessions involuntary?
4. Did the State fail to prove, by a preponderance of the evidence, that the Defendant's supposed confession was freely and voluntarily made under the totality of the circumstances?

---

[1] *State v. Jerry Lee Louis*, DeSoto County, Florida, case numbers 92-303-CF and 92-348-CF. Assistant Public Defender Tobey Hockett, personal communication, 9/19/03.

5. Should the Court suppress Defendant's coerced statements to the police because they are so highly unreliable and virtually uncorroborated?
6. Were the Defendant's due process rights violated by the failure of the police to record the entire confession?

These are the issues the Defense wants the judge to decide. The Defense has hired psychological experts to gather information and form opinions. Will the judge allow the psychologists to answer questions about these issues?

The Federal Rules of Evidence (FRE) govern the admissibility of evidence, expert testimony, and scientific evidence in the federal courts and in many state courts, with 38 states having crafted their own state evidentiary requirements based on these rules. Under the FRE, scientific or nonscientific evidence is admissible if it is relevant and not prejudicial (FRE 401 & 403). Relevant evidence is any evidence that makes a fact in issue more or less probable while nonprejudicial evidence is evidence which is more probative than it is prejudicial. (Krauss & Sales, 2003, p. 548, citation omitted)

Krauss and Sales (2003, p. 549, emphasis in original) describe the two-prong preliminary admissibility determination that a judge makes prior to the presentation of expert testimony at trial: "The judge must determine whether the *reasoning or methodology* underlying the expert testimony is scientifically valid (i.e., evidentiary reliable) and whether that *reasoning or methodology* can be applied to the facts of the case (i.e., relevant)." Under *Daubert v. Merrell Dow Pharmaceutical Inc.* (1993),[2] the trial judge must examine the scientific basis and the scientific validity of the proffered evidence and evaluate whether it assists the trier of fact (the judge or the jury) to understand or determine a fact in issue. The *Daubert* Court

---

[2] Some states, including Florida where this case was heard, continue to use the standard from *Frye v. United States* (1923): "Just when a scientific principle or discovery crosses the line between the experimental and demonstrable stages is difficult to define. Somewhere in this twilight zone the evidential force of the principle must be recognized, and while courts will go a long way in admitting expert testimony deduced from a well-recognized scientific principle or discovery, the thing from which the deduction is made must be sufficiently established to have gained general acceptance in the particular field in which it belongs."

suggested that these requirements are only met when: (a) the proffered expert scientific testimony has bearing on a factual dispute in the case, and (b) the expert testimony effectively links the scientific evidence to the facts in the case in such a way that it aids the jury in its decision making. The former of these two requirements appears to be a general relevancy concern (i.e., is the expert testimony on the scientific evidence related to an important fact in the case?), while the latter requirement is a more specific aspect of relevancy that is best described as an issue of *fit* between the scientific evidence and specific facts of the case (i.e., will the expert testimony on scientific evidence help the jurors to resolve or understand specific facts of the case?). The Court referred to this latter requirement as the helpfulness standard. (Krauss & Sales, 2003, p. 549)

With this in mind, we will consider the likely relevance of psychological testimony for each of the six legal issues raised by the Defense in the suppression hearing in the case example.

Consider the first issue: Was the Defendant in custody? Recall that in *Stansbury v. California* (1994) the U.S. Supreme Court wrote:

In determining whether an individual was in custody, a court must examine all of the circumstances surrounding the interrogation, but the ultimate inquiry is simply whether there was a formal arrest or restraint on freedom of movement of the degree associated with a formal arrest. Our decisions make clear that the initial determination of custody depends on the objective circumstances of the interrogation, not on the subjective views harbored by either the interrogating officers or the person being questioned. (pp. 321-322, citation omitted)

I would not expect the psychologist's opinion about either the suspect's or the interrogator's mental state, intent, or expectations to be relevant to a consideration of whether the suspect was in custody at a particular point in time.

Perhaps the psychologist will uncover relevant evidence about the objective circumstances at the time of the interrogation. For example, in doing a collateral interview with a relative of the defendant, the relative might tell the psychologist that she saw the suspect being patted down, searched, and held by the arm as he was placed in a police car prior to being driven to the police station for interrogation. That is likely to be relevant to this legal issue. The psychologist may not be able to testify about that in court due to a hearsay objection, but the information may nonetheless assist with the investigation and resolution of this legal issue.

The second issue asks whether the police were required to advise the Defendant of his Miranda rights, and obtain a knowing and intelligent waiver of those rights, after he was in custody. This appears to be a question of law, largely dependant on the first issue. I do not expect that psychological testimony would be relevant.

The third issue addresses whether the police failed to scrupulously honor the Defendant's right to remain silent. A comprehensive psychological evaluation might produce information that would help guide the investigation, but it is unlikely that psychological testimony would be directly relevant.

Psychological testimony is likely to be relevant to the fourth issue: Did the State fail to prove, by a preponderance of the evidence, that the Defendant's supposed confession was freely and voluntarily made under the totality of the circumstances? Clinical psychological testimony about the defendant (e.g., intelligence and personality) is relevant, as is social psychological testimony about how people respond to police interrogation. Particularly helpful is testimony about how this person (or people with similar characteristics) responded (or would be likely to respond) in this situation. Testimony about the psychological evaluation of the person, analysis of the interrogation and confession, and the person-situation interaction are all relevant. Failure to allow such testimony was considered reversible error in the case of *Boyer v. State* (2002).

What about the fifth issue: Should the Court suppress Defendant's coerced statements to the police because they are so highly unreliable and virtually uncorroborated? Recall *Crane v. Kentucky* (1986) where the question was whether the trial court could refuse to allow the Defense to present evidence that cast doubt on the trustworthiness of a confession. The U.S. Supreme Court ruled in *Crane* that such evidence must be admitted:

> The manner in which a statement was extracted is, of course, relevant to the purely legal question of its voluntariness, a question most, but not all, States assign to the trial judge alone to resolve. But *the physical and psychological environment that yielded the confession* can also be of substantial relevance to the ultimate factual issue of the defendant's guilt or innocence. Confessions, even those that have

been found to be voluntary, are not conclusive of guilt. And, as with any other part of the prosecutor's case, a confession may be shown to be insufficiently corroborated or otherwise . . . unworthy of belief. Indeed, stripped of the power to describe to the jury the circumstances that prompted his confession, the defendant is effectively disabled from answering the one question every rational juror needs answered: If the defendant is innocent, why did he previously admit his guilt? Accordingly, regardless of whether the defendant marshaled the same evidence earlier in support of an unsuccessful motion to suppress, and entirely independent of any question of voluntariness, a defendant's case may stand or fall on his ability to convince the jury that the manner in which the confession was obtained casts doubt on its credibility. (pp. 688-689, citations omitted, emphasis added)

I expect that psychological testimony would be relevant to any legally permissible challenge to the credibility of a suspect's confession.

The sixth and final legal issue in the case example regards whether the Defendant's due process rights were violated by the failure of the police to record the entire confession. I do not expect that clinical psychological testimony about this particular Defendant would be relevant, but I expect that testimony about psychological research would be relevant to this or related questions. I expect that it would be relevant that (a) research by Ofshe and Leo (1997) leads them to conclude that electronic recording of interrogations is necessary to distinguish true from false confessions, and (b) Gudjonsson (2003) reports research showing that requiring recording of police interrogations does not significantly interfere with the ability of police to do their work. The psychologist can assist the judge by providing testimony about the scientific literature that bears on this issue.

This case example illustrates that a psychologist's testimony is likely to be relevant to some, but not all, legal issues regarding a defendant's confession, and that different legal cases will generate different psycholegal questions. In some cases, a psychologist hired to gather facts relevant to one legal issue may come across information relevant to another legal issue. Rules of evidence will guide the trial judge in determining whether the expert can testify about specific findings. When the psychologist is not allowed to testify about some legal issues, the psychologist's work may indirectly assist with fair resolution of the case by providing investigatory clues.

About which legal issues are psychologists most likely to testify in disputed confession cases?

LEGAL ISSUES FOR WHICH PSYCHOLOGICAL
TESTIMONY IS EXPECTED TO BE RELEVANT

Based on my review of psychological and legal literature, and on my experience, I expect that in disputed confession cases psychologists are most likely to be asked to provide testimony relevant to the following legal issues:

- Did the State fail to prove, by a preponderance of the evidence, that the Defendant knowingly, intelligently, and voluntarily waived his or her Miranda rights?
- Did the State fail to prove, by a preponderance of the evidence, that the Defendant's supposed confession was freely and voluntarily made under the totality of the circumstances?
- Should the Court suppress the Defendant's coerced statements to the police because they are so highly unreliable and virtually uncorroborated?

Note that these questions are in the form that would be presented to the judge. The questions posed to a testifying psychologist would be in a different form, but would be designed to produce testimony that would be relevant to the question ultimately considered by the judge. The next three chapters address how a psychologist can conduct a psychological assessment and prepare testimony that would assist the trier of fact in addressing these legal issues.

— PART III —

CONDUCTING PSYCHOLOGICAL ASSESSMENTS AND PREPARING TESTIMONY

The three chapters in this part address three different legal issues. Although the legal issues are considered separately by courts, assessment issues overlap considerably. The reader is encouraged to read all three chapters even if the goal is to learn more about assessment and testimony relevant to only one of the legal issues. The Soddi Jones report (see Appendix, pp. 183-216) illustrates assessment relevant to all three legal issues.

— 8 —

ADDRESSING WAIVER OF
MIRANDA RIGHTS

LEGAL ISSUE

In *Dickerson v. United States* (2000), the U.S. Supreme Court upheld its decision in *Miranda v. Arizona* (1966). As written in *Dickerson,* "*Miranda* requires procedures that will warn a suspect in custody of his right to remain silent and which will assure the suspect that the exercise of that right will be honored." The *Dickerson* Court acknowledged what some have described as a watering down of *Miranda,* but announced that the necessity to warn suspects of their rights is alive and well: "If anything, our subsequent cases have reduced the impact of the *Miranda* rule on legitimate law enforcement while reaffirming the decision's core ruling that unwarned statements may not be used as evidence in the prosecution's case in chief."

What does *Miranda* require? The *Miranda* Court wrote:

> To summarize, we hold that when an individual is taken into custody or otherwise deprived of his freedom by the authorities in any significant way and is subjected to questioning, the privilege against self-incrimination is jeopardized. Procedural safeguards must be employed to protect the privilege, and unless other fully effective means are adopted to notify the person of his right of silence and to assure that the exercise of the right will be scrupulously honored, the following measures are required. He must be warned prior to any questioning that he has the right to remain silent, that anything he says can be used against him in a court of law, that he has the right to the presence of an attorney, and that if he cannot afford an attorney

one will be appointed for him prior to any questioning if he so desires. Opportunity to exercise these rights must be afforded to him throughout the interrogation. After such warnings have been given, and such opportunity afforded him, the individual may knowingly and intelligently waive these rights and agree to answer questions or make a statement. But unless and until such warnings and waiver are demonstrated by the prosecution at trial, no evidence obtained as a result of interrogation can be used against him. (pp. 478-479)

The requirement of a knowing and intelligent waiver comes from the following:

If the interrogation continues without the presence of an attorney and a statement is taken, a heavy burden rests on the government to demonstrate that the defendant knowingly and intelligently waived his privilege against self-incrimination and his right to retained or appointed counsel. This Court has always set high standards of proof for the waiver of constitutional rights and we re-assert these standards as applied to in-custody interrogation. Since the State is responsible for establishing the isolated circumstances under which the interrogation takes place and has the only means of making available corroborated evidence of warnings given during incommunicado interrogation, the burden is rightly on its shoulders. (*Miranda,* p. 475, citations omitted)

The requirement of a voluntary waiver comes from this passage from *Miranda:*

Whatever the testimony of the authorities as to waiver of rights by an accused, the fact of lengthy interrogation or incommunicado incarceration before a statement is made is strong evidence that the accused did not validly waive his rights. In these circumstances the fact that the individual eventually made a statement is consistent with the conclusion that the compelling influence of the interrogation finally forced him to do so. It is inconsistent with any notion of a voluntary relinquishment of the privilege. Moreover, any evidence that the accused was threatened, tricked, or cajoled into a waiver will, of course, show that the defendant did not voluntarily waive his privilege. The requirement of warnings and waiver of rights is a fundamental with respect to the Fifth Amendment privilege and not simply a preliminary ritual to existing methods of interrogation. (p. 476)

The warnings need not be delivered just like in *Miranda,* and they need not be presented in the same order (*California v. Prysock,* 1981). The prosecution bears the burden of proving that a defendant knowingly and intelligently waived his or her Miranda rights (*Tague v. Louisiana,* 1980). When a Miranda waiver is challenged, its validity is based on an analysis of the totality of the circumstances (*Dickerson v. United States,* 2000), including factors related to the suspect's capacities, the suspect's mental state at the time of waiver, the circumstances and setting, police procedures, and interactions among all these factors (Grisso, 2003).

PARSING "KNOWING, INTELLIGENT, AND VOLUNTARY"

We will consider the knowing, intelligent, and voluntary prongs separately, and then together. Grisso (2003; see Frumkin & Garcia, 2003) cites cases in which the Court's decision about whether the *knowing* criterion was met were based solely on the suspect's capacities (*United States ex rel. Simon v. Maroney,* 1964) or solely on inadequate reading of the rights by the police (*State v. Prater,* 1970), but he writes that courts usually consider both factors in deciding whether a waiver was done knowingly (e.g., *West v. United States,* 1968).

Grisso (2003) illustrates that state courts are divided about whether the *intelligent* criterion means that something more than mere understanding is required. An example where it did is the California case of *In re Patrick W.* (1978, pp. 738-739):

> although the minor showed understanding of the Miranda admonitions as explained to him by the deputies he would not, of course, have been likely to fully comprehend the meaning and effect of his statement: for example, its use in his case to refute an expert's opinion concerning the minor's diminished mental capacity to commit the crime charged. To those who argue that the same thing can be said of an adult whose confession is used against him, the simple answer is that the courts have always given more zealous protection to minors' rights, under both criminal law and civil, because of their relative helplessness when dealing with adults by reason of immaturity. We therefore hold that the minor's confession in the present case was inadmissible on the totality of the circumstances present. (citations omitted)

In contrast, Illinois' Supreme Court held in *People v. Bernasco* (1990, p. 964), that

> If intelligent knowledge in the *Miranda* context means anything, it means the ability to understand the very words used in the warnings. It need not mean the ability to understand far-reaching legal and strategic effects of waiving one's rights, or to appreciate how widely or deeply an interrogation may probe, or to withstand the influence of stress or fancy; but to waive rights intelligently and knowingly, one must at least understand basically what those rights encompass and minimally what their waiver will entail. Here, defendant was found not to understand fundamental terms contained in the Miranda warnings of his rights, not to have been able to form an intent to waive those rights, and not to have a normal ability to understand questions and concepts. Such findings, if borne out by the evidence, are sufficient to warrant the conclusion that defendant did not waive his Miranda rights knowingly and intelligently, and hence to justify suppressing his confession.

In considering whether a suspect's waiver of Miranda rights is *voluntary*, it may be necessary to first consider whether there is any coercive police activity. Note that the following are two distinct determinations of voluntariness: whether the suspect voluntarily waived his or her Miranda rights, and whether the suspect's confession was voluntary. The first addresses whether "the accused was threatened, tricked, or cajoled into a waiver" (*Miranda*, p. 476) of his or her rights, including the right to remain silent and the right to have an attorney present when questioned (which is the subject of this chapter). In the second, the court considers "the totality of circumstances to determine whether a confession had been made freely, voluntarily and without compulsion or inducement of any sort" (*Withrow v. Williams*, 1993, p. 689) (which is the subject of the next chapter).

Although the Supreme Court's findings in *Colorado v. Connelly* (1986) addressed the voluntariness of a confession, they may be suggestive about how courts would consider determinations of the voluntariness of waivers. The *Connelly* Court wrote: "We hold that coercive police activity is a necessary predicate to the finding that a confession is not 'voluntary' within the meaning of the Due Process Clause of the Fourteenth Amendment" (p. 167). "The voluntariness determination . . . is designed to determine the presence of police coercion" (p. 168).[1] Considering the *Connelly* decision, along with the fact that Miranda warnings were developed as a safeguard against coercive police activity, a finding that a waiver was involuntary would likely require *some* police coercion. Once any police coercion is established, then situational (e.g., location) and personal (e.g., psychosis) factors would be considered in the totality of the circumstances.

It may be that any police questioning that would require Miranda warnings – because it qualified as being custodial interrogation – would meet the minimal requirement for establishing that there was police coercion. The *Connelly* Court wrote:

> Absent police conduct *causally related to the confession,* there is simply no basis for concluding that any state actor has deprived a criminal defendant of due process of law. Respondent correctly notes that as interrogators have turned to more subtle forms of psychological persuasion, courts have found the mental condition of the defendant a more significant factor in the voluntariness calculus. But this fact does not justify a conclusion that a defendant's mental condition, by itself and apart from its relation to official coercion, should ever dispose of the inquiry into constitutional voluntariness. (p.164, citations omitted, emphasis added)

Of course, in any *custodial* interrogation there is some police conduct that is causally related to the confession, as noted in the dissent in *Ashcraft v. Tennessee* (1944, p. 161):

> The Court bases its decision on the premise that custody and examination of a prisoner for thirty-six hours is 'inherently coercive.' Of course it is. And so is custody and examination for one hour. Arrest itself is inherently coercive, and so is detention. When not justified, infliction of such indignities upon the person is actionable as a tort. Of course such acts put pressure upon the prisoner to answer questions, to answer them truthfully, and to confess if guilty. (pp. 160-161)

Once we recognize that police coercion does not equal police wrongdoing, it is hard to imagine a custodial interrogation that would not involve some coercive acts by the police – efforts to get a suspect to move from saying "I didn't do it" to saying "I did it."

---

[1] This case is discussed further in the next chapter.

The upshot is that inquiries into the voluntariness of a waiver, like those of whether the waiver was done knowingly and intelligently, will typically involve consideration of the person, the situation, and the person in the situation.

REUNITING "KNOWING, INTELLIGENT, AND VOLUNTARY"

In *Moran v. Burbine* (1986) the Supreme Court wrote that when a court is to decide whether a waiver was made voluntarily, knowingly, and intelligently,

> the inquiry has two distinct dimensions. First, the relinquishment of the right must have been voluntary in the sense that it was the product of a free and deliberate choice rather than intimidation, coercion, or deception. Second, the waiver must have been made with a full awareness of both the nature of the right being abandoned and the consequences of the decision to abandon it. Only if the totality of the circumstances surrounding the interrogation reveals both an uncoerced choice and the requisite level of comprehension may a court properly conclude that the Miranda rights have been waived. (p. 421, citations omitted)[2]

We will use this succinct description to structure the psychologist's role, after a brief consideration of youths and other special populations.

Is a different approach necessary for juveniles? No. In *Fare v. Michael C.* (1979), the Court wrote:

> This totality-of-the-circumstances approach is adequate to determine whether there has been a waiver even where interrogation of juveniles is involved. We discern no persuasive reasons why any other approach is required where the question is whether a juvenile has waived his rights, as opposed to whether an adult has done so. (p. 725)

Nevertheless, police may be required to do something more than a rote reading and explanation of rights for some suspects, including children, adolescents, and people with mental illness or mental deficiencies (Oberlander, N. E. Goldstein, & A. M. Goldstein, 2003, p. 339; cf. *People v. Higgins,* 1993).

---

[2]   The Court did not define the "requisite level of comprehension."

PARSING "PERSONAL
AND SITUATIONAL VARIABLES"

We will consider personal and situational variables separately, and then together. Grisso (2003, p. 154) lists the following as leading cases that have provided courts with lists of *personal characteristics* to consider when determining the capacities of suspects to waive Miranda rights: *Coyote v. United States,* 1967; *Fare v. Michael C.,* 1979; *Johnson v. Zerbst,* 1938; and *West v. United States,* 1968. These yield the following personal characteristics: "age, intelligence, education, amount of prior experience with police, physical condition, background, and conduct." Oberlander et al. (2003, p. 338) present a similar list, which also includes "language ability, literacy, . . . mental illness, and experience with the police and the court system." No such list is intended to be exhaustive.

Oberlander et al. (2003, p. 338) list situational factors courts have considered:

> who was present at the interrogation, the physical arrangements of the interrogation, police strategies for interrogation, number of times the Miranda warning was given, method of delivery (e.g., silently, aloud, from a wall poster, from a piece of paper or small card, read by a law enforcement officer, read by the defendant, read together), time elapsed between the warning and the interrogation, and the methods law enforcement officers used to assess the suspect's comprehension of the warning (e.g., no methods, signing an acknowledgment that the warning was given, inquiring whether the suspect waives each element of the warning, waiving each element in writing, paraphrasing each element of the warning).

As with personal characteristics, no such list is intended to be exclusive.

REUNITING "PERSONAL
AND SITUATIONAL VARIABLES"

At a suppression hearing, a judge decides (among other things) whether a particular person in a particular situation at a particular time made a knowing, intelligent, and voluntary waiver of his or her Miranda rights. A psychologist's testimony is likely to be considered relevant if it helps the judge make that determination.

Although it deals with psychiatrists testifying before a jury in an insanity case, the following description from *Ake v. Oklahoma* (1986, p. 80) is useful:

> The assistance of a psychiatrist may well be crucial to the defendant's ability to marshal his defense. In this role, psychiatrists gather facts, through professional examination, interviews, and elsewhere, that they will share with the judge or jury; they analyze the information gathered and from it draw plausible conclusions about the defendant's mental condition, and about the effects of any disorder on behavior; and they offer opinions about how the defendant's mental condition might have affected his behavior at the time in question. They know the probative questions to ask of the opposing party's psychiatrists and how to interpret their answers. Unlike lay witnesses, who can merely describe symptoms they believe might be relevant to the defendant's mental state, psychiatrists can identify the elusive and often deceptive symptoms of insanity and tell the jury why their observations are relevant. Further, where permitted by evidentiary rules, psychiatrists can translate a medical diagnosis into language that will assist the trier of fact, and therefore offer evidence in a form that has meaning for the task at hand. Through this process of investigation, interpretation, and testimony, psychiatrists ideally assist lay jurors, who generally have no training in psychiatric matters, to make a sensible and educated determination about the mental condition of the defendant at the time of the offense.

This couples nicely with the finding in *Jenkins v. United States* (1962) that some psychologists are qualified to render expert testimony in the field of mental disorder.

But that's not all. Some psychologists, by virtue of their knowledge, training, and experience, are able to assist the court in each of the following areas:

1. Gather and analyze information regarding "the physical and psychological environment in which the [waiver] was obtained" (*Crane v. Kentucky,* 1986, p. 684).
2. Assess the defendant's current mental status, including intelligence, memory, reading comprehension, listening comprehension, and psychopathology.
3. Reconstruct the defendant's mental state at the time of the waiver (similar to the type of assessment in insanity and other

mental-state-at-the-time-of-the-offense evaluations; see, e.g., Rogers & Shuman, 2000).

4. Assist the judge in understanding interactions among the above.

ASSESSMENT PROCEDURES

First, the psychologist reviews all available information regarding the *events* that occurred immediately before, during, and after the waiver. The attorney (either the defense or the prosecution) retaining the psychologist's services should provide all relevant materials, including waiver forms, electronic (audio or video) recordings and transcripts, and depositions. In some cases where the waiver was not recorded, records of the detectives' procedures in prior cases may be useful for estimating the likely procedure. Prior to any contact with the defendant, the expert should develop as clear an understanding of the circumstances and events as possible, from points of view other than that of the defendant. Also prior to the face-to-face evaluation, the attorney should provide the expert with records (e.g., school records, medical and psychological reports, etc.) regarding the *defendant.*

The second step is to conduct a current psychological evaluation of the defendant. Although the crucial question involves the defendant's mental state at the time of the waiver, standard psychological assessment procedures are designed to assess a person's *current* mental state, intellectual ability, reading ability, and so on. The psychologist should request relevant records from the referring attorney prior to meeting with the defendant, and may request additional records based on information obtained during the psychological assessment. As with other forensic psychological assessments, a history and mental status provide useful information, which can be supplemented by a psychiatric screening instrument such as the Brief Symptom Inventory (BSI) or the Symptom Checklist 90-R (SCL-90-R),[3] by a structured diagnostic interview (see Rogers, 2001), and/or (if the subject's reading comprehension level is sufficient)[4] by an objective test of psychopathology such as the Personality Assessment Inventory (Morey,

---

[3] The BSI and SCL-90-R are both available via http://assessments.ncspearson.com/assessments/

[4] If the subject's reading comprehension level is below the reading level of a significant number of the test items, and if the subject's listening comprehension level is at or above the level of the test items, then it may be useful to employ an oral administration of an objective test of psychopathology.

1991) or the Minnesota Multiphasic Personality Inventory-2 (Butcher et al., 1989). The person's intellectual ability can be measured with a full-scale age-appropriate intelligence test such as the Wechsler Intelligence Scale for Children – Fourth Edition (Wechsler, 2003). A neuropsychological screening test such as the Screening Test for the Luria-Nebraska Neuropsychological Battery (Golden, 1987) can be used to assist in determining whether more specific neuropsychological testing should be performed. If interview and/or test data suggest psychopathology, testing for feigning or exaggeration of symptoms should be considered; for example with the Structured Interview of Reported Symptoms (SIRS; Rogers, Bagby, & Dickens, 1992). If cognitive deficits are suggested, then testing for exaggeration or feigning should be conducted with an instrument such as the Word Memory Test (Green, 2003) or the Test of Memory Malingering (TOMM; Tombaugh, 1996). See Rogers (1997) regarding assessment of response style.

Reading and listening ability, particularly reading comprehension and listening comprehension, can be measured via subtests from achievement batteries such as the Woodcock-Johnson Tests of Achievement-III (WJ-III; Maher & Woodcock, 2001) or the Wechsler Individual Achievement Test – Second Edition (The Psychological Corporation, 2001). I am more familiar with the WJ-III; the following subtests can assist in assessing the defendant's skills relevant to Miranda waiver: Letter-Word Identification, Reading Fluency, Story Recall, Understanding Directions, Passage Comprehension, Story Recall-Delayed, Oral Comprehension, and Reading Vocabulary. Administration of those subtests allows scoring of the following clusters: Oral Language, Listening Comprehension, Broad Reading, and Reading Comprehension. If the defendant wrote out a statement/confession, then it would also be useful to score the Writing Fluency and Writing Samples subtests, which would allow scoring of the Written Expression composite. These subtests allow comparison to group norms and they provide a mechanism for computing an age level and a grade level for the various skills measured. Although it is currently not recommended that a psychologist attempt to describe a person's intelligence as comparable to that of, say, a 9 year old, it is useful and understandable to report that a person's reading or oral comprehension skills are at, say, a third-grade level.

The immediately preceding paragraphs address general psychological assessment of a person's current skills, abilities, and so forth. It is also important to more specifically assess the person's current functional abilities relevant to Miranda waiver. Two complementary procedures are employed: forensic assessment instruments (FAIs) and direct questioning of the defendant's understanding of the rights listed on the local waiver form.

Forensic assessment instruments are specialized assessment tools that have been developed in response to the demands of assessments for legal competencies. They are designed to provide standardized, quantitative methods for observing and describing behaviors that are directly relevant to legal questions about human competencies and capacities (Grisso, 2003). At the time of this writing, the Instruments for Assessing Understanding and Appreciation of *Miranda* Rights (herein abbreviated IAUAMR; Grisso, 1998) are the FAIs of choice for psychological assessments relevant to waiving Miranda rights.

It is important to recognize that the IAUAMR are psychological tests that *are directly relevant to* the legal question but *are not tests of* the legal question. The legal question is whether the defendant gave a knowing, intelligent, and voluntary waiver of his or her Miranda rights prior to questioning by the police. The IAUAMR assess understanding and appreciation at a different (typically later) time and in a different interpersonal situation (a psychological evaluation, not an interrogation). Of course, no test given today can directly assess what a person did or did not know last week or last year.

It is also important to recognize that the IAUAMR are not given in isolation. Intelligence and achievement tests (mentioned previously) allow the psychologist to compare the defendant's scores to those of a normative population and report, for example, that the defendant has below-average intelligence and reads at a sixth-grade level. The IAUAMR extends this type of comparison to sets of stimuli that are more directly relevant to the legal issue, allowing, for example, assessment of current understanding of words from a typical Miranda warning. Use of intelligence and achievement tests without the IAUAMR might be challenged as missing the point because the stimuli are not directly relevant to the legal issue. Use of the IAUAMR without intelligence and achievement tests might be challenged as insufficient due to the brevity of the tests in the IAUAMR. Use of the IAUAMR in combination with intelligence and achievement tests provides ample assessment of a person's current capacity to understand and appreciate concepts and ideas, including those relevant to Miranda rights.[5] Further description of the IAUAMR can be found in Grisso (2003). An example of its use is the Soddi Jones evaluation provided as an appendix (pp. 183-216).

Because Miranda rights differ from jurisdiction to jurisdiction, it is important to augment the structured approach of the forensic assessment instrument with direct questioning using the local waiver form. If possible, a copy of the actual waiver form signed by the defendant can be used. Based on information obtained prior to meeting with the defendant, the psychologist can present the information to the defendant as it was presented by law enforcement officers, either orally or in written form, and ask the defendant to explain his or her current understanding of the words and concepts. It may be necessary to repeat the instruction that at this point in the evaluation the psychologist is interested in the defendant's *current* understanding.

As direct questioning regarding the defendant's current understanding of the local Miranda waiver form is completed, the psychologist can shift the assessment toward the third task, reconstructing the defendant's mental state at the time of the waiver. The psychologist can point to the copy of the waiver form and ask the defendant to describe in detail events that occurred prior to, during, and after the waiver form was completed. Cognitive Interview (Fisher & Geiselman, 1992) techniques may help the defendant remember more details without contaminating the interview. The psychologist should first employ open-ended questions and get as much information as possible about the circumstances, events, and police procedures.

It can be productive to question a defendant in stages adapted from the procedure developed for Critical Incident Stress Debriefing (CISD; Everly & Mitchell, 1997). After introducing the process, the psychologist asks the defendant to first describe the factual events as they would have been recorded by a television camera, with no thoughts or feelings added on. Next, the defendant is asked to describe how he or she was thinking as events unfolded. Then the defendant is asked to describe his or her emotional feelings, and finally, to describe why he or she said and did what he or she said and did at the time.

---

[5] Another reason for utilizing the IAUAMR as part of an assessment battery (rather than in isolation) is that the IAUAMR include no assessment of response style (e.g., malingering).

Along the way, the psychologist may have received some information from the defendant about his or her mental state at the time of the Miranda waiver. After the defendant has replayed events in the fact, thought, feeling, and why-did-you-do-that phases, the psychologist asks the defendant in what ways, if any, his or her mental state was different at the previous time (the waiver) from the present (the psychological evaluation). Again, the psychologist should begin with open-ended questions, and then eventually ask more specific questions, such as whether the defendant had consumed alcohol or street drugs or was taking any prescribed medicine.

The psychologist should ask the defendant what he or she understood about the waiver at the time of the waiver, including whether the defendant believed it was mandatory to talk to the police and if not, why he or she chose to do so. If the defendant believed that it was to his or her benefit to talk to the police, how did he or she think it would help, and what contributed to that opinion? Was there anything that the police said or did that encouraged the defendant to waive his or her rights? If so, what, and why was that effective? Did the defendant plan to talk to the police all along, or did he or she initially plan not to and then change his or her mind? If so, why did the defendant change his or her mind and decide to talk to the police? It is best to pose these *why* questions after the defendant has gone through the phases of describing *what* happened.

Because the psychologist has reviewed information about the waiver prior to meeting with the defendant, the psychologist may recognize that there are discrepancies between various accounts of what happened or, if the waiver procedure was electronically recorded, between the defendant's account and the recorded events. It is important to recognize that it is not the psychologist's job to resolve factual disputes, that is, to decide who is telling the truth or what really happened. Nevertheless, it may be useful to clarify whether there is indeed a discrepancy. This should only be done after the psychologist has completed the task of eliciting the defendant's recollection of events. When that is complete, the psychologist can ask the defendant whether he or she has read documents regarding the police officers' version of what happened, or whether the defendant has had that information conveyed to him or her by other means. If so, the psychologist can ask whether the defendant is already aware of any discrepancies between what he or she says happened and what the police say.

After that step, the psychologist can choose whether to question the defendant about discrepancies identified by the psychologist. For example, if the defendant says that he or she agreed to talk to the police in order to get a reduced sentence, and the police say that they made no such promise, the psychologist can ask the defendant to describe as specifically as possible what the police officers said. The psychologist should carefully note what the defendant says the police officer said, and what the defendant thought about what the police officer said.

At the conclusion of the face-to-face evaluation (which might involve more than one session), the psychologist should have a clear assessment of the person's current mental state; a detailed account of the person's recollection of events occurring before, during, and after the waiver; the defendant's description of how and why his or her mental state may have been different at the time of the waiver; objective measurements of the defendant's current understanding of his or her rights; the defendant's description regarding what he or she understood at the time of the waiver; and the defendant's description of why he or she waived his or her rights.

After completing the face-to-face evaluation of the defendant, the psychologist can address the fourth and final task of the evaluation. The psychologist has assessed the defendant's current mental state, and has gathered information directly from the defendant and (via records review and/or interview) from law enforcement officers regarding the physical and psychological environment in which the waiver was obtained. The psychologist can now consider interactions among these factors in an attempt to reconstruct the defendant's mental state at the time of the waiver. As stated previously, this process is comparable to that of a psychologist reconstructing a defendant's mental state at the time of the offense in order to address legal questions such as insanity. Based on knowledge, training, and experience, the psychologist can help the judge understand the defendant's mental state at the time of the waiver, which aids the judge in determining whether the defendant made a knowing, intelligent, and voluntary waiver.

— 9 —

ADDRESSING THE
VOLUNTARINESS OF A CONFESSION

When a defendant has been charged with a crime and has made a statement to the police, his or her defense attorney may wish to have that statement suppressed. If the statement is suppressed, the statement could not be presented to the jury, and fruits of the statement (evidence that was acquired as a result of information obtained in the statement) may also be inadmissible. The U.S. Supreme Court has explained that one of the purposes of the safeguards prescribed by the Miranda decision was to free courts from the task of scrutinizing individual cases to try to determine, after the fact, whether particular confessions were voluntary (*Berkemer v. McCarty,* 1984). But a signed Miranda waiver is no guarantee that a confession was given voluntarily, in large part because police use trickery to extract confessions from at-least-initially unwilling suspects (Leo, 1992, 1996a, 1996b, 2001b). Therefore, some courts, including *Massey v. State* (2003), have determined that a defendant's claim that his or her confession was induced by police trickery is sufficient legal grounds to require an evidentiary hearing to determine whether the confession should be suppressed. The legal issue to be considered by the judge at the suppression hearing might be presented as follows: Did the State fail to prove, by a preponderance of the evidence, that the Defendant's supposed confession was freely and voluntarily made under the totality of the circumstances?

What do courts consider in the totality-of-the-circumstances analysis? As described in *Schneckloth v. Bustamonte* (1973), courts determine the factual circumstances surrounding the confession, assess the psychological impact on the accused, and evaluate the legal significance of how the accused reacted. The decisions do not turn on the presence or absence of a single controlling criterion, but reflect a careful scrutiny of all the surrounding circumstances, including both the characteristics of the accused and the details of the interrogation.

> Some of the factors taken into account have included the youth of the accused, his lack of education, or his low intelligence, the lack of any advice to the accused of his constitutional rights, the length of detention, the repeated and prolonged nature of the questioning, and the use of physical punishment such as the deprivation of food or sleep. (p. 226, citations omitted)

Coercive psychological techniques such as lying and trickery by the police are relevant factors to consider. Overt threats or promises of leniency might be sufficient alone to lead to a statement being suppressed, but more subtle implications of lenient or harsh treatment would be considered along with other factors. Additional factors can be derived from the cases reviewed in Chapter 6 and from state cases. There is no exhaustive list; courts consider any and all factors relevant to the voluntariness of the statement.

As mentioned in the previous chapter, there must be some element of police coercion for a confession to be ruled involuntary (*Colorado v. Connelly,* 1986). The *Connelly* case was rare in that Connelly initiated the contact with the police and the police did nothing to induce him to confess. Whenever the police initiate contact with a defendant and ask questions, there is likely to be some element of coercion (see the dissent in *Ashcraft v. Tennessee,* 1944, and see the discussion about that in Chapter 8).

The ultimate issue has been defined in psychological terms: "Is the confession the product of an essentially free and unconstrained choice by its maker? If it is, if he has willed to confess, it may be used against him. If it is not, if his will has been overborne and his capacity for self-determination critically impaired, the use of his confession offends due process" (*Culombe v. Connecticut,* 1961, p. 602). Courts do not look to experts to decide whether a particular defendant's will was overborne, due to the inherent subjectivity of such a question. Rather, psychologists can provide useful information about the person, the situation, and the person-situation interaction.

The assessment procedure parallels that described in Chapter 8, with an important difference: the relevant time is not the relatively brief time period when the defendant waived his or her Miranda rights, but the longer period extending throughout the course of the interrogation. The psychologist can assist the Court by performing an assessment that results from performing the following tasks:

1. Gather and analyze information regarding "the physical and psychological environment in which the confession was obtained" (*Crane v. Kentucky,* 1986, p. 684).
2. Gather and analyze information about the interrogation techniques employed by the police.
3. Assess the defendant's current mental status, including intelligence, memory, reading comprehension, listening comprehension, personality, and psychopathology.
4. Reconstruct the defendant's mental state during the confession.
5. Assist the judge in understanding the effect of the interrogation techniques on the defendant throughout the interrogation.

We will consider each of these assessment tasks in turn.

 Gather and analyze information regarding the physical and psychological environment in which the confession was obtained.

In *Crane v. Kentucky* (1986, p. 686) the trial court did not allow the defense to present evidence to the jury about "the size and other physical characteristics of the interrogation room, the length of the interview, and various other details about the taking of the confession." The U.S. Supreme Court reversed and remanded the case, noting that evidence surrounding a confession bears on both the confession's voluntariness and its credibility. Courts must allow such evidence to be presented to the judge to determine voluntariness (the subject of this chapter), and to the jury to determine its credibility (the subject of the next chapter).

In gathering information about the physical and psychological environment in which the confession was obtained, the psychologist should attend to where and how the police and the suspect came into contact. Who initiated contact? Did the police approach the suspect, or did the suspect approach them? At what point did the police tell, show, or take actions to suggest that the suspect was not free to go? What conversations, if any, took place at the location where the police and suspect first came into contact, during transport to the police station, in the hallway, and so on? How much time elapsed between the time when the police and suspect first came into contact and when the Miranda waiver form was signed? What happened during that time?

Was a statement taken in a room designed for interrogation and confession? Kassin (1997) describes typical interrogation rooms and explains how the characteristics of the room are designed to help the police assert power and control over the suspect. Was the interrogation room similar to the typical room that Kassin describes?

Information about the physical and psychological environment can be gleaned from the recording of the interrogation, if it was recorded; from the interrogators via their reports, notes, and depositions; and from questioning the defendant. The psychologist should note discrepancies, if any, between these data sources. Generally, the psychologist should refrain from choosing to believe one source over another. It is often useful to construct a time line which includes the initial contact between the police and the suspect, along with any documented times (e.g., when the Miranda waiver form was signed, when polygraph testing began and ended, when a partial recording began and ended, when the post-confession narrative concluded, when the suspect was booked into jail). One "clean" copy of this original time line should be maintained, with only the most accurately documented information noted.

 Gather and analyze information about the interrogation techniques employed by the police.

As the psychologist gathers information about the interrogation techniques employed by the police, it is important for the psychologist to know what he or she seeks. As described in earlier chapters, that information comes from reading interrogation manuals such as Inbau et al. (2001), from social psychology, and from applied social science literature such as Gudjonsson (2003) and Leo (1992). To the best extent possible, considering the completeness of the record, the psychologist can attempt to reconstruct the interrogation procedure using a copy of the time line described earlier. Again, the information can be gleaned from the recording of the interrogation, if it was recorded; from the interrogators via their reports, notes, and depositions; and from questioning the defendant.

Perhaps the most detailed analysis of interrogation techniques in individual cases was conducted in Pearse's unpublished 1997 doctoral thesis, as described by Gudjonsson (2003, pp. 75-114). The Police Interviewing Analysis Framework (PIAF) provides a microanalysis of all that takes place within the police interview/interrogation. Gudjonsson (2003, p. 114) concludes: "The PIAF has . . . succeeded in analyzing, measuring, and displaying the nature and type of tactics employed." The study is considered to be exploratory rather than confirmatory; one weakness is that the analysis involves some subjectivity. Despite limitations, the "findings support the main hypothesis that people may well break down in interview because of the application of police pressure and manipulation" (Gudjonsson, 2003, p. 112).

 Assess the defendant's current mental status, including intelligence, memory, reading comprehension, listening comprehension, personality, and psychopathology.

Assessment begins with procedures and techniques similar to those described in the previous chapter to conduct a general psychological assessment of a person's current mental state, skills, abilities, and so forth. Again, the psychologist should request relevant records from the referring attorney prior to meeting with the defendant, and may request additional records based on information provided during the psychological interview. As with other forensic psychological assessments, a history and mental status provide useful information, which can be supplemented by a psychiatric screening instrument, a structured diagnostic interview, and/or by an objective test of psychopathology. A full-scale intelligence test and a neuropsychological screening test should be utilized. If results of any of these assessments suggest impairment, then tests for exaggeration or feigning should be employed. Reading and listening ability, particularly reading comprehension and listening comprehension, can be measured via subtests from achievement batteries (see the more detailed description in the previous chapter for examples of all of these assessment procedures).

Are there any forensic assessment instruments (FAIs) that are potentially useful for assessments relevant to the voluntariness of a confession? Yes. There are some FAIs that address related issues, and some instruments that address directly relevant issues.

The instruments that assess related issues are those that assess understanding and appreciation of Miranda rights (discussed in the previous chapter) and those that assess competence to proceed to trial, such as the Fitness Interview Test – Revised (FIT-R; Roesch et al., 1998),[1] the MacArthur Competence Assessment Tool – Criminal Adjudication (MacCAT-CA; Poythress et al., 1999), or the Evaluation of Competency to Stand Trial – Revised (ECST-R; Rogers, Tillbrook, & Sewell, 2004). All of these instruments provide standardized assessment of current skills or abilities and allow comparison to a normative group (DeClue, 2003b; Grisso, 2003). None was designed specifically to assist with assessment of a person's vulnerability to manipulative interrogation procedures. Particularly when such instruments have already been administered to assess other forensic issues, the psychologist should consider whether the results bear on the issue of voluntariness of a confession.

In considering a person's vulnerability to the pressure of interrogation, three personality constructs have been considered to be directly relevant: *interrogative suggestibility, compliance,* and *acquiescence.* We will examine each of these constructs and consider ways to measure them.

Interrogative Suggestibility

Interrogative suggestibility is defined as

> The extent to which, within a closed social interaction, people come to accept messages communicated during formal questioning, as the result of which their subsequent behavioral response is affected.
>
> This definition comprises five interrelated components which form an integrated part of the interrogative process:
>
> 1. a social interaction;
> 2. a questioning procedure;
> 3. a suggestive stimulus;
> 4. acceptance of the stimulus; and
> 5. a behavioral response. (Gudjonsson, 2003, p. 345)

Neither the concept of interrogative suggestibility nor the tools to measure it are new. Experiments to measure interrogative suggestibility via misleading questions were performed in America (Cattell, 1895)

---

[1] In administering the FIT-R, the examiner asks the defendant a few questions about his or her questioning by the police.

and Europe (Binet, 1900, 1905) 100 years ago (Gudjonsson, 2003, p. 344). Today, the theoretical model with the most research support is that of Gudjonsson and Clark (1986; Gudjonsson, 2003) and the most empirically validated instruments for measuring interrogative suggestibility are the Gudjonsson Suggestibility Scales (GSSs; GSS 1 and GSS 2; Gudjonsson, 1984, 1987, 1997, 2003). We will consider implications of the theoretical model and then explore the measurement instruments.

The Gudjonsson-Clark model describes two distinct types of suggestibility: one emphasizes the impact of leading or suggestive questioning on testimony, and the other relates to the extent to which interrogators are able to get interviewees to "shift" (change) unwanted but perhaps accurate answers by challenge and negative feedback. "An interrogator who communicates negative feedback to a suspect, witness, or victim, may through an interrogative pressure shift unwanted, but perhaps true, responses in favor of untrue or distorted ones" (Gudjonsson, 2003, p. 347). The model recognizes three components as necessary for the suggestibility process: *uncertainty, interpersonal trust,* and *expectations.* People enter into the interrogation process with individual differences in each of these components, which affect their vulnerability to the process, and interrogators take steps to increase uncertainty, enhance interpersonal trust, and alter expectations.

People with low intelligence or memory problems are generally more uncertain about the answer to interrogators' questions and are therefore more prone to change their answers in response to negative feedback. If an interrogator succeeds in getting a suspect to doubt his or her memories, that enhances the likelihood that the suspect will change his or her answers to the interrogator's questions.

Suspects who generally have greater interpersonal trust are more prone to believe that the interrogators' intentions are genuine and that there is no trickery involved in the questioning. Interrogators who promote trust and use subtle leading questions are more likely to succeed in getting an uncertain suspect to change his or her responses.

Uncertainty and interpersonal trust are necessary but not sufficient to get people to yield to suggestions, because a person could just say "I don't know" in response to the interrogator's questions. People are less likely to do so, and therefore more likely to accept the interrogator's cues to change their answers, if they believe that:

1. they must provide a definite answer,
2. they should know the answer to the question, and
3. they are expected to know the answer and be able to give it.

The theory postulates that most people would be susceptible to suggestions if the necessary conditions of uncertainty, interpersonal trust, and heightened expectations are present. The extent to which interviewees yield to suggestion is a function of their cognitive appraisal of the interrogative situation and the coping strategies they are able to adopt. A coping strategy that helps interviewees resist suggestions involves being able to look objectively and critically at the situation and not commit oneself to an answer unless one is absolutely sure of the facts. A coping strategy that is amenable to suggestion involves an unrealistic appraisal of the situation and the reluctance to admit the fallibility of one's memory when uncertain. (Gudjonsson, 2003, p. 350)

Can individual differences in interrogative suggestibility be measured reliably? Yes, they can, using the Gudjonsson Suggestibility Scales, which

were developed for two different purposes. First, the scales were intended to be used for research in order to further our understanding of interrogative suggestibility and its mediating variables and mechanisms. Second, the scales were intended for forensic and clinical applications. The primary application was to establish an instrument that could identify people who were particularly susceptible to erroneous testimony during questioning. In other words, the emphasis was on the measurement of individual differences. (Gudjonsson, 2003, p. 362)

GSS 1 and GSS 2 have very similar norms and can be used interchangeably. The tests have impressive reliability, measured in terms of internal consistency, alternate-form, test-retest, and inter-rater reliability (Gudjonsson, 2003, pp. 364-366).

In administering either of the GSSs, the examiner reads a narrative paragraph to the subject and asks the subject to report all that he or she can recall, immediately and after a delay of about 50 minutes. Then the subject is asked 20 questions, 15 of which are subtly misleading. The subject is then told that he or she made a number of errors (whether he or she really did or not) and it is therefore necessary to ask all the questions once more. Responses are objectively scored in several ways, including *Yield 1, Shift, Yield 2, Total Suggestibility,* and *Confabulation.* Yield 1 refers to the number of suggestions (leading questions) to which the subject yields prior to negative feedback. Shift refers to the number of times there has been a distinct change in the subject's answers following negative feedback. Yield 2 refers to the number of suggestions to which the subject yields after negative feedback. Total Suggestibility is the sum of Yield 1 and Shift; it gives an indication of the subject's overall level of suggestibility. Confabulation refers to the number of times the subject provides major distortions and/or fabrications while recounting the GSS stories.

Because some of the research regarding interrogative suggestibility also involves the distinct concepts of compliance and acquiescence, we will introduce those concepts and then consider the research collectively.

Compliance

According to the Gudjonsson-Clark model, suggestibility implies personal acceptance of the information provided, but *compliance* does not. Broadly, compliance refers to the tendency of a person to go along with – comply with – propositions, requests, or instructions, in order to achieve some immediate interpersonal gain. The compliant person is fully aware that his or her responses are being influenced. The person may disagree with the proposition or request made, but he or she nevertheless reacts in a compliant way. Gudjonsson (1989, 1997, 2003) construes compliance as having two major components: (a) an eagerness to please and the need to protect one's self-esteem when in the company of others, and (b) avoidance of conflict and confrontation with others, particularly those perceived to be in a position of authority. Compliance can be conceptualized as either a personality trait or as a behavioral response to a given situation.

The Gudjonsson Compliance Scale (GCS; Gudjonsson 1989, 1997, 2003) has been developed to measure the personality trait of compliance. The GCS is intended to compliment Gudjonsson's work into interrogative suggestibility.

> It focuses on two different types of behavior. First, when interviewed by the police, some individuals are prone to comply with requests

and obey instructions that they would rather not do, for instrumental gain, such as termination of a police interview, release from custody, escaping from a conflict and confrontation or eagerness to please another person. Secondly, some individuals are susceptible to pressure from others to commit offenses (*i.e.,* they can be coerced into committing a crime). (Gudjonsson, 2003, p. 371)

The GCS is a 20-item paper-and-pencil test with two factors: (a) uneasiness or fear of people in authority and avoidance of conflict and confrontation, and (b) eagerness to please. Subjects rate their behavior in terms of how they *generally* react to interpersonal pressure and demands from others.

Compliance, as measured by the GCS, is conceptualized as a personality trait rather than a situation-bound behavior pattern. Subjects are asked to rate their behavior in terms of how they generally react to interpersonal pressure and demands from others. Test-retest reliability is adequate (Gudjonsson, 2003, p. 372). Compliance, as measured by the GCS, appears to be positively correlated with social desirability, state anxiety, trait anxiety, and dysfunctional coping, and negatively correlated with angry verbal and physical reactions to provocation (see Gudjonsson, 2003, pp. 372-373, for a review of several studies). Gudjonsson (2003, p. 373) concludes:

High compliance is associated with an attempt by the individual to reject the reality of the stressful event and withdraw effort from challenging the stressor and achieving [his or her] own goal. This suggests that compliant individuals avoid a proper appraisal of the stressful event, pretend that everything is fine, and withdraw effort from achieving their own goals or doing what they really want.

Acquiescence

Acquiescence refers to the tendency of a person to answer questions in the affirmative, regardless of the content. It can be construed as a personality trait related to submissiveness and eagerness to please, but it may be more related to intellectual and educational factors than to temperament or personality variables (Gudjonsson, 2003, pp. 376-379). People with IQs in the mentally retarded range have been found to be prone to acquiesce (Sigelman et al., 1981). Acquiescence can be measured by way of an item-reversal technique, counting how often a person agrees with both items in matched pairs of logically opposite items or statements (Winkler, Kanouse, & Ware, 1982).[2]

Research

Now we consider the research on interrogative suggestibility, compliance, and acquiescence. Gudjonsson (2003, pp. 378-379) summarizes research into the constructs as follows:

> The evidence indicates that suggestibility and compliance are poorly correlated [with each other] and that there is a weak, but significant, relationship between suggestibility and acquiescence. There is no significant relationship between acquiescence and compliance. . . . In one study . . . there was a small but significant negative correlation between compliance and Full Scale IQ. In contrast, both acquiescence and suggestibility have been found to have modest negative correlations with intelligence.

In real-life studies with people who claim to have made false confessions, such people had higher suggestibility and compliance scores than the average forensic patient. In contrast, people who had resisted interrogators' suggestions had lower than average suggestibility and compliance scores. Consistent with theory, people who claimed to have made coerced-internalized false confessions scored higher on suggestibility than those who claimed to have made coerced-compliant false confessions (see Gudjonsson, 2003, pp. 404-410 for a review of these studies). In distinguishing between suggestibility and compliance, there is some evidence that Yield 1 measures suggestibility, and Shift

> seems more akin to the concept of compliance than Yield 1, because people are making a conscious decision to alter their answers in an attempt to improve their performance. . . . The most impressive findings relate to the ability of the scales to differentiate between defendants who allege that they made a false confession and those who made no self-incriminating admissions during police interrogation, and the finding that the GSS 1 differentiated successfully between coerced-internalized and other type of false

---

[2] A form of acquiescence was hilariously illustrated by Sacha Baron Cohen (as Bruno) interviewing Los Angeles fashion mavens on episode 4 of Home Box Office's Da Ali G show. His interviewees blithely answered Bruno's questions by describing their own fashion shows in blatantly contradictory terms.

confessor. . . . Interrogative suggestibility correlates with a number
of cognitive and personality measures, including those measuring
intellectual functioning, memory, self-esteem, anxiety, assertiveness,
locus of control, and field dependence. Of particular importance seems
to be the ability of the person to cope with the demands, expectations,
and pressures of the interrogative situation. (Gudjonsson, 2003, p.
413)

It is important to keep in mind that such studies show differences
between groups, and

there are clear individual differences within the respective two groups.
For example, not all of the alleged false confessors proved highly
suggestible or compliant. . . . This raises an important point, which
should always be carefully considered by the psychologist or
psychiatrist when carrying out a forensic assessment in cases of
alleged false confession. The suspect's ability to resist the police
interviewer's suggestions and interrogative pressure, when these are
present, is undoubtedly due to the combination of situational and
interrogational factors on the one hand, and the suspect's mental state,
motivation, personality, and coping style on the other. (Gudjonsson,
2003, p. 406)

No test score, and no combination of test scores, tells whether a
given defendant gave a true or a false confession (or a partially true and
partially false confession), or whether a given confession should be
deemed to have been voluntary or coerced. While scores on tests
measuring interrogative suggestibility, compliance, and acquiescence
are all potentially helpful for understanding a person's vulnerability to
interrogation procedures, such scores should not be interpreted or
conveyed as if they had talismanic significance. A comparison to other
forensic issues may help to illustrate this point. A person with a low IQ
score is more likely to be considered incompetent to proceed to trial
than a person with a high IQ score, but the IQ score alone does not
determine competency. A person with schizophrenia is more likely to
be judged to have been insane at the time of the offense than a person
with no mental illness, but the diagnosis of schizophrenia does not end
the investigation into mental state at the time of the offense. Similarly,
a person with high scores on tests measuring interrogative suggestibility,
compliance, and/or acquiescence may or may not have confessed
voluntarily. In the context of a comprehensive assessment, such scores

help to describe the person's strengths and vulnerabilities, but the scores do not tell us what happened at some point in the past.

 Reconstruct the defendant's mental state during the confession.

As mentioned previously, this process is similar to the process of reconstructing a defendant's mental state at the time of an alleged offense, which psychologists routinely address as we conduct evaluations relevant to insanity (see Rogers & Shuman, 2000). Relevant information comes from an assessment of the person's current mental state (see previous section), data regarding the person's mental state at other points in time (e.g., previous test scores, results of previous psychological assessments), data about the setting and the interrogation procedures used, and data about other factors that would be likely to affect a person's mental state (e.g., alcohol or drug use, medication, sleep deprivation, family stress, fear, etc.). The psychologist will want to consider what was going on in the person's life around the time of the interrogation. There are a multitude of physical, psychological, and social factors that can affect a person's mental state, and all are relevant to this inquiry. For defendants who have a mental illness, the psychologist should seek reliable data about the degree to which the person was suffering from symptoms before, during, and after the interrogation. As Gudjonsson (2003, p. 314) notes, "Any information obtained from the accused must, whenever possible, be supported or corroborated by other evidence, because it is essentially self-serving."

There is a forensic assessment instrument that can help psychologists gather information about why a person confessed: the Gudjonsson Confession Questionnaire – Revised (GCQ-R; Gudjonsson & Sigurdsson, 1999; Gudjonsson, 2003, pp. 628-630). As hypothesized, studies with this instrument show that

> internalized false confessors reported experiencing greater *internal pressure* to confess during the interrogation than compliant false confessors, including experiencing a greater feeling of guilt about the offense. . . . Secondly, the internalized false confessors scored higher than the compliant false confessors on a *drug intoxication* factor. This suggests that being under the influence of alcohol or drugs at the time of the alleged offense, or during the police interrogation, makes suspects more susceptible to believing that they

have committed an offense of which they are innocent. (Gudjonsson, 2003, pp. 210-211)

Use of the GCQ-R can help a defendant articulate why he or she confessed, although, as it is when simply asking the defendant why he or she confessed, there are no guarantees that the defendant's responses will be truthful.

 Assist the judge in understanding the effect of the interrogation techniques on the defendant throughout the interrogation.

Whether requested by the defense, the prosecution, or the judge, the psychologist's primary role as an expert witness is to assist the judge (Committee on Ethical Guidelines for Forensic Psychologists, 1991). As Gudjonsson (2003, p. 315) notes, "When leading questions have been asked by the interrogators and persuasive manipulation and pressure [have been] employed, then these have to be related to the accused's personality and mental state, as well as to the circumstances of the situation." By virtue of our knowledge, training, and experience, psychologists who have studied the psychology of interrogation and confession can help judges understand these interactions.

Focusing on confessions generally (not just false confessions), Gudjonsson (2003, p. 157) summarizes research into why subjects confess as follows:

> The available evidence indicates that suspects confess due to a combination of factors, rather than to one factor alone. Three general factors appear to be relevant, in varying degree, to most suspects. These relate to an *internal* pressure (e.g., feelings of remorse, the need to talk about the offense), *external* pressure (e.g., fear of confinement, police persuasiveness), and perception of *proof* (e.g., the suspects' perceptions of the strength of evidence against them).

After psychologists identify the defendant's vulnerabilities, they can help the judge recognize how interrogators have exploited those weaknesses, if they have; how interrogators have manipulated information to alter the suspect's perceptions, if they have; and how interrogators have manipulated external pressures, if they have. Of course, it is up to the judge to render the ultimate decision about whether a confession was illegally coerced.

— 10 —

ADDRESSING THE
RELIABILITY OF A CONFESSION

The reliability of a confession can be challenged at a suppression hearing and at trial. In a suppression hearing, the legal issue presented to the judge by the defense may take a form similar to the following: Should the Court suppress defendant's coerced statements to the police because they are so highly unreliable[1] and virtually uncorroborated? At trial, the defense may argue that the jury should give no weight to the defendant's statements to police during interrogation because they are unreliable, and the defense may attempt to elicit testimony from witnesses to support that argument. The prosecution may attempt to elicit testimony to the contrary.

The defense's right to present evidence relevant to the reliability of a confession is guaranteed by the Sixth and Fourteenth Amendments (*Crane v. Kentucky,* 1986, pp. 688-689, citations omitted):

> The manner in which a statement was extracted is, of course, relevant to the purely legal question of its voluntariness, a question most, but not all, States assign to the trial judge alone to resolve. But the physical and psychological environment that yielded the confession can also be of substantial relevance to the ultimate factual issue of the defendant's guilt or innocence. Confessions, even those that have been found to be voluntary, are not conclusive of guilt. And, as with any other part of the prosecutor's case, a confession may be shown to be insufficiently corroborated or otherwise . . . unworthy of belief.

---

[1] As used here, "unreliable" does not necessarily mean false. In simple terms, it means "You can't count on it' or "You don't know what it means" or "uncertain."

Indeed, stripped of the power to describe to the jury the circumstances that prompted his confession, the defendant is effectively disabled from answering the one question every rational juror needs answered: If the defendant is innocent, why did he previously admit his guilt? Accordingly, regardless of whether the defendant marshaled the same evidence earlier in support of an unsuccessful motion to suppress, and entirely independent of any question of voluntariness, a defendant's case may stand or fall on his ability to convince the jury that the manner in which the confession was obtained casts doubt on its credibility.

Therefore the defense can present evidence of both the process and the content of a confession that suggest inaccuracy of the confession. And some appellate courts, including *Boyer v. State* (2002, p. 419), have specifically held that trial courts must allow testimony by "an expert on interrogation techniques and false confession phenomena."

Courts recognize that the average juror is not aware of the frequency of false confessions, or of their causes. For example, in *Smith v. United States* (1954, p. 153, citation omitted), the Court noted that "the experience of the courts, the police and the medical profession recounts a number of false confessions voluntarily made. . . . This experience with confessions is not shared by the average juror." Therefore, an expert witness should be allowed to educate the jury about the suspected causes of false confessions.

A psychologist serving as an expert witness can present testimony as follows:

1. Some people falsely confess to some crimes some times.
2. Some interrogation procedures increase the risk of false confessions.
3. Some personal factors make some people more vulnerable to police influence than others.
4. There are procedures recommended by social scientists and law enforcement agencies to avoid false confessions.
5. There are procedures recommended by social scientists and law enforcement agencies to recognize false confessions.

For Items 2 through 5, the psychologist can then describe factors in the instant case that are present, and those that are not present.

Some people falsely confess to some crimes some times.

Psychologists who have studied the psychology of interrogations and confessions are aware that some people falsely confess to some crimes some times, and that the frequency of false confessions, though unknown and presumed to be small, is not infinitesimal. Such psychologists have some understanding about the social processes that can contribute to a false confession, about the psychological vulnerabilities that make some people more vulnerable to giving a false confession than others, about proper procedures to reduce the risk of a false confession, and about proper procedures for gathering data to assess the reliability of a confession. The average juror may believe that false confessions occur less frequently than they actually do, may lack knowledge about who is most vulnerable to giving a false confession, and may have little or no knowledge about the social processes that contribute to false confessions. Therefore, psychologists can play an important role in confession cases by educating the jury about false confessions.

Psychologists who consult on confession cases should be familiar with the clinical and research literature on false confessions, and should be prepared to convey this information to the jurors. Earlier chapters of this book should provide a good starting point for amassing this knowledge, and the reader is encouraged to go to the primary sources to enhance knowledge about who confesses and why. The information in Chapter 6 should help psychologists appreciate the legal context regarding confessions, but there is no substitute for consultation with an attorney, especially one who is experienced in working on confession cases in the local jurisdiction.

 Some interrogation procedures increase the risk of false confessions.

The legal and psychological literatures provide lists of procedures that are considered to increase the risks of a false confession.[2] While no list is exhaustive, the following should be considered:

---

[2] This list is compiled from the psychological literature summarized in Chapters 1 through 4 and the legal literature summarized in Chapter 6. Remember that some of the same procedures that could increase the likelihood that a guilty person would confess could also increase the risk that an innocent person would confess (Ofshe & Leo, 1997).

- whether the accused initiated contact with the law enforcement officials
- the location of the interrogation (e.g., the coercive atmosphere of a station-house setting)
- whether the police isolated the suspect from others
- whether the accused initially denied guilt
- how the police responded to the accused's denial of guilt
- what part, if any, did the interrogator's prior relationship with the suspect play in eliciting the statement
- whether the police made direct or implied threats that not cooperating or confessing might lead to a more severe sentence
- whether the police made direct or implied promises that cooperating and/or confessing might lead to a more lenient sentence
- whether the police made direct or implied promises that the suspect's cooperation and/or confession would be conveyed to another party (such as the prosecutor, judge, or jury) that would subsequently be in a decision-making position regarding the case
- whether the police made direct or implied promises that the suspect would be able to go home (sooner) if he or she cooperated and/or confessed
- whether the police made direct or implied threats that the suspect would go home later (perhaps not until the next day or later) if he or she did not cooperate and/or confess
- whether the police made statements calculated to delude the suspect as to his or her true position
- whether the police (firmly) stated that the evidence against the suspect was overwhelming (and resistance was futile)
- whether the suspect was given the opportunity to sleep or eat
- the length of the interrogation
- the timing of the interrogation (e.g., late at night)
- whether the police lied to the suspect, or otherwise employed trickery or dishonesty
- whether the police exaggerated the amount of evidence against the suspect
- whether the police exaggerated the certainty of the evidence against the suspect
- whether the police fabricated documents

- whether the police lied to or otherwise misled the suspect about the results of a polygraph examination
- whether the police exaggerated the certainty of the results of a polygraph examination
- whether the police advised the suspect of his or her Constitutional rights
- how the police advised the suspect of his or her Constitutional rights, and how they ascertained that he or she understood them and made a knowing, intelligent, and voluntary waiver of them
- whether the police sought out the suspect's vulnerabilities and attempted to exploit them
- whether the police suggested moral justifications for the offense
- whether the police suggested psychological excuses for the offense
- whether the police minimized the moral seriousness of the offense
- whether the police minimized the legal seriousness of the offense
- whether the police suggested that the offense might have occurred by accident, in self-defense, or unintentionally
- whether the police suggested that it would be in the suspect's best interest to confess
- whether the police suggested that it would be in the best interest of another person (e.g., victim, co-defendant) for the suspect to confess
- whether the police directly or indirectly suggested that the result of a confession would be that the suspect would receive therapy
- whether the police directly or indirectly suggested that the result of a confession would be that the victim would be able to receive therapy
- whether the police refused to accept the suspect's denial of guilt
- whether the police (either purposefully or inadvertently) provided details of the crime to the suspect (in the process of interrogating him or her)
- whether the police took steps to enhance their power, control, and/or authority while interrogating the suspect
- whether the police took steps to encourage the suspect to think that one or more interrogators were the suspect's friends and were trying to help him or her

- whether the police interrupted the suspect as he or she attempted to answer questions
- whether the suspect was encouraged to respond to forced-choice questions
- whether the suspect was subjected to a barrage of questions (by multiple interrogators)
- whether the police asked (or demanded) the suspect to explain fabricated evidence (e.g., how do you explain that your fingerprints were found on the weapon?)
- whether the police suggested that the suspect's memory might be faulty
- whether the police suggested that the suspect might have committed the crime even though he or she does not remember having done it
- whether the police asked the suspect to (close his or her eyes and) imagine what he or she might have done
- whether the police asked the suspect to imagine how the guilty person might have committed the crime
- whether the police used any techniques involving (guided) imagery
- whether the police positively reinforced admissions and/or negatively reinforced denials
- whether the police used touch to soothe or control the suspect
- whether the police applied emotional pressure to encourage the suspect to confess
- whether the police conducted a careful, detailed, post-admission interview (i.e., elicited a detailed post-admission narrative)

Social psychology research such as that of Asch (1956), Festinger (1957), Freedman, Wallington, and Bless (1967), Milgram (1983; see also Blass, 2000), and Nel, Helmreich, and Aronson (1969), helps to explain why such techniques work, and gives a broader context for understanding why people react to interrogation techniques in ways that the general public would not expect (Fulero, 2004; Wakefield & Underwager, 1998).

It is not expected that the use of one or two such procedures would lead most innocent suspects to confess, but a combination of such procedures could lead to a false confession, particularly for vulnerable suspects. Techniques that question or challenge a suspect's memory, or techniques such as guided imagery that could influence a suspect's memory, particularly enhance the risk of an internalized false confession. The risk of a compliant false confession is particularly enhanced when interrogators use combinations of techniques that stress the certainty of the evidence (including exaggerating the certainty of evidence or fabricating evidence) against the suspect *and* minimize the moral and/ or legal seriousness of the defendant's actions *and* suggest or imply an advantage of confessing.

 Some personal factors make some people more vulnerable to police influence than others.

The legal and psychological literatures provide lists of personal characteristics that are considered to increase the risks of a false confession.[3] While no list is exhaustive, the following should be considered:

- low intelligence
- learning disability
- youthful age and/or immaturity
- lack of experience
- lack of education
- mental disorder (e.g., schizophrenia) affecting reality testing
- mental disorder (e.g., Alzheimer's disease) affecting memory
- psychoactive substance use (e.g., drunk or under the influence of hallucinogens) around the time of the interrogation or around the time of the alleged offense[4]
- withdrawal symptoms at the time of the interrogation or at the time of the alleged offense[5]
- dependent personality
- anxiety disorder

---

[3]   This list is compiled from the psychological literature summarized in Chapters 1 through 4 and the legal literature summarized in Chapter 6.

[4]   Psychoactive substance use around the time of the interrogation can impair the subject's ability to make decisions and to resist influence tactics. Psychoactive substance use around the time of the alleged offense can impair the subject's memory and thereby increase vulnerability.

[5]   Withdrawal symptoms around the time of the interrogation can impair the subject's ability to make decisions and to resist influence tactics. Withdrawal symptoms around the time of the alleged offense can impair the subject's memory and thereby increase vulnerability.

- suggestibility
- recent bereavement
- language barriers
- medical condition

The reader is encouraged to see the two previous chapters regarding psychological assessment procedures.

 There are procedures recommended by social scientists and law enforcement agencies to avoid false confessions.

This is discussed in Chapter 4. The following list is adapted from Ofshe and Leo (1997):

1. Interrogators should electronically record (audio- or videotape) the entire interrogation.
2. All interviews that result in a confession should include a detailed post-admission narrative.
3. After the conclusion of the interrogation (including the post-admission narrative), investigators should check to see whether the details provided by the suspect conform to the actual evidence in the case. Detectives should perform further investigation as needed to confirm or disconfirm the suspect's statement.

It is not just social scientists who recognize that some suspects falsely confess in response to police interrogations, and it is not just social scientists who have offered descriptions of how police should conduct interrogations in order to decrease the risk of obtaining a false confession. In the 2002 *FBI Law Enforcement Bulletin*, Napier and Adams acknowledge that some suspects falsely confess in response to police interrogation, and they caution that "Professional officers view a single false confession as one too many" (Paragraph 4). In their view, fundamental interview and interrogation principles can safeguard confessions by compiling solid, incriminating evidence. They present five interview principles to reduce the risk of false confessions.

First, investigators[6] should avoid over-reliance on behavioral cues and gut instincts, and should investigate all viable leads capable of

---

[6] Napier and Adams use "investigator" rather than "interrogator."

identifying additional suspects and eliminating wrongly identified suspects.

Second, investigators should recognize that

certain individuals possess traits that make them overly susceptible to police interrogation techniques, thereby leading to coerced confessions. These impressionable traits include youthfulness, a low or borderline intelligent quotient (IQ), mental handicap, psychological inadequacy, recent bereavement, language barrier, alcohol or other drug withdrawal, illiteracy, fatigue, social isolation, or inexperience with the criminal justice system. . . . Such vulnerabilities as reduced mental capabilities, the ability to withstand pressure, bereavement, mental illness, age, or other personal traits that may increase suggestibility require special care when using questioning techniques. Investigators should place the suspect's vulnerability in context, adapt the investigative approach, and fully document any adaptations. (Paragraphs 8, 10)

Third, investigators should avoid contaminating the interview.

To avoid contaminating a suspect's subsequent admissions and unnecessarily revealing investigative knowledge, investigators should initiate the criminal involvement phase of questioning by using only open-ended questions, which avoid the pitfalls of leading or informing suspects. These questions begin with such phrases as "Describe for me. . . . ," "Tell me about. . . . ," and "Explain how. . . ." These questions force suspects to commit to a version of events instead of simply agreeing with the investigator; they also prevent disclosing investigative knowledge. Because suspects may provide a wealth of information in this free narrative form, open-ended questions make successful lying difficult. If, however, suspects decide to lie, open-ended questions provide a forum. This aspect of the open-ended question technique may help investigators because every lie forecloses avenues by which suspects may later try to defend themselves. Investigators must receive answers to open-ended questions without any type of judgment, reaction, or interruption. By allowing suspects to tell their stories without interruption, investigators fulfill the basic purpose of an interview – to obtain information. Additionally, investigators benefit from committing suspects to a particular position, which may contain information that later becomes evidence of guilt or provides a connection to the crime, crime scene, or victim. The questioning process does not become contaminated when investigators initiate the interview with open-ended questions. Investigators have not told suspects the details of the crime or subsequent investigation and, thereby, have preserved the evidence. After listening to the narrative responses to the open-ended question, skilled investigators will probe with additional open-ended questions and will ask direct, closed questions later. (Paragraphs 15-17)

Napier and Adams (2002) also recommend against the use of crime-scene photographs during interrogation because they contaminate the interviewee's knowledge.

Fourth, when investigators use techniques designed to elicit a partially false confession, such as suggesting that the suspect committed the alleged crime by accident, they subsequently work to obtain a true and accurate confession. "From the original admission of guilt, experienced investigators . . . [strive] to obtain a fuller, more accurate description of the suspect's criminal behavior" (Paragraph 23).

Fifth, investigators should eschew the use of threats and promises such as suggestions that "remaining silent will lead to greater penalties, but confessing to a minimized scenario will result in reward" (Paragraph 25), that confessing will help the suspect avoid the death penalty, or that if the suspect does not confess, then the investigation and prosecution will extend to a third party such as his or her brother or sister or child. "Some critics accurately have identified these tactics as being coercive enough to make innocent people confess to a crime that they did not commit" (Paragraph 25). Although Napier and Adams (2002) recommend against the use of *blatant* threats and promises, they appear to recommend the use of "subtle references offered for interpretation as the suspect chooses" (Paragraph 27). My reading of this section of Napier and Adams' article is that they recommend that officers use whatever interrogation techniques they believe will help them get an initial admission, as long as it does not contaminate the suspect's knowledge and as long as the tactics used will not result in the confession being suppressed. Once a suspect makes an initial admission, though, "Investigators must accept the admission, return to the basics of the investigation, and obtain a statement that comports to the reality of the crime" (Paragraph 28).

There are procedures recommended by social scientists and law enforcement agencies to recognize false confessions.

This is described succinctly by Napier and Adams (2002) in text that continues directly from the quote in the preceding paragraph:

> Likewise, investigators must go well beyond the "I did it" admission. They must press for minute details to tie suspects to the crime scene to disclose their active participation in the crime. Corroboration anchors the most secure confession. Some suspects may not readily provide information to support their involvement in a crime for fear of exposing the true nature of their evil acts. However, a suspect's corroboration, by providing details known to only a few individuals, solidifies a confession. Evidence linking such details as the location of the body, the weapon, or the fruits of the crime provide a superior foundation for preventing the retraction of a confession or one otherwise successfully challenged in court. (Paragraphs 28-29)

Ofshe and Leo (1997, p. 239) recommend that confession evidence should only be admissible when the accused's guilt is corroborated by independent evidence:

> Police officers should be trained (1) to seek clear-cut corroboration for every confession; and (2) to recognize that a suspect's failure to satisfy this requirement is a red flag that he may be innocent. . . . Only awareness that false confessions happen and reliance on objective standards for evaluating a confession statement will allow police to stop themselves from making the all too frequent mistake of arresting an innocent suspect. . . . The decision to admit a confession should be based not only on voluntariness but also on the fit between a defendant's post-admission narrative and the facts of the crime. . . . The only trustworthy evidence of a defendant's guilt or innocence that comes from interrogation is his post-admission narrative of the crime. Because confession statements are sometimes evidence of guilt and sometimes evidence of innocence, jurors should be instructed to rely on the fit between the defendant's narrative and the facts of the crime when deciding how to classify and weigh confession evidence.

SUMMARY OF THIS CHAPTER

I am not in any way suggesting that psychologists or other social scientists should replace juries or do juries' jobs. I do suggest that psychologists who study the psychology of interrogations and confessions have special knowledge that can help juries do their jobs.

When there is a clear and accurate record of the entire interrogation, psychologists can help identify the presence of personal and social factors, if any, that increase the risk of a false confession. Psychologists can also help to understand how social and personal factors interact. For example, Ofshe and Leo (1997) describe how some people with low intelligence are vulnerable to making stress-compliant false confessions even in the absence of overtly coercive threats or promises.

When there is not a clear and accurate record of the entire interrogation, psychologists can help the jury understand how this decreases the reliability of a confession. One key way is that it makes it impossible to know whether and to what extent interrogators (perhaps to some extent inadvertently) provided crime-scene details to the suspect prior to the suspect confessing.

Psychologists can help juries understand the importance of the post-admission narrative, and how the lack of a post-admission narrative undermines the reliability of a confession.

Do courts admit such testimony? Fulero (2004) writes that testimony about the phenomenon of false confessions, social psychological testimony about the police interrogation procedures that are commonly used, clinical psychological testimony about personality or clinical factors that might be linked to confessions, and specific clinical testimony about a particular defendant, are likely to pass muster, while testimony that purports to determine if a particular confession is true or false is not.

Are law enforcement agencies likely to view psychologists who testify in disputed-confession cases as friends or enemies? I believe that will depend more on the policies and procedures of the law enforcement agency than it will depend on which side (defense or prosecution) requested the psychologist's services. In cases where law enforcement personnel electronically recorded the entire interrogation, carefully informed the suspect of his or her Constitutional rights, ensured that the suspect understood those rights and gave a voluntary waiver, used legally permissible techniques to encourage a suspect to confess, began with open-ended statements and avoided contaminating the suspect's knowledge of the crime scene, continued the interrogation beyond the "I did it" statement to obtain a detailed statement regarding particulars of the crime, compared the defendant's statement to the actual details of the crime, and conducted further investigation to confirm or disconfirm the subject's statement, the psychologist's testimony about the reliability of the interrogation will reflect that the law enforcement workers did their jobs properly, without increasing the risk of a false confession.

Of course, even when law enforcement officers do their jobs well, some suspects will have personal characteristics that make them more vulnerable to making a false confession, and the testifying psychologist will point this out. In such cases, the psychologist would also testify that the law enforcement officers showed that they recognized the suspect's vulnerabilities and took steps to document the suspect's level of understanding of his or her rights, the reason he or she waived his or her rights, the reason why he or she chose to confess, and the fact that the suspect ultimately provided details that matched the crime scene and were not provided to the suspect during the course of the interrogation.

On the other hand, law enforcement officers are likely to see psychologists as being the enemy when the law enforcement officers have not done their jobs well. Once the psychologist has testified, the jury will be likely to see failure to electronically record the entire interrogation and/or to take a detailed post-admission narrative as the glaring deficiencies they are. In the short run, psychologists who testify in disputed-confession cases may be viewed with antipathy by law enforcement officers who may feel attacked for not having done their jobs well enough. In the long run, such testimony is likely to force law enforcement officers to gather confession evidence in a more reliable way, so that fewer innocent people are arrested and convicted. This will free up some resources so that additional guilty people may be arrested and convicted.

— Synopsis —

In the first chapter of this book we learned that it has been clearly established (e.g., through DNA evidence) that some people falsely confess to crimes some times. In subsequent chapters, we have come to understand why some people falsely confess. We have seen that there are ways to reduce the risk of false confessions, and there are ways to recognize false confessions when they occur. Finally, we have seen that there are roles for psychologists to play in disputed-confession cases regarding Miranda waiver, voluntariness of a confession, and reliability of a confession. Recent court decisions suggest that at least in some jurisdictions there may be increasing demand for well-prepared psychologists to assist the courts in confession cases:

- A defendant's claim that his or her confession was induced by police trickery is sufficient legal grounds to require an evidentiary hearing to determine whether the confession should be suppressed (*Massey v. State*, 2003).
- Trial courts must allow testimony by "an expert on interrogation techniques and false confession phenomena" (*Boyer v. State*, 2002, p. 419).

How will such testimony impact the judicial system?

For the past 17 years I have engaged in the independent practice of forensic psychology. I have been the contract psychologist for several law enforcement agencies. I have also conducted psychological evaluations and provided testimony in criminal forensic cases at the request of the defense, the prosecution, or the judge. Based on this experience, it is my opinion that law enforcement officers do not always conduct interrogations in a way that ensures that the resulting confessions are as reliable as they could be. As interrogations and confessions are held up to careful scrutiny, flawed interrogations leading to unreliable confessions will be recognized for what they are. Psychologists' assessments and testimony contribute to that scrutiny.

A psychologist who has studied the psychology of interrogations and confessions can assist the court when a particular interrogation or confession is held up to careful scrutiny. The psychological assessment and analysis will not directly address whether a confession is true or false, but it will assist the consideration of the reliability of a confession. In some cases, police will have conducted a flawed interrogation of an innocent suspect. Scrutiny of the interrogation and confession will reveal that the confession is unreliable. That could lead the judge to suppress a confession or it could lead the jury to give little weight to the confession, either of which could contribute to the release of an innocent person. In other cases, police will have conducted a flawed interrogation of a guilty suspect. Again, scrutiny of the interrogation and confession will reveal that the confession is unreliable. That could lead the judge to suppress a confession or it could lead the jury to give little weight to the confession, either of which could contribute to the release of a guilty person.

In the short run, psychologists' testimony may sometimes enhance the cause of justice and may at times help someone get away with murder. In the long run, psychologists' testimony is likely to lead law enforcement officers to gather confession evidence in a consistently more reliable way, which will enhance liberty and justice for all.

— Appendix —

Sample Report of a Psychological Assessment Addressing Miranda Waiver, Voluntariness of a Confession, and Reliability of a Confession

Gregory DeClue, PhD

Diplomate in Forensic Psychology, American Board of Professional Psychology

16443 Winburn Place
Sarasota, FL 34240-9228
Voice/Fax (941) 951-6674
gregdeclue@mailmt.com

Florida Psychology License
Number PY0003427
Certified Sex Therapist
http://gregdeclue.myakkatech.com

Re: State of Florida v. Soddi Jones[1]

Case Number: 2003-CF-2426

SAMPLE REPORT OF PSYCHOLOGICAL ASSESSMENT

Name: **Soddi Jones**

Date of Birth: 6/16/59

Dates of Assessment: 12/30/03, 1/5/04, 1/27/04, & 1/28/04

Date of Report: 2/1/04

IDENTIFYING INFORMATION AND REASON FOR REFERRAL

Soddi Jones is a 44-year-old male who was arrested and charged with sexual offenses. This evaluation was ordered to assist in his defense. Assistant Public Defender Stephen Swiftmud assisted with scheduling the evaluation and provided background materials. Mr. Swiftmud

---

[1] This sample report is based on an amalgam of actual reports, which may result in some inconsistencies. All names and identifying information have been changed. Professor Charles Patrick Ewing (and perhaps others) use "SODDI" (an acronym for Some Other Dude Did It) to characterize a class of legal defenses. This report is written as if it were prepared at the request of defense counsel. Parts of the report may not be admissible in court in some jurisdictions.

requested that I address issues relevant to waiver of Miranda rights and issues relevant to the interrogation and confession.

METHOD

Wechsler Adult Intelligence Scale-III (WAIS-III)
Screening Test for the Luria-Nebraska Neuropsychological Battery (LNNB-ST)
Woodcock-Johnson Tests of Achievement-III (WJ-III)
[Effort tests][2]
Instruments for Assessing Understanding and Appreciation of Miranda Rights (IAUAMR)
Personality Assessment Inventory (PAI)
Minnesota Multiphasic Personality Inventory-2 (MMPI-2)
Structured Interview of Reported Symptoms (SIRS)
Gudjonsson Suggestibility Scale (GSS)
Psychological interview
Review of available records including State's Discovery Exhibit; transcript of depositions of Lieutenant R and Deputy A; videotape of interview with Soddi Jones (and transcript thereof); psychological evaluation of Mr. Jones by GW, PhD, on 11/3/03; and medical records at the jail

NOTICE

This evaluation took place in a private room at M County Jail. I explained to Mr. Jones that I would be conducting a psychological evaluation of him and that I would be preparing a report that would go to the defense attorney. I further explained that, if the attorney believed the evaluation would be helpful to his case, the attorney would be likely to release it to the judge and the prosecutor. Mr. Jones showed understanding of this and agreed to participate in the evaluation under those conditions.

INTERVIEW

Mr. Jones was oriented to person, place, and time, and was in adequate contact with immediate reality. His speech was clear and

---

[2] In order to decrease the risk that details could be used to assist in coaching people on how to dissimulate on effort tests in the future, I have elected not to include description of effort tests in this sample report.

coherent. His mood was calm and appropriate to the situation. [Further mental status and most social history deleted.]

Mr. Jones said that he was arrested once before, about 18 years ago, for burglary, in Alabama. He said he served two prison sentences for two counts, "six years and three years, stacked. I did six years in prison and three years' parole." He said he has not been arrested any other times and that he has not been in jail any other times.

Mr. Jones described past use of mood-altering substances. He said he smoked marijuana "probably about twice a week" and drank "about a quart of beer . . . about twice a week." He acknowledged smoking cocaine "about once a month."

When asked if he had ever been treated for an alcohol or drug problem, he said, "No. Well, I was going to Coastal Recovery Crisis Center. I think I always get let go because there isn't anything wrong." He said he estimates he has been at the Crisis Center "about four or five" times. When asked if it's usually when he has been doing drugs, he said, "It's when I'm feeling bad. Haven't been doing drugs."

When asked if he has a mental-health problem, he said, "Uh, yeah, sure." He said that he is taking medication now. When asked what kind, he said, "I don't know the names of them. I forget them. All I know is Benadryl for a cold and sleep. Codeine, Cogentin, something like that. When I was at Coastal Recovery, I took some Haldol."

When asked if the medicine helps him, he said, "Yes." When asked how it helps him, he said, "Helps me get to sleep and helps my muscle spasms."

When asked to describe the muscle spasms further, he said, "Like stiffness. It could come from me working out or it could come from my past injuries." When asked further about those, he said, "Back, lower back injuries. Broke both of my legs." When asked how he broke his legs, he said, "One by jumping off a roof, and one I got hit by a car, got run over by a car."

When asked about any other past medical problems, he said, "No, I had stitches in my left knee." In response to questions, he said he had been active in sports, including "wrestling, a little bit of football, played basketball." He said he was on the wrestling team at K High School, and he said, "I always wanted to go back to school, though, 'cause my mind goes to sleeping."

Mr. Jones said that he has no medical problems at this time. When asked the names of his current medication, he said, "Benadryl, Cogentin." He said he does not take medicine when he is not in jail.

Medical Records at the Jail

Medical records include:

8/12/97, 1:15 a.m.
Arresting officer and Cpl. M states that subject made statements of harming self and also had placed a knife to his abdomen when officer was trying to arrest him. He denied any medical or psychiatric problems or meds. Denied wanting to hurt himself – but inmate would not look at me when talking with me even when I requested he do so.

8/18/97
Psychiatry. Reports last psych hosp was 1 month ago @ Crisis Stabilization Unit on 10th Street. He denies substance abuse. Inmate denies report that held knife to his stomach and threatened self harm @ time of his arrest. Prior suicide attempts include jumping off roof which broke his right leg in several places 6 years ago. Has also had thoughts of stepping in front of traffic. Hit by car at age 12 years when he was riding bike. Claims to have + auditory hallucinations which he "ignores." He denies need for psychotropic medication. He denies SI or HI.

10/6/03
Psychiatry. Has previously been in CSU – very poor historian. Reports hx aud halluc. States he "asked a few people to kill him." Speech is low, soft. Will request records from last hosp.

10/15/03
Psychiatry. Patient states he has + command auditory hallucinations to kill self but he is not responding to them. Will change Artane to Benadryl [for] EPS. Appears to have poverty of thought content. Completed 11th grade.

10/27/03
Psychiatry. Patient much more lucid on exam.

11/3/03
Psychiatry. Inmate with improved reality testing 0 SI. 0 HI. 0 aud halluc. Calm, pleasant. Recommend transfer to 4 E.

11/10/03
Psychiatry. Inmate reports he still has some aud halluc "but not as often." Denies SI or HI. 0 side effects from meds reported. Vague responses. Will increase Prolixin. ? Thought blocking.

11/17/03

Psychiatry. Inmate reports + aud halluc "all the time – just a lot of shouting and cussing." He denies SI or HI. More verbal. Appears to have more linear, organized thought process. Agrees to Prolixin Decanoate as he is only intermittently compliant with meds. Requests transfer to 4 E which is recommended.

12/29/03

Psychiatry. Inmate has been in adjustment cell approx. 4 weeks. He reports + aud halluc. "They just talk about stuff. They're not telling me to kill myself." Trial next month on charges of sexual battery. Affect very flat. 0 further episodes of EPS since Artane was increased and so will increase Prolixin Decanoate for continued psychotic symptoms.

Mr. Jones is currently prescribed Prolixin, Artane, and Benadryl. Records appear to indicate that he is taking his medication regularly. This was confirmed orally by a nurse.

PSYCHOLOGICAL TESTING

Ability

The WAIS-III is a standardized, objective test of intelligence. Results follow:

Vocabulary	5	Picture Completion	4
Similarities	8	Digit Symbol Coding	3
Arithmetic	5	Block Design	7
Digit Span	6	Matrix Reasoning	8
Information	6	Picture Arrangement	6
Comprehension	7		

	IQ	%ile
Verbal IQ	77	6
Performance IQ	73	4
Full Scale IQ	73	4

The above test scores appear to provide an accurate appraisal of Mr. Jones' current intellectual functioning. Scores may be lowered somewhat by his psychotic symptoms. The Verbal, Performance, and Full Scale IQ scores are all in the borderline range.

Neuropsychological Screening

The Screening Test for the Luria-Nebraska Neuropsychological Battery (LNNB-ST) is a standard screening test for neuropsychological impairment. Mr. Jones' raw score on the LNNB-ST was four. The cutoff score on this instrument is eight. This suggests that if Mr. Jones were given a full neuropsychological battery he would not score in the impaired range.

Achievement

The Woodcock-Johnson Tests of Achievement-III (WJ-III) is used to assess skills in areas such as reading, writing, and arithmetic. In Florida public schools it is the most widely used instrument of its type. Although it is not meaningful to compare an adult's IQ scores to those of a child (such as saying a 44-year-old man has the IQ of an 11-year-old child), it is meaningful to compare an adult's WJ-III scores to those of a child (such as saying he reads at a sixth-grade level, or that his reading level is comparable to that of an 11-year-old child). Mr. Jones' WJ-III scores follow:

Achievement Tests	AE[3]	GE	Clusters	AE	GE
Letter-Word Identification	13-1	7.5	Oral Language	9-1	3.7
Reading Fluency	10-9	5.4	Listening Comprehension	10-4	4.8
Story Recall	12-3	7.2	Broad Reading	11-8	6.3
Understanding Directions	8-5	2.9	Reading Comprehension	11-5	6.2
Writing Fluency	10-4	4.9	Written Expression	10-6	5.0
Passage Comprehension	11-9	6.7			
Writing Samples	11-0	5.6			
Oral Comprehension	12-1	7.1			
Reading Vocabulary	11-2	5.9			

The above test scores appear to provide an accurate appraisal of Mr. Jones' current achievement. Most of these skills are at a fourth-to sixth-grade level, comparable to those of a 9- to 11-year-old child.

Effort on Cognitive Tests

I administered two tests designed to assess whether or not the subject is giving his best effort. On both of these tests Mr. Jones achieved near-

---

[3] AE is the age equivalent, expressed as "year-month." GE is the grade equivalent, expressed as "year.month."

perfect scores. That shows that he was giving his best effort on these tests, and it suggests that he may have been giving his best effort on other cognitive tests, including the intelligence and achievement tests, and on forensic assessment instruments such as the IAUAMR and the GSS (see below).

Understanding and Appreciation of Miranda Rights

These tests were given because they include information relevant to waiver of Miranda rights and because they have well-established norms.

Comprehension of Miranda Rights (CMR)

Development of the CMR began with several objectives: (a) To measure understanding of the four primary Miranda warnings by way of paraphrased response; (b) to develop a standard and reliable method for administering the procedure and obtaining responses; (c) to provide examinees with every possible opportunity to reveal what they understood the warnings to mean; (d) to develop an objective scoring system; and (e) to develop criterion definitions for scoring of responses that would represent the consensus of opinion of a panel of attorneys and psychologists concerning the essential meaning of each of the Miranda warnings. (Grisso, 1998, p. 9)[4]

Mr. Jones earned a score of 8 out of 8 on the CMR. He showed the ability to say in his own words what the Miranda rights mean.

Comprehension of Miranda Rights Recognition (CMR-R)

The purpose of the CMR-R is to assess an examinee's understanding of each Miranda warning by his or her ability to recognize whether or not the particular pre-constructed sentence has the same meaning as the Miranda warning statement. It consists of presentation of the Miranda warning statements with corresponding statements that the examinee must identify as the "same" as or "different" from the Miranda warning statements. All presentations of warnings and items are both oral and in writing on stimulus pages in the test easel. (Grisso, 1998, p. 31)

---

[4] From *Instruments for Assessing Understanding & Appreciation of Miranda Rights* (Manual; pp. 9, 31, 35, 45), by T. Grisso, 1998, Sarasota, FL: Professional Resource Press. Copyright © 1998 by Professional Resource Exchange, Inc. Reprinted with permission.

Mr. Jones earned a CMR-R score of 5 out of 12. His ability to *recognize* whether statements about rights were similar or different was no better than chance.

Comprehension of Miranda Vocabulary (CMV)

The CMV measure "is an objective method for assessing an individual's understanding of six critical words that appear in standard Miranda warnings" (Grisso, 1998, p. 35).

Mr. Jones did not show understanding regarding the words "consult" and "entitled." He did show understanding of the words "attorney," "interrogation," "appoint," and "right." His score was 8 out of 12 on the CMV. For comparison, 72% of adult offenders in the normative group scored higher than that on the CMV.

Function of Rights in Interrogation (FRI)

The FRI was developed to assess subjects'

appreciation of the significance of Miranda rights in the context of interrogation. . . . A grasp of the significance of this right requires at least an understanding of the role of the lawyer as an advocate and a sense of the types of questions which police might ask. The FRI is designed to assess this functional grasp of the warnings as differentiated from an understanding of single words and of Miranda phrases. (Grisso, 1998, p. 45)

Mr. Jones earned a raw score of 17 out of 30 on the FRI. For comparison, 98% of adult offenders in the normative group scored 19 or higher on the FRI.

Interpretation of IAUAMR Scores

Mr. Jones' scores on the Instruments for Assessing Understanding and Appreciation of Miranda Rights (IAUAMR) show that he currently has basic understanding of his Miranda rights. This understanding may be more due to background knowledge than to the ability to understand explanations of his rights. He shows little ability to distinguish between pairs of sentences that sound somewhat similar but have very distinct meanings. Mr. Jones' lack of ability to appreciate the meaning and impact of Miranda rights was particularly evident on the FRI, which involves application of the rights to a realistic scenario.

Mr. Jones' performance on the IAUAMR suggests the following:

- He shows some background awareness of the basic Miranda rights.
- He understands some of the key words in the Miranda rights, including "attorney" and "right."
- He does not show the ability to detect important differences between sentences that sound somewhat similar but have different meanings.
- He does not show the ability to make decisions based on his rights.

Personality/Psychopathology

Two standard, objective self-report instruments were administered, the Personality Assessment Inventory (PAI) and the Minnesota Multiphasic Personality Inventory-2 (MMPI-2). Given Mr. Jones' reading scores, there was a possibility that he might have difficulty with some items, particularly on the MMPI-2. I was present throughout the course of the testing, and when he asked for the meanings of words I provided simple, dictionary-type definitions (e.g., brood = worry). This occurred approximately twice on the PAI and approximately six times on the MMPI-2.

Mr. Jones answered all 344 items of the PAI. The PAI provides a number of validity indices which are designed to provide an assessment of factors that could distort the results of testing. Mr. Jones showed mild elevations on scales designed to assess inconsistency and infrequency. He showed a great elevation on a scale designed to assess negative impressions and he showed a very low score on a scale designed to assess attempts to give a positive impression. His scores on PAI malingering indices were elevated, suggesting that he may have been attempting to exaggerate problems. Mr. Jones' PAI profile is considered invalid.

Mr. Jones answered all 567 items on the MMPI-2. As with the PAI, validity scales suggest over-endorsement of problems.

More data from the PAI and MMPI-2 are presented below, in a subsection titled "Yea Saying."

Response Style

The SIRS is a structured interview which was designed to assess response styles, including feigning or exaggeration of symptoms. The SIRS has been used in a variety of populations to distinguish subjects who have been instructed to feign psychiatric problems from people with genuine psychiatric disorders. This test has been effectively utilized with mentally retarded people to distinguish nonmalingerers from malingerers (Hayes, Hale, & Gouvier, 1998).[5]

The SIRS has eight primary scales to detect feigning or exaggeration of symptoms. Mr. Jones' scores on four of the scales were in the definite range. His scores on the other four scales were in the probable range. The SIRS manual includes the following recommendation for interpretation when three or more scales are in the probable range:

> This combination of elevated scores is characteristic of individuals who are feigning a mental disorder and is rarely seen in clients responding truthfully.

More consideration of Mr. Jones' performance on the SIRS is presented below, in a subsection titled "Yea Saying."

Yea Saying

Both the SIRS and the PAI consist largely of statements for which a "true" response would suggest the presence of (or exaggeration of) psychological symptoms. Analysis of the PAI indicated that Mr. Jones achieved the highest coefficient of fit for the "all very true" profile[6] and the second highest coefficient of fit for the "all mainly true" profile. This suggests the possibility that his responses may have been influenced by what is referred to in psychological testing as "yea saying." This is a response style in which the respondent says "yes" or "true" to many items, irrespective of their content.

Unlike the original MMPI, the MMPI-2 includes a scale which assesses yea-saying directly. According to Pope, Butcher, and Seelen

---

[5]   Hayes, J. S., Hale, D. B., & Gouvier, W. D. (1998). Malingering detection in a mentally retarded forensic population. *Applied Neuropsychology, 5*(1), 33-36.

[6]   That is, his profile was more similar to a profile derived from answering all items "very true" than to any other profiles including, for example, psychiatric patients with a diagnosis of psychosis, people with major depression, or people instructed to exaggerate symptoms of mental illness while responding to the inventory.

(1993), the True Response Inconsistency (TRIN) Scale was designed to assess the tendency for some individuals to respond in an inconsistent manner by endorsing many items in the same direction (either true or false). The TRIN scale is made up of 20 pairs of items to which the same response is semantically inconsistent. According to Pope et al., MMPI-2 TRIN T scores greater than or equal to 80 indicate inconsistent responding because of "yea saying." Mr. Jones' score on TRIN was significantly elevated, with a T score of 93.

Suggestibility

Mr. Jones' responses on the PAI, SIRS, and MMPI-2 show a readiness to acknowledge psychological problems and a pattern of "yea saying." During the SIRS, Mr. Jones often responded "Sure" to questions posed, including some experiences which are, to most people, obviously rare if not impossible – though the examiner asks the questions in a neutral tone, as if a positive response would not be surprising. This raises a question about whether Mr. Jones might be prone to answer questions in a way which is highly influenced by demand characteristics, including intentional or unintentional influences by the person asking the question. To assess this in Mr. Jones, I administered the Gudjonsson Suggestibility Scale (GSS).[7]

The GSS was designed to assess two aspects of interrogative suggestibility.[8] With the first type, "The emphasis is on the impact of leading or suggestive questioning. . . . The second relates to the extent to which interrogators are able to 'shift' unwanted but perhaps accurate answers by challenge and negative feedback" (Gudjonsson, 1992, p. 116).

Administration of the GSS produces several scores.[9] *Immediate Recall* gives an indication of the subject's attention, concentration, and

---

[7] For an independent review of the GSS, see Thomas Grisso's *Evaluating Competencies: Forensic Assessments and Instruments* (1986). Grisso reviewed the early validation studies on the GSS and concluded, "Construct validation research with the GSS has placed the forensic examiner in a good position to use GSS scores when considering questions of an examiner's decreased resistance to suggestion or subtle pressure in interrogations by law enforcement officers" (p. 147).

[8] "Interrogative suggestibility" is defined as "the extent to which, within a closed social interaction, people come to accept messages communicated during formal questioning, as the result of which their subsequent behavioral response is affected" (Gudjonsson & Clark, 1986, p. 84).

[9] See Gudjonsson, 1992, pages 134 to 136.

memory capacity. The mean (average) score for people of average IQ is about 21, with a standard deviation of 6. A score of 11 falls at the 5th percentile rank for normal subjects (i.e., it falls outside the normal range). The mean score for forensic patients is about 15, with a standard deviation of 8. Mr. Jones' score on Immediate Recall is 9, indicative of poor attention, concentration, and/or short-term memory capacity.

Yield 1 refers to the number of suggestions the subject yields to on the GSS prior to negative feedback. The mean for normals is about 4, with a Standard Deviation of 3. A Yield 1 score of 9 or above falls outside the normal range (i.e., the 95th percentile rank). Forensic patients, including court referrals, typically obtain a Yield 1 score of between 6 and 7, SD of 3.5. Mr. Jones' score on Yield 1 is 11, indicating significant vulnerability to even mildly leading questions.

Shift refers to the number of times there has been a distinct change in the subject's answers following negative feedback.[10] The mean for normals is about 2.5, with a standard deviation of 2.2. A score of 7 or above falls outside the normal range. The mean score for forensic patients, including court referrals, is about 4, with a standard deviation of 3. Mr. Jones' score on Shift is 10, indicating an exceptionally high tendency to change his answers when given even mild or subtle negative feedback.

Yield 2 is the number of suggestions accepted after interrogative pressure. Typically, Yield 2 is about 1 point higher than Yield 1, which means that a score of 10 or above falls outside the normal range. Mr. Jones' score on Yield 2 is 11, indicative of significant vulnerability to even mildly leading questions following negative feedback.

A *Total Suggestibility* score can be derived by adding scores on Yield 1 and Shift. The mean for normals is about 7, with a standard deviation of 5. A score of 15 or above falls outside the normal range (i.e., 95th percentile rank). The mean for forensic patients, including court referrals, is about 10, with a standard deviation of 5.5. Mr. Jones' Total Suggestibility score is 21, indicative of marked suggestibility.

Also scored on the GSS is *Confabulation.* This refers to problems in memory processing where people replace gaps in their memory with

---

[10] After a short narrative about a robbery is read to the subject and the subject tells as much as he can remember (Immediate Recall), the subject answers 20 questions, 15 of which are leading questions (Yield 1). The subject is then told, firmly, "You have made a number of errors. It is therefore necessary to go through the questions once more, and this time try to be more accurate." The same 20 questions are asked again, and changes in the subjects' responses produce the Shift score.

imaginary experiences which they believe to be true. This includes any pieces of information which have been added to the story, or major distortions in the story's content. The mean is about 0.5; 3 or more confabulations falls outside the normal range. Mr. Jones' score on Confabulation is 3, indicating that he makes up information to fill knowledge or memory gaps significantly more than average.

GENERAL IMPRESSIONS

Soddi Jones is a 44-year-old male who currently scores in the borderline range of intelligence. His IQ score is at the 4th percentile, which means that approximately 96% of adults in the United States score higher on IQ tests than he does. It appears that he attempted to do his best on the effort tests, and that suggests he was giving his best efforts on intelligence and achievement tests and on other tests. School records were not available at the time of this report.

Mr. Jones has a history of severe mental illness, with psychotic symptoms, including auditory hallucinations. He is currently being treated with antipsychotic medication while in jail. He continues to show some symptoms of mental illness, including symptoms which prompted Dr. GW to suggest that he may be mentally retarded. Current testing produced IQ scores a little above the cutoff for mental retardation, but he shows cognitive difficulties that appear to result from a combination of low intelligence and a psychotic disorder that is not fully controlled by current medication.

Psychodiagnostic testing was invalid. Although the possibility of conscious malingering is not entirely ruled out, the TRIN score from the MMPI-2, the coefficient of fit with the All Very True and All Mainly True profiles on the PAI, and the various scores on the GSS suggest the following: He has poor concentration, short-term memory, and understanding, leading to confabulation; he tends to say "yes" or "sure" in response to questions; he acquiesces to leading questions; and he changes his answers when faced with negative feedback from questioners.

PSYCHOLEGAL ISSUES

Mr. Jones' attorney asked that I identify and analyze data relevant to the following three issues:

1. Whether Mr. Jones knowingly, intelligently, and voluntarily
    waived his Miranda rights.
2. Whether Mr. Jones' statements to the police were freely and
    voluntarily made.
3. Whether Mr. Jones' statements to the police were highly
    unreliable and virtually uncorroborated.

These will be considered in order.

Whether Mr. Jones Knowlingly, Intelligently and
Voluntarily Waived His Miranda Rights

Personal Factors

Mr. Jones has a documented history of mental illness, including
psychosis. Current psychological testing shows an IQ score in the
borderline range; approximately 96% of adults in the United States
score higher than Mr. Jones scored. Most of his reading and
communication skills are at a third- to sixth-grade level, comparable to
those of a 9- to 11-year-old child.

Testing about Mr. Jones' *current* understanding and appreciation
of Miranda rights shows some background understanding about Miranda
rights. However, he does not show the ability to detect important
differences between sentences that sound somewhat similar but have
different meanings. Overall, Mr. Jones does not show the ability to
make decisions based on his rights.

Mr. Jones' scores on the GSS suggest that he would be more
vulnerable to influence than most people. This is likely due to his mental
illness, his low functional intelligence, and perhaps also to personality
factors not specifically identified in the testing.

Situational Factors

Mr. Jones did not approach the police to confess a crime. When I
asked him about his arrest, he told me, "They come to my house. Me
and my wife were sitting in the back of the pickup truck in the driveway.
They said they wanted to talk to me downtown. . . . They put handcuffs
on me. I said, 'Am I under arrest?' They said, 'No.'. . . He put me in the
car. From that point on, it was a total nightmare."

On page 6 of the transcript of Mr. Jones' statement to the police,
Mr. Jones reports that he cannot read the rights because the print is too
small. On page 3 he shows that he does not understand the meaning of

the word "voluntarily," which is consistent with test scores. Detective T then asks Mr. Jones questions about whether he was forced or threatened to go to the police station, and whether he was promised anything for going there. He gives one-word responses. He does not say in his own words why he went to the police station, or what his understanding is regarding why the police brought him there.

He shows understanding of what it means to swear to tell the truth (pages 4-5).

Mr. Jones gives mostly one-word responses as his rights are read to him (pages 6-8).

Although Mr. Jones has been told that he has the right to remain silent, when he is asked whether he has to talk to the police, he answers "Yes" (page 8). He then gives one-word responses to further questions about this, but never clearly shows understanding that he does not have to talk to the police.

Although Mr. Jones has been told that he has the right to have an attorney present, when he is asked whether he has the right to have an attorney or a lawyer in the room with him if he wants one, he says, "No" (pages 8-9). He then gives one-word responses to further questions about this, but never clearly shows understanding that he has the right to have an attorney present.

Mr. Jones clearly agrees to talk to the police (page 9). He apparently signs and initials a waiver form. *After* he signs the form, and *after* Detective T changes the subject by asking Mr. Jones how long he has been married, Mr. Jones is given the opportunity to ask questions "on this." He has no questions (pages 8-9).

Person-Situation Interaction

The Probable Cause Affidavit indicates that Mr. Jones made statements to detectives "after he was read Miranda from issued card." I found no indication from the PCA or from the videotape that officers attempted to compensate for his mental illness and low functional intelligence. That is, they did not make appropriate adjustments to make sure that he understood the Miranda warnings.

Whether Mr. Jones' Statements to the Police Were Freely and Voluntarily Made

A recent Florida case, *Grasle v. State,* 779 So.2d 334, 336 (Fla. 2nd DCA 2000) includes "Test for voluntariness of confession asks whether, under the totality of circumstances, the confession was a product of coercive police conduct." In cases such as *Colorado v. Connelly*, 479 U.S. 157 (1986), where the defendant approaches the police and requests to confess to a crime, self-coercion due to mental illness would not render a confession involuntary. To be considered involuntary for legal purposes, there would have to be some actions by the police to influence the defendant to confess. *Grasle* lists the following factors for consideration: the defendant's vulnerability, age, and maturity; the location of the interrogation; whether the accused initiated contact with the law enforcement officials; what part, if any, did the interviewer's relationship with the defendant play in inducing the confession; and whether a confession has been elicited by the direct or implied promise of leniency.

The following factors are listed in *State v. Sawyer*, 561 So.2d 278 (1990): whether the confession was given in the coercive atmosphere of a station-house setting; whether the police suggested the details of the crime to the suspect; whether the suspect was subjected to a barrage of questions during predawn hours and not given an opportunity to sleep or eat; whether psychological coercion was applied; whether the police made threats, promises of leniency, or made statements calculated to delude the suspect as to his or her true position; and whether the police made threats of harm.

In *State v. Cayward*, 552 So.2d 971 (1989), *review dismissed*, 562 So.2d 347 (Fla.1990), the second district court of appeals ruled that (a) police action in fabricating laboratory reports and exhibiting them to defendant during interrogation in attempt to secure confession violated defendant's constitutional right to due process, and (b) presentation of false scientific documents overstepped line of permitted police deception.

Which of these factors, if any, arose in the present case?

The Defendant's Vulnerability, Age, and Maturity

The results of this evaluation show that Mr. Jones was especially vulnerable due to functionally low IQ and mental illness, but not due to youth.

The Location of the Interrogation; Whether the Confession Was Given in the Coercive Atmosphere of a Station-House Setting

The transcript lists the location as B, Florida. On the videotape, the setting appears to be an interrogation room at a law enforcement station house. Two of the interrogators had handguns visible during the interrogation.

Whether the Accused Initiated Contact With the Law Enforcement Officials

Mr. Jones told me that he did not initiate the contact. He said that he had no intention to confess to a crime. This appears to be consistent with the records.

- And of course, the detective got you here. . . . "Yes." (p. 3 lines 9-11)

What Part, if Any, Did the Interviewer's Relationship With the Defendant Play in Inducing the Confession?

- No prior relationship was evident.

Whether a Confession Has Been Elicited By the Direct or Implied Promise of Leniency; Whether the Police Made Threats, Promises of Leniency, or Made Statements Calculated to Delude the Suspect as to His or Her True Position

- You know we want to clear this up for you. (p. 38 line 3)
- With all our hearts, this is what we want. We want to help. Believe it or not we're really here to help you, and we're also here to help C. (p. 38 lines 8-11)
- You want help, don't you? . . . Okay. The way I can help you is in many different ways. Okay. But the only way that I can help you, okay, is by getting all the truth out. . . . There's going to be a charge on this. Okay. I mean, there's no if, ands, or buts. There's going to be a charge. . . . Do you want anybody who looks at this in the future to say, you know what, he made a mistake but he told the truth about it, and let's move on. . . . Okay. The other side of that coin is, he made a mistake. He only gave us about half the truth. How much of a break are we going to give him? . . . I'm sure somewhere down the road there's going to be some counseling involved for you. . . . That's what we're trying to do, to get you some help. (p. 38 line 23 to p. 40 line 18)
- And I want to help you sort this out because I think it's in your interest. (p. 53 lines 24-25)

Whether the Police Suggested the Details of the Crime to the Suspect

- C came in and told the detective that you had been having sex with her. That's what she said. (p. 8 line 25; p. 9 lines 1-2)
- C has told this detective that you have been putting your penis into her vagina for the last two years, and that the last time was last Saturday. . . . Saturday before, week before. (p. 11 lines 7-15)
- She also said that after you're done having sex with her, you would get off of her. . . . She said the liquid would come out . . . and you would wash it off. (p. 11 lines 21-25; p. 12 line 1)
- She said it happened 500 times. Do you think it happened 500 times? (p. 33 lines 24-25)
- How did – was she laying – how was she laying? Was she laying on her stomach or was she laying on her back? (p. 34 lines 15-17)
- She said you put it in. (p. 36 line 2)
- She had her legs spread. (p. 36 lines 16-17)
- Which hand did you take to spread her panties over to the side? (p. 36 lines 22-23)
- So she spread her panties over to the side and then you was there and you were pushing in? (p. 37 lines 1-2)
- She said this started two years ago. (p. 37 line 23)
- And she said it's basically every, I guess every weekend. (p. 43 lines 5-6)
- [Additional details were suggested as the interview progressed.]

Whether the Suspect Was Subjected to a Barrage of Questions During Predawn Hours and Not Given an Opportunity to Sleep or Eat

- Tape began at 12:50 a.m. Mr. Jones reports that he got about four or five hours of sleep the night before. (page 134)

Whether the Police Made Threats of Harm

- Not identified.

Whether Psychological Coercion Was Applied

Law Enforcement Officers who train interrogators (e.g., Inbau, Reid, & Buckley, 1986) and psychologists who study the psychology of confessions (e.g., Gudjonsson, 1992; Kassin, 1997; Wrightsman &

Kassin, 1993) identify various psychological techniques that interrogators can employ as they attempt to elicit confessions. While these techniques may or may not be considered *illegally* coercive in a particular case, psychologists classify them as being coercive or manipulative tactics, in that they are deliberately employed to influence the subject to confess.

Specific themes are recommended to manipulate a suspect into confessing. For example, "It is advisable, whenever possible, to point out the relative insignificance of the offense in terms of how much worse it could have been" (Inbau et al., 1986, p. 127). Psychologists analyzing confessions include this in the "soft sell" technique of *minimization*, "in which the detective tries to lull the suspect into a false sense of security (Kassin, 1997, p. 223). In another approach, *maximization*, "the interrogator uses 'scare tactics' designed to intimidate a suspect believed to be guilty" (Kassin, 1997, p. 223).

> To summarize, maximization communicates an implicit threat of punishment, whereas minimization implies an offer of leniency. Yet, although trial judges exclude confessions elicited by *explicit* threats and promises, they often admit into evidence those prompted by *implicit* threats and promises. For all intents and purposes, these commonly used techniques circumvent laws designed to prohibit the use of coerced confessions. Indeed, Inbau et al. (1986, p. 320) were quick to reassure their readers that "although recent Supreme Court opinions have contained derogatory statements about 'trickery' and 'deceit' as interrogation devices, no case has prohibited their usage." (p. 224)

Although some authors (Inbau & Reid, 1962) have identified as many as 16 overlapping strategies, for convenience we will consider the following five (overlapping) themes.

Minimization. This technique suggests or implies to the suspect that the crime is minor, the punishment is minor, the likelihood of being punished is low, the likelihood of an alternative to punishment (such as treatment) is high, and so on.

- I mean, if it only happened once or twice (inaudible) I understand. (p. 34 lines 2-3)

Maximization. This technique suggests or implies that there is much evidence to prove that the suspect is guilty, the punishment will be severe (unless the suspect confesses), and so forth. (See below regarding false scientific documents.)

Misleading Statements/Lies:

- Soddi, the only thing I want to figure out here is whether or not you ever put your penis against her vagina. (p. 10 lines 11-13)
- Now, Soddi, we want to help you on this. (p. 30 line 24)
- I'll help you here, but you've got to help us. (p. 33 line 3)
- Soddi, we want to help you here, but you've got to tell us for us to help, you know that. (p. 33 lines 22-23)
- I wrote the word failed. You know why I wrote that? I can see from that chair how nervous you got when he asked you those specific questions. (p. 42 lines 5-7)
- That's implied. Any more is implied in a statement like that. (p. 60 lines 1-2)
- What's going to happen is she's going to grow up, she's going to marry someone that's going to molest their kids. It's a routine. It doesn't stop. (p. 60 lines 18-21)
- If I go over there and find out that you were continuing to lie to us and I come back over here, we can't help you any more. (p. 70 lines 8-10)
- We're not in any way trying to trick you. (p. 91 line 14)
- But before you can get help, you have to come to terms with what you did and be totally honest. (p. 116 lines 15-16)

Rapport/Emotional Appeal. With this technique the interrogators attempt to create an atmosphere of camaraderie, sympathy, friendship, and so on.

- I understand. I understand. . . . I understand. . . . I understand. (p. 6 lines 14, 20, and 23. [Similar comments elsewhere during interrogation.]
- [Interrogators used physical distance and touch to imply concern (evident in videotape, not transcript).]
- Well, you go by Sodderich, or do you go by – "Soddi." (p. 7 line 25; p. 8 line 1)
- Trust me, I've been doing this for a lot of years. (p. 18 lines 13-14)
- Now I think that you're man enough to tell this detective exactly what happened. You know why I say that? Because he's got to

help you find a way to save face, if you wish, with you know, with your wife and your family. Okay. All right. We've got to help you, you know. (p. 31 lines 12-19)

- You did a wonderful thing by saying, yeah, this is what happened. Okay. Wonderful thing. (p. 38 lines 12-14)
- I believe you. I believe it was a mistake and I believe that you're sorry. I really do. I can look and see that in your eyes. (p. 41 lines 22-25)
- But you know what? That means you have a conscience. . . . And I truly believe this will never happen again. (p. 42 lines 8-9, 13)
- But all three of us are males here, aren't we? . . . You know, and if you've got a stiff penis, you want to put it inside, right? (p. 52 lines 15-20)
- If I find myself in bed with two women, and one was sound asleep, I would roll over and tap on the other one's shoulder. That's the way guys are. (p. 65 lines 19-22)
- It's the opposite in my house. I'm the bad guy in my house. (p. 76 lines 17-18)
- My dad was a sign painter. I know all about it. (p. 100 lines 23-24)
- He'll take good care of you. (p. 149 line 20)

Imagination/Altered State of Consciousness. This technique involves either of two tactics, or both. Interrogators may suggest that the suspect committed a crime while in an altered state of consciousness, such as being drunk, and therefore has limited or no memory of the act. Alternatively, interrogators may actually attempt to induce an altered state of consciousness by encouraging the suspect to relax and imagine/ visualize having committed the crime.

- And do me a favor. Take a deep breath. Seriously. . . . Another one. A deep breath. . . . Take another deep breath. . . . You're not being totally honest with us because you're confusing yourself. We need you to just relax and let it go. And let it go (inaudible) do. Because when you let it go, you will find that the words come out of your mouth, because it's the truth. You don't have to think. You don't have to replay it in your mind. (Inaudible) that. Just let it go. . . . If I'm not getting honesty from you, I have to believe everything she tells me. So why don't we just start with the facts. How many times did you have sex with her, sexual intercourse, dick in the vagina, how many times? . . . At least half a dozen (inaudible) according to her. (p. 92 line 3 to p. 93 line 21)

Whether False Scientific Documents Were Fabricated and Exhibited to Defendant

- The first thing I'm going to do, I want to establish your truth pattern. (p. 19 lines 14-15)
- When you answer those questions as you just have, I'll get your truth pattern. (p. 20 lines 16-17)
- But I do need one example of your lie pattern in that chart. (p. 20 lines 20-21)
- After we have established your truth pattern, and (inaudible), then we'll run your test. (p. 21 lines 8-9)
- I've got this strap (inaudible) measure the respiratory system. (p. 21 lines 24-25)
- I've got a blood pressure cuff that's going to go on your arm. It's going to measure pulse and changes in blood pressure. (p. 22 lines 6-8)
- This is going to measure the galvanic skin response. (Inaudible) little finger that's going to measure pulse and changes in blood volume. (p. 22 lines 12-14)
- We're going to calibrate the equipment and then we'll get started. (p. 22 lines 16-17)
- Three times I get your truth pattern, one time I get your lie pattern. (p. 22 lines 24-25)
- Well, when you did lie (inaudible) that second time around we got a good lie pattern. (p. 23 lines 17-19)
- I'll calibrate the equipment. (p. 26 lines 6-7)
- I'll calibrate the equipment. (p. 27 line 10)
- Would you like to jot some numbers down? . . . Can you see those numbers? . . . Okay. (Inaudible) .010. And the other one is .9860. And then .2330, .7670. Cumulative total is .282, .97 (inaudible). That's what (inaudible) cumulative total. (p. 28, lines 17-18, 22, 25; p. 29 lines 1-3)
- I'm going to show you what this is all about. . . . You see this? Can you see this? . . . (Inaudible) is the question, did you ever put your penis against C's vagina. . . . You know, against the lips of the vagina. The truthful score is .0140 and the deceptive or lie score is .9860. . . . R2 is the question, did you ever put your penis into C's vagina. Of course, if you put it into it, then that's sexual intercourse, isn't it? . . . I mean, that's having sex. The .2330 is a truthful column and .7670 is a deceptive column. Now, the combined total for the test is .0282 truthful, and it's .9718

deceptive or lie. All right. Soddi, what this says is, when you answered the questions, when you said no about putting your penis either against or into, you have lied to me. (p. 29 line 4 to p. 30 line 23)

- There's another way to look at this. We're going to do an analysis and we're going to do. . . . The red ones are, putting your penis against her vagina and putting your penis into her vagina. Okay? (p. 31 line 22 to p. 32 line 7)
- Soddi, let me ask you, because in thinking about that, you know, when we looked at the numbers you're .76 deceptive on the penetration. The penetration is actually this one, and this one, and this one. And you see how much greater it is? I mean, on this last chart it really went up, which would say to me, you know, if you put your penis, the head of your penis – because you had a hard on, right? . . . (p. 51 lines 3-12, *while pointing to and drawing Mr. Jones' attention directly to the "scientific" document*)
- We started with her telling her side of the story. We got talking to you. You denied everything. . . . Took this test that proved you were lying. . . . You admitted you did it. (p. 121 lines 16-22)

During the course of the interrogation, one of the officers identified a polygraph machine as a lie detector, conducted a polygraph exam of Mr. Jones, told Mr. Jones that the machine showed that he was lying, showed Mr. Jones computer-generated documents, and claimed that those documents proved that Mr. Jones was lying and that he had committed the crime.

Are these *false* scientific documents? Yes. The "test" is premised on the assumption that it would be meaningful if Mr. Jones showed greater physiological reactions to the two questions "Did you ever place your penis against C's vagina?" and "Did you ever place your penis into C's vagina?" than to the three questions "In your life, did you ever make even one mistake?" "In your life did you ever violate even one law?" and "In your life did you ever tell even one lie?" The "test" is further premised on the assumption that if Mr. Jones showed greater physiological reactions to the questions about capital sexual battery than to innocuous questions about ordinary human imperfections, then that would prove that he was lying. The "test" is based on the assumption that any person would show greater physiological reactions when answering any question with a lie than when answering any question with the truth. That is demonstrably false.

Are these false *scientific* documents? Yes. The description of the material shown to the defendant indicates that the interrogators deliberately cloaked the "test" in terms designed to bolster its impact by giving it the appearance of a scientific document.

Are these false scientific *documents?* Yes. In *State v. Cayward* (p. 972), the "false reports indicated that a scientific test established that the semen stains on the victim's underwear came from the defendant. The police showed the reports to the defendant as a device to induce a confession. Some time later during the interview, the defendant confessed." Here, the suspect is shown a document on a computer that falsely indicates that the probability that he is lying is .9860. There is no reason to believe that seeing the information graphically depicted on a computer document would be less impressive and misleading to the suspect than seeing it on a written page. And one of the interrogators appeared to diligently write down the data on a piece of paper, thereby producing a written document presumably containing the same false information.

Regarding the psychological impact of presenting the suspect with these false documents, I concur with the court in *State v. Cayward* (p. 974):

> It may well be that a suspect is more impressed and thereby more easily induced to confess when presented with tangible, official-looking reports as opposed to merely being told that some tests have implicated him. If one perceives such a difference, it probably originates in the notion that a document which purports to be authoritative impresses one as being inherently more permanent and facially reliable than a simple verbal statement.

The *State v. Cayward* court also considered the following practical problem (p. 974):

> Unlike oral misrepresentations, manufactured documents have the potential of indefinite life and the facial appearance of authenticity. A report falsified for interrogation purposes might well be retained and filed in police paperwork. Such reports have the potential of finding their way into the courtroom.

That problem – extended life of fabricated documents – occurred at least twice in this case. First, the confidential report of the polygraph examiner includes (on page 2):

The scoring algorithm determines the posterior probability of truth. . . .
Statistically, scores greater than .7000 are definite. The numerical
scores produced by the scoring algorithm were:

	Truth Probability	Deception Probability
Relevant Question #1	.0140	.9860
Relevant Question #2	.2330	.7670
Combined Total	.0282	.9718

Based on the software scoring algorithm analysis, Soddi Jones was
deceptive in answering the relevant questions during the polygraph
exam. Soddi Jones was apprized of the deceptive results of the
polygraph exam and he admitted that last Saturday he had sex with
[victim] and that he rubbed his penis against her bare vagina.

The second instance of extended life of fabricated documents is
found on page 7 of the Police Department Supplemental Report. "The
results according to the computer polygraph examination were as
follows: Question #1 Did you ever place your penis against [vic-
tim's] vagina? Answer no. Truth probability .0140, deceptive probability
.9860. . . . "

Did the police *intentionally* fabricate a scientific document and
exhibit it to the defendant during the interrogation? It is clear that the
interrogators used the false document to try to elicit a confession. I do
not know what was in the minds of the interrogators as they produced
the false scientific document and exhibited it to the suspect – specifically,
whether they knew that it was false. In my opinion, a reasonably well-
trained forensic psychologist would recognize that the document was
bogus.[11] Most modern law enforcement agencies utilize psychological
consultants, and therefore have ready access to professional guidance
regarding such issues. Certainly, the law enforcement agency should
have known that the purported scientific report was bogus.

---

[11] This is so basic that it was included in the curriculum and laboratory procedures when I
taught college courses in introductory psychology in the 1970s. This is also current. For
example, ongoing research into the polygraph by the U.S. Department of Defense was
discussed at the May 2002 Council of Police Psychological Services Conference on
Pigeon Key, Florida. Anyone familiar with scientific research on the polygraph would
recognize that the claims were impossible and the purported scientific document was
bogus. See DeClue, G. (2003a). The Polygraph and Lie Detection. *Journal of Psychiatry
and Law, 31,* 361-368. (book review)

Summary Regarding Whether
Statements Were Made Voluntarily

In cases such as *Grasle* and *Sawyer,* judges have identified numerous factors that should be weighed in considering whether a confession was a product of coercive police conduct. As I analyze the available data in this case, it is my opinion that some of these factors were present and some were not.

In *Cayward,* the court distinguished between police making false *verbal* assertions versus manufacturing false documents, and appeared to indicate that the latter form of deception renders a confession involuntary *per se.* As I analyze the data in this case, it is my opinion that Mr. Jones was shown false scientific documents as a device to induce a confession. From a psychological perspective, I find no reason to believe that Mr. Jones would be less vulnerable to this coercive tactic because a computer document rather than paper document was used, and I find no reason to believe that the impact of the documents on the suspect would be lessened if the interrogators believed the blatantly false document to be true.

Whether Mr. Jones' Statements to the Police
Were Highly Unreliable and Virtually Uncorroborated

In considering this question, five points need to be addressed.

1. Some people falsely confess to crimes some times.
2. Some interrogation procedures increase the risk of false confessions.
3. Some personal factors make some people more vulnerable to police influence than others.
4. There are procedures recommended by social scientists and law enforcement agencies to avoid false confessions.
5. There are procedures recommended by social scientists and law enforcement agencies to recognize false confessions when they occur.

As courts and the general public have come to recognize the accuracy of DNA evidence, it is now universally accepted that some people falsely confess to some crimes some times. We can consider case-specific data for points 2 through 5.

Some Interrogation Procedures
Increase the Risk of False Confessions

The following procedures may have increased the risk of a false confession in this case:

- Contact with the police was initiated by the police, not by the accused.
- The interrogation began after midnight, and Mr. Jones said that he had only gotten about 4 hours sleep the night before.
- The interrogation took place in a station-house setting, which courts recognize to be coercive.
- The police took steps to enhance their power, control, and/or authority while interrogating the suspect by interviewing him in a small room while they were armed.
- The police isolated Mr. Jones from others.
- The police failed to take Mr. Jones' mental illness and low functional intelligence into account when they advised him of his Constitutional rights, and they failed to effectively ascertain whether he understood those rights.
- Mr. Jones initially denied guilt.
- The police did not accept Mr. Jones' statement that he was not guilty. They encouraged him to submit to a polygraph test, saying that it would "clear him."
- The police lied to the suspect and employed trickery via the polygraph test.
- The police exaggerated the certainty of the evidence against the suspect, specifically, the polygraph results.
- The police fabricated documents which falsely claimed that the polygraph test proved that he was lying.
- The police demanded that the suspect explain the fabricated polygraph "evidence."
- The police made direct or implied promises that the suspect's cooperation and/or confession would be conveyed to another party (such as the prosecutor, judge, or jury) that would subsequently be in a decision-making position regarding the case: "The way I can help you is in many different ways. Okay. But the only way that I can help you, okay, is by getting all the truth out. . . . There's going to be a charge on this. Okay. I mean, there's no if, ands, or buts. There's going to be a charge. . . . Do you want anybody who looks at this in the future to say, you know what, he made a mistake but he told the truth about it, and let's move on. . . . Okay. The other side of that coin is, he made a mistake.

He only gave us about half the truth. How much of a break are we going to give him?" (pp. 38-39).

- The police sought out the suspect's vulnerabilities and attempted to exploit them, for example, saying, "I think you're man enough to tell this detective exactly what happened. You know why I say that? Because he's got to help you find a way to save face with your wife and family."

- The police suggested psychological excuses for the offense: "But all three of us are males here, aren't we? . . . You know, and if you've got a stiff penis, you want to put it inside, right?" (p. 52) and "If I find myself in bed with two women and one was sound asleep, I would roll over and tap on the other one's shoulder. That's the way guys are" (p. 9).

- The police minimized the moral seriousness of the offense: "I believe it was a mistake and I believe that you're sorry. I really do. I can look and see that in your eyes" (p. 41).

- The police minimized the legal seriousness of the offense, for example, by saying, "She said it happened 500 times. Do you think it happened 500 times? How many times do you think it happened? I mean, if it only happened once or twice, I understand. That would be different than 500, wouldn't it?" (pp. 33-34).

- The police suggested that it would be in the suspect's best interest to confess: "And I want to help you sort this out because I think it's in your interest" (p. 53).

- The police suggested that it would be in the best interest of another person (i.e., the victim) for the suspect to confess: "What's going to happen [if you don't confess] is she's going to grow up, she's going to marry someone that's going to molest their kids. It's a routine. It doesn't stop" (p. 60).

- The police suggested that the result of a confession would be that the suspect would receive therapy: "I'm sure somewhere down the road there's going to be some counseling involved for you. . . . That's what we're trying to do, to get you some help" (p. 40).

- The police took steps to encourage the suspect to think that one or more interrogators were the suspect's friends and were trying to help him, for example, "We want to help you on this" (p. 30) and "We want to help you here, but you've got to tell us for us to help" (p. 33).

- The police interrupted the suspect as he attempted to answer questions.

- The police used techniques involving guided imagery: "And do me a favor. Take a deep breath. . . . Another one. A deep breath. . . . Take another deep breath. . . . You're not being totally honest with us because you're confusing yourself. . . . Just let it go. . . . If I'm not getting honesty from you, I have to believe everything she tells me. So why don't we just start with the facts. How many times did you have sex with her, sexual intercourse, dick in the vagina, how many times? . . . At least half a dozen (inaudible) according to her" (pp. 92-93).
- The police positively reinforced admissions and negatively reinforced denials.
- The police applied emotional pressure to encourage the suspect to confess.
- The suspect was encouraged to respond to forced-choice questions, for example, "Was she laying on her stomach or was she laying on her back?" (p. 34).
- The police provided details of the crime to the suspect in the process of interrogating him, for example: "She said it happened last Saturday night on the kitchen table" (p. 34).
- The police failed to conduct a careful, detailed, post-admission interview.

Some Personal Factors Make Some People More Vulnerable to Police Influence Than Others

The following personal factors may have increased the risk of a false confession in this case:

- low intelligence
- mental disorder (psychotic disorder)
- suggestibility

There Are Procedures Recommended by Social Scientists And Law Enforcement Agencies to Avoid False Confessions

[Although information relevant to this topic *could* be included in a written report, I typically do not do so (though I do prepare testimony). If one wanted to include this in a written report, one could utilize relevant information from Chapter 10 of this text and state whether such procedures were followed in the given case. If such procedures were not used, one could show how that could have contributed to a false confession in this case.]

There Are Procedures Recommended by
Social Scientists and Law Enforcement Agencies to
Recognize False Confessions When They Occur

[Again, I typically do not include such information in my written reports (but I do prepare testimony). One could include relevant information from Chapter 10 of this text and state whether such procedures were followed in the given case. If such procedures were not used, one could describe how that prevents one's ability to rule out the possibility of a false confession in this case.]

FINAL NOTE

Some people wonder why an innocent person would confess to a crime. Mr. Jones said that he is such a person; here is how he explained it to me. "We got to the police station. . . . They said, 'We have allegations from your daughter that you've been sexually abusing her.' I said I didn't do it. . . . The detective told me everything she said, from how it happened, when it happened. Well, the only story he told me was the last Saturday. He went over detail by detail what took place. . . . He says the only way we can settle this is a polygraph. I said, 'Do I need a lawyer?' He said, 'No.' " Mr. Jones said that after using the restroom he submitted to a polygraph.

Mr. Jones continued, "He did it four times. There was questions I was supposed to say no to for yes and questions I was supposed to say yes to for no. By the last time, I was confused. This was like two, three in the morning. I hadn't slept. The chair is real uncomfortable. . . . He said, 'See this right here? You failed the test.' All I seen was like the commercial on TV where they show these scales with different colors. I asked this other detective, 'Do I go home now?' He said, 'No, you got to answer some more questions.' I knew I wasn't going home. In Alabama they beat the confession out of me and I figured that's what they were gonna do this time."

He said, "They kept on telling me, 'we know you did this, you failed the polygraph test.' The polygraph guy, I asked if I could use the restroom. He said, 'No, you got to answer some more questions.' I said, 'Do I need a lawyer before we go on with this?' He said, 'No, you don't need no lawyer.' There was a camera in the corner and he said they were taping it. . . . It seemed like every time I was saying no, he was getting louder and louder. I told him I needed to use the bathroom. He said this question ain't gonna last much longer."

He continued, "Another man, some kind of cop, come in. . . . There was a point in time where I broke down and told him what he told me in the office. It was a total nightmare. They done got me to the point where I was scared to death. It was way late, four or five in the morning. I was tired, sleepy, and just flat wore out. It was to the point where I thought the only way I was gonna get out of there was if I told them what they wanted me to say."

Gregory DeClue, PhD, ABPP

REFERENCES

DeClue, G. (2003a). The polygraph and lie detection [Book review]. *Journal of Psychiatry and Law, 31,* 361-368.

Grisso, T. (1986). *Evaluating Competencies: Forensic Assessments and Instruments.* New York: Plenum.

Grisso, T. (1998). *Instruments for Assessing Understanding & Appreciation of Miranda Rights* (Manual). Sarasota, FL: Professional Resource Press.

Gudjonsson, G. (1992). *The Psychology of Interrogations, Confessions and Testimony.* New York: Wiley.

Gudjonsson, G. H., & Clark, N. K. (1986). Suggestibility in police interrogation: A social psychological model. *Social Behavior, 1,* 83-104.

Hayes, J. S., Hale, D. B., & Gouvier, W. D. (1998). Malingering detection in a mentally retarded forensic population. *Applied Neuropsychology, 5*(1), 33-36.

Inbau, F. E., & Reid, J. E. (1962). *Criminal Interrogation and Confession.* Baltimore, MD: Williams & Wilkins.

Inbau, F. E., Reid, J. E., & Buckley, J. P. (Eds.). (1986). *Criminal Interrogation and Confessions* (3rd ed.). Baltimore, MD: Williams & Wilkins.

Kassin, S. M. (1997). The psychology of confession evidence. *American Psychologist, 52*(3), 221-233.

Pope, K. S., Butcher, J. W., & Seelen, J. (1993). *The MMPI, MMPI-2, and MMPI-A in Court: A Practical Guide for Expert Witnesses and Attorneys.* Washington, DC: American Psychological Association.

Wrightsman, L. S., & Kassin, S. M. (1993). *Confessions in the Courtroom.* Newbury Park, CA: Sage.

CASES CITED

Colorado v. Connelly, 479 U.S. 157 (1986).

Grasle v. State, 779 So.2d 334, 336 (Fla. 2nd DCA 2000).

State v. Cayward, 552 So.2d 971 (1989), *review dismissed,* 562 So.2d 347 (Fla. 1990).

State v. Sawyer, 561 So.2d 278 (1990).

— References —

American Psychological Association. (2002). Ethical Principles of Psychologists and Code of Conduct. *American Psychologist, 57,* 1060-1073.

Asch, S. E. (1956). Studies of independence and conformity: A minority of one against a unanimous majority. *Psychological Monographs, 70*(Whole No. 416).

1998 Australia Prize: Professor Sir Alec Jeffreys (UK). Retrieved January 5, 2005, from https://sciencegrants.dest.gov.au/SciencePrize/Pages/Doc.aspx?name=previous_winners/Aust1998Jeffreys.htm

Baldwin, J., & McConville, M. (1980). *Confessions in Crown Court Trials. Royal Commission on Criminal Procedure Research Study No. 5.* London: HMSO. (Cited in G. Gudjonsson. [2003]. *The Psychology of Interrogations and Confessions: A Handbook.* West Sussex, England: Wiley.)

Bedau, H. A., & Radelet, M. L. (1987). Miscarriages of justice in potentially capital cases. *Stanford Law Review, 41,* 21-179.

Binet, A. (1900). *La Suggestibilite.* Paris: Doin. (Cited in G. H. Gudjonsson. [2003]. *The Psychology of Interrogations and Confessions: A Handbook.* West Sussex, England: Wiley.)

Binet, A. (1905). La science du temoignage. *Annee Psychologique, 11,* 128-136. (Cited in G. H. Gudjonsson. [2003]. *The Psychology of Interrogations and Confessions: A Handbook.* West Sussex, England: Wiley.)

Blass, T. (Ed.). (2000). *Obedience to Authority: Current Perspectives on the Milgram Paradigm*. Mahwah, NJ: Lawrence Erlbaum Associates.

Borum, R., Otto, R., & Golding, S. (1993). Improving clinical judgment and decision making in forensic evaluation. *Journal of Psychiatry and Law, 21,* 35-76.

Butcher, J. N., Dahlstrom, W. G., Graham, J. R., Tellegen, A. M., & Kaemmer, B. (1989). *MMPI-2: Manual for Administration and Scoring.* Minneapolis: University of Minnesota Press.

Cattell, J. M. (1895). Measurements of the accuracy of recollection. *Science, 2,* 761-766.

Committee on Ethical Guidelines for Forensic Psychologists. (1991). Specialty guidelines for forensic psychologists. *Law and Human Behavior, 15*(6), 655-665.

Connors, E., Lundregan, T., Miller, N., & McEwan, T. (1996). *Convicted by Juries, Exonerated by Science: Case Studies in the Use of DNA Evidence to Establish Innocence after Trial.* Washington, DC: National Institute of Justice.

DeClue, G. (2002). Feigning does not equal malingering. *Behavioral Sciences and the Law, 20,* 717-726.

DeClue, G. (2003b). Toward a two-step model for assessing adjudicative competence. *Journal of Psychiatry and Law, 31,* 305-317.

Ekman, P., O'Sullivan, M., & Frank, M. G. (1999). A few can catch a liar. *Psychological Science, 10*(3), 263-266.

Everly, G. S., & Mitchell, J. T. (1997). *Critical Incident Stress Management (CISM): A New Era and Standard of Care in Crisis Intervention.* Ellicott City, MD: Chevron.

Festinger, L. (1957). *A Theory of Cognitive Dissonance.* Evanston, IL: Row Peterson.

Fisher, R. P., & Geiselman, R. E. (1992). *Memory Enhancing Techniques for Investigative Interviewing: The Cognitive Interview.* Springfield: Charles C. Thomas.

Freedman, J., Wallington, S., & Bless, E. (1967). Compliance without pressure: The effect of guilt. *Journal of Personality and Social Psychology, 7,* 117-124.

Frumkin, I. B., & Garcia, A. (2003). Psychological evaluations and the competency to waive *Miranda* rights. *The Champion, 27*(9), 12-23.

Fulero, S. M. (2004). Expert psychological testimony on the psychology of interrogations and confessions. In G. D. Lassiter (Ed.),

Interrogations, Confessions, and Entrapment (pp. 247-263). New York: Kluwer Academic/Plenum.

Golden, C. J. (1987). *Screening Test for the Luria-Nebraska Neuropsychological Battery.* Los Angeles, CA: Western Psychological Services.

Green, P. (2003). *Green's Word Memory Test for Windows: User's Manual.* Edmonton, Canada: Green's Publishing (http://www.wordmemorytest.com/).

Grisso, T. (1986). *Evaluating Competencies: Forensic Assessments and Instruments.* New York: Plenum.

Grisso, T. (1998). *Instruments for Assessing Understanding and Appreciation of Miranda Rights* (Manual). Sarasota, FL: Professional Resource Press.

Grisso, T. (2003). *Evaluating Competencies: Forensic Assessments and Instruments* (2nd ed.). New York: Plenum.

Gudjonsson, G. H. (1984). A new scale of interrogative suggestibility. *Personality and Individual Differences, 5,* 303-314.

Gudjonsson, G. H. (1987). A parallel form of the Gudjonsson Suggestibility Scale. *British Journal of Clinical Psychology, 26,* 215-221.

Gudjonsson, G. H. (1989). Compliance in an interrogation situation: A new scale. *Personality and Individual Differences, 10,* 535-540.

Gudjonsson, G. H. (1997). *The Gudjonsson Suggestibility Scales Manual.* Hove, England: Psychology Press.

Gudjonsson, G. H. (2003). *The Psychology of Interrogations and Confessions: A Handbook.* West Sussex, England: Wiley.

Gudjonsson, G. H., & Clark, N. K. (1986). Suggestibility in police interrogation: A social psychological model. *Social Behavior, 1,* 83-104. (Cited in G. H. Gudjonsson. [2003]. *The Psychology of Interrogations and Confessions: A Handbook.* West Sussex, England: Wiley.)

Gudjonsson, G. H., & Sigurdsson, J. F. (1999). The Gudjonsson Confession Questionnaire – Revised (GCQ-R): Factor structure and its relationship with personality. *Personality and Individual Differences, 27*(5), 953-968.

Inbau, F. E., Reid, J. E., & Buckley, J. P. (Eds.). (1986). *Criminal Interrogation and Confessions* (3rd ed.). Baltimore, MD: Williams & Wilkins.

Inbau, F. E., Reid, J. E., Buckley, J. P., & Jayne, B. C. (2001). *Criminal Interrogation and Confessions* (4th ed.). Gaithersburg, MD: Aspen.

Jayne, B. C. (1986). The psychological principles of criminal interrogation. An appendix. In F. E. Inbau, J. E. Reid, & J. P. Buckley (Eds.), *Criminal Interrogation and Confessions* (3rd ed., pp. 327-347). Baltimore, MD: Williams & Wilkins.

Jeffreys, A., Wilson, V., & Thein, S. L. (1985). Hypervariable 'minisatellite' regions in human DNA. *Nature, 314*, 67-73.

Kassin, S. M. (1997). The psychology of confession evidence. *American Psychologist, 52*(3), 221-233.

Kassin, S. M. (1998). More on the psychology of false confessions. *American Psychologist, 53*(3), 320-321.

Kassin, S. M., & Kiechel, K. L. (1996). The social psychology of false confessions: Compliance, internalization, and confabulation. *Psychological Science, 7,* 125-128.

Kassin, S. M., & McNall, K. (1991). Police interrogations and confessions: Communicating promises and threats by pragmatic implication. *Law and Human Behavior, 21,* 469-484.

Kassin, S. M., & Neumann, K. (1997). On the power of confession evidence: An experimental test of the fundamental difference hypothesis. *Law and Human Behavior, 21,* 469-484.

Kassin, S. M., & Wrightsman, L. S. (1985). Confession evidence. In S. M. Kassin & L. S. Wrightsman (Eds.), *The Psychology of Evidence and Trial Procedure* (pp. 67-94). Beverly Hills, CA: Sage.

Krauss, D. A., & Sales, B. D. (2003). Forensic psychology, public policy, and the law. In I. B. Weiner (Series Ed.) & A. M. Goldstein (Vol. Ed.), *Handbook of Psychology: Vol. 11. Forensic Psychology* (pp. 543-560). New York: John Wiley & Sons.

Lassiter, G. D., & Geers, A. L. (2004). In G. D. Lassiter (Ed.), *Interrogations, Confessions, and Entrapment* (pp. 197-214). New York: Kluwer Academic/Plenum.

Leo, R. A. (1992). From coercion to deception: The changing nature of police interrogation in America. *Crime, Law, and Social Change, 18,* 35-59.

Leo, R. (1996a). Inside the interrogation room. *Journal of Criminal Law and Criminology, 86,* 266-303.

Leo, R. (1996b). *Miranda's* revenge: Police interrogation as a confidence game. *Law and Society Review, 30,* 259-288.

Leo, R. (2001a). False confessions: Causes, consequences, and solutions. In S. D. Westervelt & J. A. Humphrey (Eds.), *Wrongly Convicted: Perspectives on Failed Justice* (pp. 36-54). New Brunswick, NJ: Rutgers University Press.

Leo, R. (2001b). Questioning the relevance of *Miranda* in the Twenty-First Century. *Michigan Law Review, 99*(5), 1000-1029.

Leo, R. A., & Ofshe, R. J. (1998). The consequences of false confessions: Deprivation of liberty and miscarriages of justice in the age of psychological interrogation. *Journal of Criminal Law and Criminology, 88,* 429-496.

Leo, R. A., & Ofshe, R. J. (2001). The truth about false confessions and advocacy scholarship. *Criminal Law Bulletin, 37*(4), 293-370.

Leo, R. A., & Thomas, G. C. (Eds.). (1998). *The Miranda Debate: Law, Justice, and Policing.* Boston: Northeastern University Press.

Maher, N., & Woodcock, R. W. (2001). *Woodcock-Johnson III Tests of Achievement Examiner's Manual.* Itasca, IL: Riverside.

Mann, S., Vrij, A., & Bull, R. (2004). Detecting true lies: Police officer's ability to detect suspect's lies. *Journal of Applied Psychology, 89,* 137-149.

Markman, S. J., & Cassell, P. G. (1988). Protecting the innocent: A response to the Bedau-Radelet study. *Stanford Law Review, 41,* 121-160.

McConville, M. (1993). *Corroboration and Confessions: The Impact of a Rule Requiring That No Conviction Can Be Sustained on the Basis of Confession Evidence Alone. The Royal Commission on Criminal Justice Research Study No. 36.* London: HMSO. (Cited in G. Gudjonsson. [2003]. *The Psychology of Interrogations and Confessions: A Handbook.* West Sussex, England: Wiley.)

Melton, G. B., Petrila, J., Poythress, N. G., & Slobogin, C. (1997). *Psychological Evaluations for the Courts* (2nd ed.). New York: Guilford.

Milgram, S. (1983). *Obedience to Authority: An Experimental View.* New York: Harper/Collins.

Morey, L. (1991). *Personality Assessment Inventory Professional Manual.* Lutz, FL: Psychological Assessment Resources.

Napier, N. R., & Adams, S. H. (2002). Criminal confessions: Overcoming the challenges. *FBI Law Enforcement Bulletin, 71*(11). Retrieved June 11, 2003, from http://www.fbi.gov/publications/leb/2002/nov2002/nov02leb.htm#page_10

Nel, E., Helmreich, R., & Aronson, E. (1969). Opinion change in the advocate as a function of the persuasability of his audience: A clarification of the meaning of dissonance. *Journal of Personality and Social Psychology, 12,* 117-124.

Oberlander, L. B., Goldstein, N. E, & Goldstein, A. M. (2003). Competence to confess. In I. B. Weiner (Series Ed.) & A. M. Goldstein (Vol. Ed.), *Handbook of Psychology: Vol. 11. Forensic Psychology* (pp. 335-357). New York: John Wiley & Sons.

Ofshe, R., & Leo, R. (1997). The social psychology of police interrogation: The theory and classification of true and false confessions. *Studies in Law, Politics, and Society, 16,* 189-251.

Poythress, N. G., Nicholson, R., Otto, R. K., Edens, J. E., Bonnie, R. J., Monahan, J., & Hoge, S. K. (1999). *MacCAT-CA: The MacArthur Competence Assessment Tool – Criminal Adjudication, Professional Manual.* Lutz, FL: Psychological Assessment Resources.

The Psychological Corporation. (2001). *Wechsler Individual Achievement Test-Second Edition.* San Antonio, TX: The Psychological Corporation.

Radelet, M. L., Bedau, H. A., & Putnam, C. E. (1992). *In Spite of Innocence: Erroneous Convictions in Capital Cases.* Boston, MA: Northeastern University Press.

Radelet, M. L., Lofquist, W. S., & Bedau, H. A. (1996). Prisoners released from death rows since 1970 because of doubts about their guilt. *Thomas M. Cooley Law Review, 13,* 907-966.

Roesch, R., Zapf, P. A., Eaves, D., & Webster, C. D. (1998). *Fitness Interview Test* (rev. ed.). Burnaby, British Columbia, Canada: Mental Health Law and Policy Institute, Simon Fraser University.

Rogers, R. (1997). *Clinical Assessment of Malingering and Deception* (2nd ed.). New York: Guilford.

Rogers, R. (2001). *Handbook of Diagnostic and Structured Interviewing.* New York: Guilford.

Rogers, R., Bagby, R. M., & Dickens, S. E. (1992). *Structured Interview of Reported Symptoms Professional Manual.* Lutz, FL: Psychological Assessment Resources.

Rogers, R., & Shuman, D. (2000). *Conducting Insanity Evaluations* (2nd ed.). New York: Guilford.

Rogers, R., Tillbrook, C. E., & Sewell, K. W. (2004). *Evaluation of Competency to Stand Trial – Revised (ECST–R).* Lutz, FL: Psychological Assessment Resources.

Scheck, B., & Neufeld, P. (2001). DNA and innocence scholarship. In S. D. Westervelt & J. A. Humphrey, *Wrongly Convicted: Perspectives on Failed Justice* (pp. 241-252). New Brunswick, NJ: Rutgers University Press.

Scheck, B., Neufeld, P., & Dwyer, J. (2001). *Actual Innocence*. New York: Doubleday.

Sigelman, C. K., Budd, E. C., Spanhel, C. L., & Schoenrock, C. J. (1981). When in doubt say yes: Acquiescence in interviews with mentally retarded persons. *Mental Retardation, 19,* 53-58.

Sigurdsson, J. F., & Gudjonsson, G. H. (1994). Alcohol and drug intoxication during police interrogation and the reasons why suspects confess to the police. *Addiction, 89,* 985-997.

Sigurdsson, J. F., & Gudjonsson, G. H. (1996). Psychological characteristics of 'false confessors'; a study among Icelandic prison inmates and juvenile offenders. *Personality and Individual Differences, 20,* 321-329.

Simon, J. (1991). *Homicide: A Year on the Killing Streets*. Boston: Houghton Mifflin.

Tombaugh, T. N. (1996). *Test of Memory Malingering (TOMM)*. North Tonawanda, NY: Multi-Health Systems.

Wakefield, H., & Underwager, R. (1998). Coerced or nonvoluntary confessions. *Behavioral Sciences and the Law*, 16, 423-440.

Wald, M., Ayres, R., Hess, D. W., Schantz, M., & Whitebread, C. H. (1967). Interrogations in New Haven: The impacts of *Miranda*. *Yale Law Journal, 76,* 1519-1648.

Watson, J. D., & Berry, A. (2003). *DNA: The Secret of Life*. New York: Knopf.

Watson, J. D., & Crick, F. H. C. (1953). Molecular structure of nucleic acids: A structure for deoxyribose nucleic acid. *Nature, 171,* 737.

Wechsler, D. (2003). *Wechsler Intelligence Scale for Children – Fourth Edition Administration and Scoring Manual*. San Antonio, TX: The Psychological Corporation.

Winkler, J. D., Kanouse, D. E., & Ware, J. E. (1982). Controlling for acquiescence response set in score development. *Journal of Applied Psychology, 67,* 555-561.

Wrightsman, L. S., & Kassin, S. M. (1993). *Confessions in the Courtroom*. Newbury Park, CA: Sage.

— Cases Cited —

Ake v. Oklahoma, 470 U.S. 68 (1986).
Arizona v. Fulminante, 499 U.S. 279 (1991).
Arizona v. Roberson, 486 U.S. 675 (1988).
Ashcraft v. Tennessee, 322 U.S. 143 (1944).
Ashdown v. Utah, 357 U.S. 426 (1958).

Beckwith v. United States, 425 U.S. 341 (1976).
Beecher v. Alabama, 389 U.S. 35 (1967).
Beecher v. Alabama, 408 U.S. 234 (1972).
Berkemer v. McCarty, 468 U.S. 420 (1984).
Blackburn v. Alabama, 361 U.S. 199 (1960).
Boulden v. Holman, 394 U.S. 478 (1969).
Boyer v. State, 825 So.2nd 418 (Fla.App. 1 Dist. 2002).
Bram v. United States, 168 U.S. 532 (1897).
Brewer v. Williams, 430 U.S. 387 (1977).
Brown v. Allen, 344 U.S. 433 (1953).
Brown v. Illinois, 422 U.S. 590 (1975).
Brown v. Mississippi, 297 U.S. 278 (1936).
Butler v. McKellar, 494 U.S. 407 (1990).

California v. Beheler, 463 U.S. 1121 (1983).
California v. Prysock, 453 U.S. 355 (1981).
Chambers v. Florida, 309 U.S. 227 (1940).
Chapman v. California, 386 U.S. 18 (1967).
Chavez v. Martinez, 538 U.S. 760 (2003).

Cicenia v. Lagay, 357 U.S. 504 (1958).
Clewis v. Texas, 386 U.S. 707 (1967).
Colorado v. Connelly, 479 U.S. 157 (1986).
Colorado v. Spring, 479 U.S. 564 (1987).
Connecticut v. Barrett, 479 U.S. 523 (1987).
Coyote v. United States, 380 F.2d 305 (CA 10 1967) *cert. denied,* 389
    U.S. 992.
Crane v. Kentucky, 476 U.S. 683 (1986).
Crooker v. California, 357 U.S. 433 (1958).
Culombe v. Connecticut, 367 U.S. 568 (1961).

Darwin v. Connecticut, 391 U.S. 346 (1968).
Daubert v. Merrell Dow Pharmaceutical Inc., 509 U.S. 579 (1993).
Davis v. North Carolina, 384 U.S. 737 (1966).
Davis v. United States, 512 U.S. 452 (1994).
Dickerson v. United States, 530 U.S. 428 (2000).
Doyle v. Ohio, 426 U.S. 610 (1976).
Duckworth v. Eagan, 492 U.S. 195 (1989).
Dunaway v. New York, 442 U.S. 200 (1979).

Edwards v. Arizona, 451 U.S. 477 (1981).
Escobedo v. Illinois, 378 U.S. 478 (1964).

Fare v. Michael C., 442 U.S. 707 (1979).
Fikes v. Alabama, 352 U.S. 191 (1957).
Frazier v. Cupp, 394 U.S. 731 (1969).
Frye v. United States, 293 F. 1013 (D.C. Cir. 1923).

Gallegos v. Nebraska, 342 U.S. 55 (1951).
Gideon v. Wainwright, 372 U.S. 335 (1963).
Gonzalez v. State, 4 S.W.3d 406 (Tex. App.-Waco 1998).
Greenwald v. Wisconsin, 390 U.S. 519 (1968).

Haley v. Ohio, 332 U.S. 596 (1948).
Hardy v. United States, 186 U.S. 224 (1902).
Harris v. New York, 401 U.S. 222 (1971).
Harris v. South Carolina, 338 U.S. 68 (1949).
Harrison v. United States, 392 U.S. 219 (1968).
Haynes v. Washington, 373 U.S. 503 (1963).

Hoffa v. United States, 385 U.S. 293 (1966).
Hopt v. Territory of Utah, 110 U.S. 574 (1884).

Illinois v. Perkins, 496 U.S. 292 (1990).
In re Gault, 387 U.S. 1 (1967).
In re Patrick W., 148 Cal.Rptr 735 (1978).

Jackson v. Denno, 378 U.S. 368 (1964).
Jenkins v. Delaware, 395 U.S. 213 (1969).
Jenkins v. United States, 307 F.2nd 637 (1962).
Johnson v. New Jersey, 384 U.S. 719 (1966).
Johnson v. Zerbst, 304 U.S. 458 (1938).

Kent v. Porto Rico, 207 U.S. 113 (1907).

LaValle v. Delle Rose, 410 U.S. 690 (1973).
Lee v. Mississippi, 332 U.S. 742 (1948).
Lego v. Twomey, 404 U.S. 477 (1972).
Leyra v. Denno, 347 U.S. 556 (1954).
Lisenba v. California, 314 U.S. 219 (1941).
Lynumn v. Illinois, 372 U.S. 528 (1963).
Lyons v. Oklahoma, 322 U.S. 596 (1944).

Malinski v. New York, 324 U.S. 401 (1945).
Massey v. State, 820 So.2d 1003 (Fla.App. 4 Dist. 2003).
Massiah v. United States, 377 U.S. 201 (1964).
Mathis v. United States, 391 U.S. 1 (1968).
McNabb v. United States, 318 U.S. 332 (1943).
McNeil v. Wisconsin, 501 U.S. 171 (1991).
Michigan v. Harvey, 494 U.S. 344 (1990).
Michigan v. Jackson, 475 U.S. 625 (1986).
Michigan v. Mosley, 423 U.S. 96 (1975).
Michigan v. Tucker, 417 U.S. 433 (1974).
Miller v. Fenton, 474 U.S. 104 (1985).
Mincey v. Arizona, 437 U.S. 385 (1978).
Minnick v. Mississippi, 498 U.S. 146 (1990).
Miranda v. Arizona, 384 U.S. 436 (1966).
Mooney v. Holohan, 294 U.S. 103 (1935).
Moore v. Dempsey, 261 U.S. 86 (1923).
Moran v. Burbine, 475 U.S. 412 (1986).

New York v. Quarles, 467 U.S. 649 (1984).
North Carolina v. Alford, 400 U.S. 25 (1970).
North Carolina v. Butler, 441 U.S. 369 (1979).

Opper v. United States, 348 U.S. 84 (1954).
Oregon v. Bradshaw, 462 U.S. 1039 (1983).
Oregon v. Elstad, 470 U.S. 298 (1985).
Oregon v. Hass, 420 U.S. 714 (1975).
Oregon v. Mathiason, 429 U.S. 492 (1977).
Orozco v. Texas, 394 U.S. 324 (1969).

Pate v. Robinson, 383 U.S. 375 (1966).
Patterson v. Illinois, 487 U.S. 285 (1988).
Payne v. Arkansas, 356 U.S. 560 (1958).
People v. Bernasco, 562 N.E.2d 958 (Illinois, 1990).
People v. Higgins, 278 N.E.2d 68 (1993).
Pierce v. United States, 160 U.S. 355 (1896).
Procunier v. Atchley, 400 U.S. 446 (1971).

Reck v. Pate, 367 U.S. 433 (1961).
Rhode Island v. Innis, 446 U.S. 291 (1980).
Rogers v. Richmond, 365 U.S. 534 (1961).

Schneckloth v. Bustamonte, 412 U.S. 218 (1973).
Shea v. Louisiana, 470 U.S. 51 (1985).
Sims v. Georgia, 385 U.S. 538 (1967).
Smith v. Illinois, 469 U.S. 91 (1984).
Smith v. United States, 348 U.S. 147 (1954).
Solem v. Stumes, 465 U.S. 638 (1984).
Spano v. New York, 360 U.S. 315 (1959).
Sparf v. United States, 156 U.S. 51 (1895).
Stansbury v. California, 511 U.S. 318 (1994).
State v. Prater, 77 Wn.2d 526, 463 P.2d 640 (1970).
State v. Scales, 518 N.W.2d 587 (Minnesota, 1994).
Stein v. New York, 346 U.S. 156 (1953).
Stephan v. State, 711 P.2d 1156 (Alaska, 1985).
Stroble v. California, 343 U.S. 181 (1952).
Swenson v. Stidham, 409 U.S. 224 (1972).

Tague v. Louisiana, 444 U.S. 469 (1980).
Taylor v. Alabama, 457 U.S. 687 (1982).
Texas v. Cobb, 532 U.S. 162 (2001).
Thomas v. Arizona, 356 U.S. 390 (1958).
Thompson v. Keohane, 516 U.S. 99 (1995).
Townsend v. Sain, 372 U.S. 293 (1963).
Turner v. Pennsylvania, 338 U.S. 62 (1949).

United States v. Bayer, 331 U.S. 532 (1947).
United States v. Carignan, 342 U.S. 36 (1951).
United States ex rel. Bilokumsky v. Tod, 263 U.S. 149 (1923).
United States ex rel. Simon v. Maroney, 228 F.Supp. 800 (1964).
United States v. Hale, 422 U.S. 171 (1975).
United States v. Mitchell, 322 U.S. 65 (1944).
United States v. Washington, 431 U.S. 181 (1977).
Upshaw v. United States, 335 U.S. 410 (1948).

Wainwright v. Greenfield, 474 U.S. 284 (1986).
Ward v. Texas, 316 U.S. 547 (1942).
Watts v. Indiana, 338 U.S. 49 (1949).
West v. United States, 399 F.2d 467 (5th Cir. 1968), *cert. denied,* 393 U.S. 1102 (1969).
White v. Texas, 310 U.S. 530 (1940).
Withrow v. Williams, 507 U.S. 680 (1993).
Wong Sun v. United States, 371 U.S. 471 (1963).
Wyrick v. Fields, 459 U.S. 42 (1982).

Ziang Sun Wan v. United States, 266 U.S. 1 (1924).

— Subject Index —

— Author Index —

Adams, S. H., 41-42, 174-177
Aronson, E., 172
Asch, S. E., 172
Ayres, R., 37

Bagby, R. M., 148
Baldwin, J., 37, 39
Bedau, H. A., 5, 38
Berry, A., 4
Binet, A., 158-159
Blass, T., 172
Bless, E., 172
Bonnie, R. J., 158
Borum, R., 55
Buckley, J. P., 10, 11-13, 24, 27, 42, 156,
    202, 203
Budd, E. C., 162
Bull, R., 12
Butcher, J. N., 148, 194

Cassell, P. G., 5
Cattell, J. M., 158
Clark, N. K., 159, 161
Committee on Ethical Guidelines for
    Forensic Psychologists, 166
Connors, E., 4
Crick, F. H. C., 3

Dahlstrom, W. G., 148
DeClue, G., 56, 158, 209
Dickens, S. E., 148
Dwyer, J., 5

Eaves, D., 158
Edens, J. E., 158

Ekman, P., 11-12
Everly, G. S., 150

Festinger, L., 172
Fisher, R. P., 150
Frank, M. G., 11-12
Freedman, J., 172
Frumkin, I. B., ix, 141
Fulero, S. M., 172, 178

Garcia, A., 141
Geers, A. L., 43
Geiselman, R. E., 150
Golden, C. J., 148
Golding, S., 55
Goldstein, A. M., ix, 144, 145
Goldstein, N. E., 144, 145
Gouvier, W. D., 194
Graham, J. R., 148
Green, P., 148
Grisso, T., 51-57, 141, 145, 149-150, 158,
    191-192, 193
Gudjonsson, G. H., 5-6, 9, 15-17, 20, 25,
    27-28, 34-38, 42-44, 135, 156-
    166, 186, 195, 202

Hale, D. B., 194
Hayes, J. S., 194
Helmreich, R., 172
Hess, D. W., 37
Hoge, S. K., 158

Inbau, F. E., 10, 11-13, 24, 27, 42, 156,
    202, 203

241